MAKING THE DIFFERENCE

GENDER, PERSONHOOD AND THEOLOGY

Elaine L. Graham

MOWBRAY

Mowbray
A Cassell imprint
Wellington House, 125 Strand, London WC2R 0BB, England
215 Park Avenue South, New York, NY 10003, USA

First published 1995

British Library Cataloguing-in-Publication Data
A catalogue record for this book is available from the British Library.

ISBN 0–264–67346–8

Printed and bound in Great Britain by Biddles Ltd, Guildford and King's Lynn

Contents

Introduction

The changing nature of relationships between women and men is one of the most remarkable features of contemporary Western society. Many women now possess a range of opportunities and expectations of which their great-grandmothers would never have dreamed; and virtually every aspect of our lives – work, legislation, politics, family life, media portrayals and sexual behaviour – reflect the transformation of attitudes and roles which has taken place in the past two generations. Many of these changes have been and remain controversial; but as the twentieth century draws to a close, issues of gender roles and relationships occupy a central place in our individual and collective concerns.

Although they have been relatively slow to respond to many of these developments, the West's religious traditions have not remained unaffected. Many of these faith-communities are experiencing renewed attention to the roles and status of women, and finding that their position is often controversial and problematic (Holm, 1994; King, 1993; Ahmed, 1992; Plaskow, 1990). In general, men have controlled and formulated the doctrines, texts and rituals of these faiths, and women have been relegated to an inferior and subordinate status. However, encouraged by the impetus of 'secular' institutions, religious groups are being required to re-examine traditional teachings pertaining to the activities and horizons of women, and the precise nature of male–female relations.

Many studies have identified a contrast between radical and egalitarian teaching in the classical traditions, which was subsequently obscured by other cultural factors that regarded women as inferior to men. Others have focused on the retrieval of forgotten women in positions of leadership and influence; or reappropriated female characters and symbolism – in worship of goddess figures, the wisdom of female prophets, shamans or healers, remembering of the folkloric wisdom of women – as an antidote to the 'androcentric' or male-dominated nature of religious imagery and authority (Holm, 1994:xii–xxii).

All these enquiries focus on a central issue: that of the precise nature of religious teaching on matters of sexual relations, family life, the status of women and the balance of male and female in religious imagery and leadership. They invite exploration of the extent to which attitudes and prospects within religious traditions reflect authentic teachings, the degree to which cultural influences permeate religious doctrine and practice, and whether religion is a liberating or oppressive force for contemporary women. Christianity has shared in these upheavals, initially in the United States and Europe, but increasingly on a global scale. Christians of all traditions are discovering that questions of gender are challenging virtually every aspect of belief and practice.

For example, one of the most significant phenomena within the Western church over the past 25 years has been the emergence of feminist theology. Fuelled by the second wave of the modern women's movement, drawing upon the theoretical and critical stances of academic feminism, and inspired by Latin American Liberation Theology, feminist theologians have achieved a remarkable body of work in a relatively short time. They have sought to establish the opportunities and validate the methods by which women, long silenced as theological subjects, may articulate their perspectives and contribute towards the reconstruction of a more 'inclusive' theological discipline (Ruether, 1992b).

Such theological developments both reflect and promote pastoral and policy concerns associated with the proper roles and relationships of women and men within the Christian church. These are concerned with the appropriate ordering of the church's ministry and practice; the validity of women's priestly ministry; the use of 'inclusive' language in liturgy; and the deployment of 'masculine' and 'feminine' attributes and characteristics in the metaphorical naming of God and God's actions in the world.

However, many of these debates conceal unexamined assumptions. One of the fundamental tenets of feminist theology has been its appeal to 'women's experience' as a corrective to androcentric tradition, and as a foundational source of knowledge upon which to base a theological reconstruction (Ruether, 1992b). Yet, with the possible exception of Pamela Dickey Young's attempt to qualify and categorize women's experience (Young, 1990), there has been little attention to the substance of such claims to a unique knowledge and experience founded on a distinction of gender. Feminist critics argue that traditional accounts of authoritative human experience are the construct of patriarchal interests, and claim the right to articulate an alternative and oppositional perspective; but this only serves to raise questions about the sources of such experience and knowledge.

Similarly, as pressure grows in many churches to transform relations between women and men from hierarchy to community, the real nature of their respective roles and functions is thrown into relief. Some versions of the relative positions of women and men may regard the formation of gender identity as determined by the straightforward logic of 'natural' imperatives; others will argue that human habitation of an already gendered culture in which women are objectified and subordinated is itself the primary site of gender differentiation. In either case, protagonists will fashion their notions of the ideal and authentic community on the basis of their assumptions about the significance and origins of gender divisions for human destiny.

In many cases, support for the greater participation of women in church life, especially in the ordained ministry, rests on a conviction that no ontological barrier exists to the equal exercise of women's pastoral and sacramental ministry. Yet many of those same advocates would assert that women do also bring a different dimension to ordained ministry and priesthood, based on 'feminine' characteristics and disposition. Such practical strategies and theological visions are founded on two distinct understandings of human nature: one of a commonality of women and men with a shared nature, and one of a radical distinctiveness of women from men, whether such difference is considered innate or socially constructed.

These are issues which concern the nature of human experience; but this is also a question of theological language. The 'maleness' of God as portrayed in traditional Christian religious language has been criticized as denying the full humanity of women, because male experience is implicitly privileged and rendered normative and superior by its exclusive use in representing the divine. It is argued that this relegates female humanity to a derivative, 'misbegotten' and subordinate status. This is an important debate, not least because it highlights the way in which theological language which draws upon gendered metaphors for God is necessarily shaped by human values concerning the acceptability of 'male' and 'female' experience for imaging and naming divine nature and activity.

At the heart of such debates is the question of the fundamental meaning and significance of *gender* in theology and Christian practice. Within the human and social sciences, analysis of gender is treated as an essential aspect of a broader analysis of the social order and human behaviour. Such theories of gender have three chief preoccupations. The first attempts to trace the formation and acquisition of *gender identity* – individual characteristics and personality traits – and to theorize about their origins. It is often associated with research into 'sex differences', which seeks to identify empirically the respective qualities of masculinity and femininity and their significance in constituting an individual's sense of self. Secondly, there are theories of *gender relations*: patterns of power, norms and roles, the cultural representation of women and men, customs, legislation and the sexual division of labour. The third focus concerns *representations of gender*: the deeper structures of our culture, and how gender helps to organize our ideas not just about women and men, but about nature and knowledge, the public and the private, rationality and science. Such theories identify the symbolic and epistemological dimensions of gender.

By contrast, within the Christian church and studies of theology, there has been little sustained or disciplined attention to the underlying nature and significance of gender, in spite of the practical and intellectual implications already noted. The substance, methods and conclusions of the critical study of gender remain unexamined – or at best misunderstood – both in terms of theological discourse and practical church policy.

Such debates therefore expose the extent to which such practical and contemporary issues are subtended by much deeper assumptions about gender as a category of human experience and human nature. However, the confusion of such questions in theological circles reveals the lack of sustained attention so far given to an analysis of the phenomenon of gender as it affects church policy, theological discourse and religious practice. Despite the ubiquity of debates about gender issues in the churches, gender as an issue in itself receives no more than superficial attention. This book represents an attempt to begin a more detailed and critical enquiry. It is a

deliberately interdisciplinary engagement with contemporary critical studies of gender, with a view to presenting such insights in
dialogue with theological studies.

Many of the debates about gender in the churches acknowledge
the challenges to Christian tradition from secular experience. However, the degree to which such information is regarded as necessarily
informing or influencing Christian policy and practice neatly encap-
sulates a perennial dilemma: to what extent are the changes around
us to be absorbed into the life of the church as evidence of God at
work in the world; or has Scripture and the accumulated teaching of
tradition provided sufficient authority to guide the affairs of the
Christian community in matters of human relationships? Thus, it is
important to see how two issues intertwine: one about the empirical
validity of information about gender difference; and another about
the appropriate response by theology and the churches to such
evidence.

This is effectively a question about the authority of secular
perspectives; but also about the nature of Christian orthodoxy, most
particularly in its openness to changing contexts and opinions. As we
shall see, the evidence about gender from the human and social
sciences provides a wealth of information on which to reflect; but the
legitimacy of theology's interaction with 'secular' sources is itself a
disputed and controversial area.

My discussion will focus on three major subject disciplines and
four thematic discussions in which critical theories from a variety of
disciplines in the human and social sciences have converged to
challenge many of the notions of the fixity and dichotomy of gender
identity and difference. They offer profound implications for our
understanding of the very foundations of human culture and identity, and I shall consider the implications of some of these for
theological studies in my concluding observations.

Interrogation of Theories of Gender

Any scholar embarking on a multi-disciplinary study from an outside
perspective will necessarily encounter material or theoretical traditions which are unfamiliar. Unfortunately, she may proceed with a
superficial or anachronistic mind-set which misinterprets or distorts
her understanding. Pastoral and practical theologians, used to working across the boundaries of the theological and human sciences,

have been accused of mishandling their sources and thus founding their social analysis or diagnoses upon flawed premises (Pattison, 1986). It is important to be aware that the enquirer does not come to the chosen disciplines innocent of theoretical, political and epistemological biases. It is not therefore the intention of this book to stand as an objective assembly of the 'facts' of gender difference, nor of the conclusive or entire findings of any discipline. It is rather undertaken as a self-conscious interrogation of some aspects of gender studies; a recognition that all subject disciplines are pluriform, with many theoretical and empirical subdivisions.

Such a process will be selective, but none the less comprehensive. A completely exhaustive account is impossible, but the material and perspectives presented are to be considered fully representative of current debates and trends. The purpose of this book is to construct some analytical framework by which such material can engage and interact with the theological disciplines, and especially pastoral and feminist theologies. The perspectives thus gained will serve as a systematic, critical and comprehensive preparation for the further project of theological analysis and enquiry.

Gender relations are connected to other dimensions of social relations; race and class in particular. Contemporary gender theorists are aware of the importance of considering the role of women and men in the light of other categories of power and difference; but the focus of this study will be primarily on gender theory. Similarly, although issues of sexuality, sexual orientation and sexual behaviour do intersect with gender, they will not be in the foreground of the discussion offered here.

In Part One, I provide an overview of the emergence of gender as an issue within the social and human sciences, and the ways in which commentators in theology and the churches have treated such evidence. Critical studies of gender have shifted over the past 30 years from concern with empirical measures of 'sex differences' to a more theoretical characterization of gender as an aspect of social relations; yet debates in theology and the churches have not moved beyond a characterization of the 'sex'/'gender' distinction that has now become out-dated. It is clear that a deeper and more critical enquiry is necessary, into the nature and extent of gender difference, its origins and dynamics, as well as the implications for policy and practice. Such an interrogation needs an interdisciplinary perspective and a sophisticated theoretical focus.

In Part Two, I examine specific subject disciplines in which critical studies of gender have been especially influential: in the development of human sexual difference, the symbolic and material division of labour, and the dynamics of individual subjectivity (personality, identity and consciousness). These raise questions of the relationship of 'nature' and 'culture', the contribution of embodied experience to gender identity and the role of the construction of scientific knowledge in the formation of cultural models of gender causation. These themes are taken up in Part Three, which draws upon a wider range of intellectual disciplines, from the history of medicine, the philosophy of science, literary and linguistic theory, ecology and the sociology of knowledge.

In Chapter Ten, I offer a new paradigm for the integration of contemporary theories of gender into theological studies and Christian practice. To regard human experience as inherently gendered requires a sophisticated and critical approach to many aspects of Christian anthropology; and it sets an agenda for further studies of religious and cultural practice as the source of gender identity, relationships and representations.

Part I
Gender Issues

1 · *What is Gender?*

But if we are to pursue the history of women's experience and of feminism there can be no retreat from a closer enquiry into subjectivity and sexual identity. For if feminism insists on the political significance of the female subject and on the urgent need to reorganise sexual differences and division, it is to convey a more generous conception of human consciousness and its effects. (Alexander, 1984:131)

Scholarship in the critical studies of gender has passed through various stages. Early interest, fuelled by social change, concentrated on identifying the historical exclusion of women from many areas of achievement, and the implicit gender stereotypes upon which such distinctions rested. Further studies of gender difference exposed many conventional characterizations of gender as unrealistically dichotomous and exaggeratedly polarized, and exploded the myth of sex differences as entirely determined by 'natural' forces. More recently, work has been informed by a variety of theoretical perspectives which have facilitated a shift towards an understanding of gender as less a set of discrete indices of difference, and more as a category of human experience. Thus, contemporary theories of gender are concerned not so much to identify and refute 'difference' as to offer a variety of conceptual processes by which all aspects of human culture – language, subjectivity, social structures, symbolic representation – reflect and maintain 'gendered' characteristics and support gender as a form of social relations.

Origins of Gender Dualism in the West

Ideas of gender in the contemporary West have been influenced by the legacy of classical Greek philosophy, most notably a binary or dualistic pattern of characterizing human traits and relationships.

Although symbolic and empirical representations of gender have traditionally portrayed it as a dichotomous phenomenon, such rigorous dualism is actually the product of human categorization. Critical accounts of the portrayal of gender in Greek philosophy – especially teachings attributed to Plato (*c.* 428–355 BCE) and Aristotle (384–322 BCE) – tend to characterize it as unremittingly dualistic, and responsible for all subsequent systems of Western thought in which male and female are dichotomous and polarized. However, closer inspection betrays a greater pluralism to the ancient Greeks' portrayal of the concepts of man and woman. Prudence Allen argues that the Greeks characterized the relative differences and similarities between women and men as operating at a number of levels: ontological status (the substance of basic human nature); reproductive function; and intellectual and moral qualities. Different philosophers argued for a unity, polarity or complementarity of the genders in any or all of these categories, and it was only over the passage of time, and largely as a result of the assimilation of Greek philosophy into early Christianity, that the Platonic and Aristotelian views of male and female as discrete and separate beings predominated. Heraclitus posited male and female as polar opposites, surmising that, as new life emerged from the union of male and female, thus all creation must be founded on such an ontological and functional division (Allen, 1985:19ff).

Gender dualism is only one element in a much more comprehensive system of Western thought; the male/female dichotomy must be seen as a guiding organizing category for other binary pairs which all mutually reinforce each other. Allen attributes the first systematic ordering of these binary pairs to Pythagoras, but the list may be rendered as follows:

Male/Female
Culture/Nature
Straight/Curved
Reason/Intuition
Public/Private
Humanity/Nature-Animality
Production/Reproduction
Subject/Object
Self/Other
Odd/Even

Universal/Particular
Mind/Body
Civilized/Primitive
Good/Bad
Master/Slave
(Plumwood, 1993:43; Allen, 1985:19)

However, these 'deep structures' of dualism may be all-pervasive, but they have their origins in particular human understandings of the nature of human agency and social organization. Plumwood equates the sources of Platonic dualism with the establishment of a discontinuity between reason and nature, which was inherently 'gendered' by virtue of the equation of free men with the culture of heroism and death. The world of men – of the spirit, culture and rationality – is effected via the denial and exclusion of the world of women and 'Others' (1993:67–103). Thus, social realities are absorbed into the accounts given by particular social groups, who rationalize their world-view by appealing to its origins in 'nature'.

Plato's views of the origins of gender are identified with two sources. Aristophanes tells the story in the *Symposium* of how humans were originally created in three varieties (male, female and hermaphrodite), who were separated into halves by Zeus, and subsequently have been on a quest for reunion: the single-sex beings in homosexual relationships, the hermaphrodites in heterosexuality. In *Timaeus*, males are the direct creations of the gods, and spend their lives attempting to return to their original home in the heavens. To fail is to fall further into the realm of material nature – and return as a woman or beast. Plato believed that all life was but a poor reflection of an ideal, transcendent realm; higher forms resembled the Ideal more adequately, and it was possible to ascend the scale. However, scholars also argue that Plato reserved a place for women amongst the Guardians in the Republic, provided they were given the education and opportunity to equip them to take their place alongside men.

Aristotle also emphasized the distinction between 'form' and 'matter', but argued, against Plato, that the two existed interdependently and hierarchically. Matter exists 'for the sake of' form, with the latter giving animation to the former. Form describes and embodies the essence of a thing in a way that matter cannot.

Aristotle's teachings on biology reflect his essentially functionalist view of the universe: that the characteristics and roles of any part of life could be explained in terms of its respective role, or function, in sustaining and maintaining the present structure. There is therefore a natural order to all things, relationships being determined by the part each element contributes to the whole. Thus, the distinction between male and female can be explained by their differentiation in reproductive function. Aristotle was a consistent advocate of sex polarity, refuting any notion that the female contributed anything to the generation of the species. The inferiority of woman is to be explained by reference to her subordinate physiology; she is to be compared with 'matter', while man resembles superior 'form'. The female is also characterized as deficient: inadequate in the elements of heat and moisture necessary for the generation of life. Hence the Aristotelian notion of the female as 'misbegotten' male, a departure from the 'true' human essence.

Early Christianity experienced a conflict between classical Greek anthropologies – of women as inherently inferior, only able to adopt masculine privilege or share the male world by denial of reproductive and biological nature – and a radical Christian rejection of male/female difference and subordination in the name of the universal and unconditional nature of salvation and grace (Galatians 3:28). In embracing forms of sexual asceticism, the earliest Christians were rejecting women's reproductive role as the all-determining indication of social position. However, for fear of causing offence, the earliest Christians also counselled conformity to the Graeco-Roman household codes; thus an ambivalence was established, which spread throughout Western civilization: of male and female as polar opposites, yet with elements of protest and resistance (Edwards, 1989:54–82; 89–101; Gossman, 1991; Maloney, 1991).

Scholastic theology of the middle ages taught that women were not directly made in the image of God, but only derived their full humanity through the man. Thomas Aquinas taught that women were ontologically unequal to men. Influenced by Aristotelian biology, he believed that females were defective males, developing as such when conditions *in utero* were unsatisfactory for the full development of male humanity. Thus only men fully represented 'true' human nature; women were merely inferior matter, not in possession of the spiritual and intellectual powers that distinguished men from the animals. Traditional Thomist theology taught that whilst women were inferior in the realm of nature, they might be generously admitted as equals into the realm of salvation by the grace of Christ (Maloney, 1991).

The emergence of modernity, identified with the propagation of rational-scientific methods of observation, the accumulation of capital, development of technological expertise and its application to social and economic organization, is often associated with the greater social control of women. Commentators characterize the so-called 'Scientific Revolution' as a period in which 'patriarchal' values, personified in Francis Bacon's characterization of (masculine) Science's appropriation of (feminine) Nature in the language of sexual domination, were consolidated (Merchant, 1990; Easlea, 1980, 1981; Jordanova, 1980). Many of the traditional spheres of comparative independence for women – such as the domestic economy, the wisdom of women healers and midwives, and centres of learning founded on religious communities – were either placed under male-dominated authority or marginalized as civil society and factory industry effected a split between the public and private realms. The subsequent association of woman with nature, matter, sexuality and domesticity further condemned women to a subordinate and marginal role, although the portrayal of women also deliberately evoked their purity and innocence, especially in the discourse of Romanticism (Ruether, 1992b; Brown and Jordanova, 1982; Bloch and Bloch, 1980).

However, although the elevation of scientific reason in the West has been equated with the subordination and oppression of women, the philosophical and political movements associated with the Enlightenment and the democratic revolutions of the eighteenth century also provided an important vocabulary of humanism and civil rights (Alexander, 1984). The first inklings of modern feminism emerged as social critics such as John Stuart Mill and Mary Wollstonecraft questioned whether the privileges accorded all men by virtue of a shared capacity to reason and self-determination should not be extended to women (Jaggar, 1983:27–39; Epstein, 1988:2–5).

Thus, both in philosophical and material terms, the development of modern society carried the seeds both of women's objectification and of their emancipation. Indeed, the first campaigns of 'first-wave'

feminism in the nineteenth century, focusing on civil rights, equality before the law, access to education and the extension of
the suffrage, frequently had recourse to the language both of
equality and of women as distinctively morally superior (Bacchi,
1990).

Critical Studies of Gender

The fixity and inevitability of gender roles came under increasing
critical scrutiny in the years after 1945. The influence of the 'second-
wave' women's movement was crucial to the transformation of
gender relations and expectations in Europe and the United States
from the early 1960s. This movement should properly be seen as
both a shift in intellectual and political understanding, but also
necessarily prompted by technological and economic change.
Women had been prominent in the wartime workforces and
although significant social policy pressure was exerted to persuade
them to return to domestic responsibilities, the overwhelming trend
for the rest of the century has been a steady expansion of paid
employment opportunities for women in all industrialized countries
(Witz, 1993). Increasingly, therefore, women found themselves
participating in the labour force to an unprecedented degree. At the
same time, the burdens of domestic labour and childbearing were
eased by technological and medical innovations. Thus, the transformation of consciousness effected by 'feminist' theory and politics in the
1960s took place in the context of material and social change.

The convictions of the women's movement were articulated and
focused by several key works, among them Betty Friedan's *The
Feminine Mystique* (1963) and Simone de Beauvoir's *The Second Sex*
(first published in 1949). The former proclaimed that a generation of
North American women were confronting 'a problem that has no
name': the suburban captivity and *ennui* of housewives who sud-
denly discover they have no self-identity independent of husband or
children, yet who have no vocabulary with which to express their
dissatisfaction. Beauvoir analysed the subordination and inferiority
of women in Western culture and philosophy in terms of a cultural
definition of maleness as normative – and culture as therefore
modelled upon 'androcentricism' – and women as alien, derivative,

or 'Other'. In their definition of a world in which men define reality, and their exposure of its exclusion and objectification of women, these critiques provided the theoretical impetus for a generation of feminist politics.

A crucial part of the second-wave women's movement was the scientific study of male–female characteristics and relationships in the name of challenging the *status quo* of women's subordination and inferiority. As in the past, when arguments from nature were used to justify the subordinate status of women, so supporters and opponents of the women's movement were now concerned to evaluate whether changes in the existing 'arrangement between the sexes' could be supported or refuted by empirical evidence. Scientific studies were conducted into so-called 'sex differences' in order to discover whether the existing arrangement between the sexes was natural and inevitable, or based on discrimination and prejudice against women.

A more detailed summary of clinical studies into the biological basis of sexual differentiation, and their scientific context, will follow in Chapter Four. Broadly, however, the studies of the 1970s and 1980s emphasized a number of points: the complexity of the 'causes' of sexual dimorphism in mammals; the initial physiological and hormonal 'bisexuality' of the fetus; and the degree of variation within any given sample, so that when 'biological sex difference' is evoked, it is more properly to be thought of as a continuum within which individuals may display a diversity of hormonal, physiological, neurological and reproductive features.

Some scientists attempted to trace the connections between biological sex and social and psychological behaviour by constructing indices of 'masculinity' and 'femininity' (Terman and Miles, 1936). Modelled on IQ testing, these studies identified several hundred personality traits distinguished as either 'masculine' or 'feminine'. An individual's score indicated the degree to which they were 'female- or male-typical'; and Terman and Miles argued that with the exception of a small sample of 'M–F deviants' (imputed to be 'inverts' or homosexuals), most individuals exhibited a strong correlation between biological sex and personality. Such tests were held to prove that gender difference – behavioural qualities of masculine and feminine – could be equated with biological sex.

However, later critics challenged such M–F testing as 'reifying' as innate and tangible qualities those personality traits that were more appropriately regarded as social conventions or constructions. They argued that it was not possible to construct a questionnaire that was able to discern fixed qualities independent of social contexts; nor were there stable unidimensional categories in which individuals displayed clearly bipolar groups of qualities (Deaux, 1987).

Given the nature of evidence from the biological sciences which suggested that natural propensities developed in some kind of interaction with cultural factors, interest in the effects of sociological and environmental influences on gender development intensified. Within the social sciences, studies proliferated which examined how society produced expectations, stereotypes and conditionings which enforced sex roles. One typical study of 'sex role stereotyping' of this time considered the influence of schooling, media and family pressures in reproducing different roles and personality traits in males and females; and prescriptive practices in the institutions of work, marriage and social policy that enforce clearly-differentiated 'male' and 'female' spheres and behaviours (Chetwynd and Hartnett, 1978; Hargreaves and Colley, 1986; see also Connell, 1987; Goffman, 1974, 1979).

However, critics also identified ways in which cultural representations of gender frequently exaggerated or reified gender difference, serving an ideological purpose in emphasizing difference rather than similarity (Connell, 1987:78–87). In this way, popular and cultural aspects of gender helped to construct a perceived reality in which human experience and the natural order were axiomatically divided into two mutually exclusive and ontologically separate halves.

Not only were 'sex differences' not as dichotomous or polarized as conventional wisdom supposed, therefore, but they were also subject to cultural conditioning. A consensus was emerging, therefore, to regard 'culture' as exerting a powerful – perhaps decisive – influence upon individuals, and that observable differences between men and women could not be attributed to the unmediated workings of 'laws of nature' alone, but to some pattern of interaction between 'nature' and 'nurture'. However, varieties of biological determinism, such as sociobiology, still endured, and I shall return to this in Chapter Four.

Sex and Gender

One quotation neatly summarizes the accumulated evidence for this first stage in the critical study of gender, and represents an influential piece of analysis: the distinction between 'sex' and 'gender', as advanced by Robert Stoller in 1968:

> With a few exceptions, there are two sexes, male and female. To determine sex one must assay the following conditions: chromosomes, external genitalia, internal genitalia, gonads, hormonal states, and secondary sex characteristics . . . One's sex, then, is determined by an algebraic sum of all these qualities, and, as is obvious, most people fall under one of the two separate bell curves, the one of which is called 'male', the other 'female'.
>
> Gender is a term that has psychological and cultural rather than biological connotations: if the proper terms for sex are 'male' and 'female', the corresponding terms for gender are 'masculine' and 'feminine', these latter may be quite independent of (biological) sex. Gender is the amount of masculinity and femininity found in a person, and obviously, while there are mixtures of both in many humans, the normal male has a preponderance of masculinity and the normal female a preponderance of femininity. (Stoller, 1968, quoted in Oakley, 1972:158–59)

Stoller's definition, and the distinction between 'sex' as natural, biological and physiological, and 'gender' as psychological and cultural, was theoretical orthodoxy for twenty years. It was of immense heuristic and political value to the emergent feminist movement, because it enabled scholars to argue that women's subordinate and secondary position was due to socially constructed, and not naturally occurring, patterns of gender division. This offered a means of refuting those 'naturalistic' arguments which rooted differences between women and men in the immutable logic of biological imperative; instead, it could attribute the foundations of gender identity to social and cultural factors.

Androgyny

The political and strategic implications of the breaking of the link between sex and gender can be seen in the rise in popularity of the notion of androgyny in the early 1970s. A social psychologist, Sandra Bem, developed the Bem Sex Role Inventory that attempted to measure individuals' predisposition to feminine or masculine characteristics. However, unlike earlier investigators of gender traits (such as Terman and Miles in the 1930s) she did not assume that masculinity and femininity were mutually exclusive. Instead, she asked respondents to identify themselves in terms of conventionally gendered qualities (feminine as tender, understanding, shy, masculine as assertive and independent) and 'neutral' features (happy, sincere). Individuals could then be marked on all three scales as independent variables, producing a personality profile that, regardless of biological sex, could be high or low in masculinity and femininity. Persons attaining a minimal deviation on M and F scores were rated as 'androgynous' (Bem, 1993; Morawski, 1987; Doyle and Paludi, 1991).

Thus, Bem claimed that 'femininity' and 'masculinity' were learned patterns of behaviour; furthermore, they could be seen as independent collections of character traits with significant overlap, rather than naturally occurring dichotomies into which individuals inevitably conformed by virtue of biological sex. Androgyny was embraced as the ideal character type of liberated women and men: exemplifying the most desirable qualities of both conventional gender types, unconstrained by stereotyping, aiming for psychic integration and wholeness (Heilbrun, 1973; Spence *et al.*, 1974; Bem, 1993:115–32).

However, androgyny was also heavily criticized, and it is interesting to note that it has virtually disappeared from social scientific and feminist debates about gender. (Sandra Bem herself has 'recanted' her original advocacy of androgyny as a feminist strategy: see Bem, 1993:115–27). Its flaws also begin to indicate some of the problems with the 'sex/gender' analysis, and provide an indication of how subsequent theories of gender have moved on to emphasize more complex perspectives.

Firstly, the notion of androgyny was itself implicitly dualistic, in that it modelled an explicit distinction between biological and physiological identity, and cultural or psychological personality. Regardless of biological sex, it was argued, one could become an 'androgynous person'; liberation was thus effectively effected via the transcendence of bodily, reproductive limitation (Firestone, 1971). However, the implication is that the 'sexed' body is a prison, a vessel from which the true person must be released to achieve psychic integration. It suggests, effectively, that 'gendered' masculine and feminine character traits are simply 'all in the mind'. As some of my later chapters will indicate, various trends within the women's movement have become dissatisfied with what they see as a 'disembodied' form of feminism that characterized equality of persons as requiring a denial of bodily and reproductive needs. Effectively, therefore, androgyny is a latter-day form of Gnosticism, in which sexuality, embodiment and physiology are denied in order to attain enlightenment. As other commentators have remarked, androgyny for the Greeks was always a vision of the perfect man, grafting feminine qualities onto himself; effectively a colonization of the feminine by the male, rather than a true integration or deconstruction of gender distinction (Elshtain, 1987; Morawski, 1987).

Secondly, the vision of the androgyne is essentially apolitical. Change is effected through psychic transformation, by the cultivation of desirable personality traits, rather than political action or social change. At a time when many supporters of the women's movement were engaging with issues of economic disadvantage and violence against women, and were campaigning for policy and legal measures to end structural discrimination against women, the concept of androgyny seemed individualistic, utopian and quietist. It failed to take account of the systematic denigration of the 'feminine' qualities – as identified by de Beauvoir and later critics – in assuming that women and men were equally placed to merge and assimilate personality traits. Thus, the extent to which Western culture rested upon a systematic denial and expulsion of qualities, activities and symbolism associated with 'the feminine' and women, also exposed the extent to which gender imbued the deepest structures of society.

Another criticism that could be levelled against androgyny – and at many of the theories of 'socialization' – was the sense in which gender identity was intimately and deeply ingrained in our psyches. It questioned whether gender identity, albeit constructed, could be changed at will – not just because 'external' factors of discrimination and oppression left us less than free agents, but also because every individual carried ambivalence and contradiction within their psychological make-up. As we shall see, this issue of the resistance to change, and why many feminist women found themselves colluding with sexism, as it were, against their better judgements, was one of the reasons for the turn to various psychoanalytic theories in critical theories of gender. However, the simple assumption of androgynous roles was believed to belie the complexity and deep-seated nature – extending to the unconscious – of gender identity.

Finally, as Sandra Bem remarks, androgyny rests on a fundamental contradiction. By embracing the tangible categories of 'masculine' and 'feminine', the androgyne is perceived to be deconstructing such a dichotomy. But is there not a risk that constant reference to these polarized qualities, however constructed they are seen to be, will merely perpetuate the dualism and serve to reify, rather than dissolve, the distinction?

> Androgyny inevitably focuses more on the individual's being both masculine and feminine than on the culture's having created the concepts of masculinity and femininity in the first place. Hence, androgyny can legitimately be said to reproduce precisely the gender polarization that it seeks to undercut, and to do so even in the most feminist of treatments. (Bem, 1993:125)

Thus, the emergence and decline of androgyny identifies some of the strengths and weaknesses of the sex/gender distinction. Of course, not all sex/gender analyses advocated androgyny, but the problems of androgyny as a resolution of gender inequality highlight some of the limitations of the sex/gender analysis: firstly, it provides little critical leverage on the notions of 'masculinity' and 'femininity' beyond their being cultural creations; secondly, it imputes a mind/body dualism in which embodied experience – however much that is regarded as culturally mediated – can play no part in the generation of gendered personhood; thirdly, it is individualistic in that it fails to account for structural patterns of *power*; fourthly, it assumes a parity or complementarity of masculine and feminine that is belied by cultural representations of gender difference founded on the feminine predicated as 'Otherness' and non-being.

From 'Sex' and 'Gender' to 'Power' and 'Difference'

As I have argued, some of the criticisms of androgyny undoubtedly emerged from developments in feminist theory and politics which emphasized the disparity in relations between women and men. Such analysis was less disposed to theorize about gender as psychosexual characteristics as to draw upon various forms of materialist theories which identified women's oppression in structural and institutional forms. Central to this strand of thinking was the notion of 'patriarchy' as a historical, social and interpersonal reality:

Patriarchy is the power of the fathers: a familial-social, ideological, political system in which men – by force, direct pressure, or through ritual, tradition, law and language, customs, etiquette, education, and the division of labor, determine what part women shall or shall not play, and in which the female is everywhere subsumed under the male . . .

Under patriarchy, I may live in *purdah* or drive a truck; . . . I may become a hereditary or elected head of state or wash the underwear of a millionaire's wife; I may serve my husband his early-morning coffee within the clay walls of a Berber village or march in an academic procession; whatever my status or situation, my derived economic class, or my sexual preference, I live under the power of the fathers, and I have access only to so much of privilege or influence as the patriarchy is willing to accede to me, and only for so long as I will pay the price for male approval. (Rich, 1976:40–41)

From 'radical' feminism, therefore, critical studies of gender received an analysis of gender relations as founded upon the sexual control and coercion of women by men. The construction of hetero-sexuality – and its supporting institutions of marriage, the family and the sexual division of labour – is a crucial feature of gender inequality and the construction of masculinity under patriarchy: men's objectification of women, through sexual harassment, violence, pornography and legal/social discrimination are believed to be endemic to male-female relations. Such divisions are 'naturalized' by depicting women as biologically predisposed to passivity and men to aggression. Women who experienced assault by men were accused of failing to control over-violent masculine instincts, and of provoking their assailants by inappropriate or irresponsible behaviour (Richardson, 1993; Jaggar, 1983).

However, alternative perspectives argue that violence against women is not an expression of uncontrollable sexual desire but of men's fear and hatred of women. This, with the analysis of hetero-sexual masculinity as founded on the denial of traits regarded as 'feminine', and the association of male-female relations with sexual coercion (Brittain, 1989), has focused critical attention on the nature of unequal power relations between women and men – and the legal, sexual and ideological means of their enforcement – as constituting the core of gender divisions.

Further shifts away from gender understood as individualized character traits, towards analyses of the systemic and structural patterns of differentiation, have also emerged from studies of the economic and material conditions of women and men. Analyses of women in the labour market have attributed inequalities not to innate differences in ability but to structural forces which systematically marginalize women (Witz, 1993; Glendinning and Millar, 1992). Critics emphasize the importance of regarding women's position in the labour market as a result of gender stereotyping in public and private spheres. Women's prospects in paid work were conditioned by the real and perceived responsibilities of their domestic roles. The cultural expectation that women were more 'naturally' suited to maternal and caring responsibilities was held to inform a series of factors that shaped occupational destiny, from differences in educational opportunity, gender segregation in the workforce, the assumption of burdens such as 'care in the community', to lack of status in the workplace (Charles, 1993:54–102; Witz, 1993).

Globally, the phenomenon of the 'feminization of poverty' (Elson and Pearson, 1989; Wallace and Marsh, 1993; Charles, 1993:157–90) underlines the structural and cumulative factors of women's lesser status. Women's vulnerability in the labour market is compounded by their secondary position in the family and the state,   as well as within the paid economy itself. Studies of men and masculinities have also identified how important work and relations in the workplace are for the construction of particular forms of male identity (Cockburn, 1983; Morgan, 1992:120–40).

Contemporary Theories of Gender

Thus, contemporary critical enquiries into gender – identity, relations and representations – have moved from empirical studies of difference towards a broader analysis of social order and human behaviour of which gender is an integral element. This represents a shift away from addressing the extent to which women are 'hidden from history', to measuring and refuting gender difference as an absolute, innate and polarized phenomenon, and now to theorizing gender as a pattern of relations between women and men. This has been in many senses a self-reflexive shift. Contemporary theories of gender have themselves been influenced by the intellectual and political movements which have emerged in response to the challenges to, and transformations of, conventional gender roles over the past 30 years. In the case of four such movements which represent the most influential contemporary trends within theories of gender, they are advancing further the critiques of established notions of subjectivity, power and cultural meanings in the name of the wider enquiry into gender.

The Interdisciplinary Nature of Theories of Gender

I have already identified the roots of critical studies of gender as resting in the primarily clinical tests of 'sex differences' in psychology, and the investigations into the constituent elements comprising 'normal' and 'abnormal' sexual differentiation in the biological sciences. Since then, the scope of academic enquiry has become more widely established within a broad range of academic disciplines, including anthropology, psychology, biological sciences, sociology and social theory, history, philosophy and cultural studies. Some of the debates within these areas will be explored in Parts Two and Three.

However, there is also a substantial body of material which seeks an integrated and multidisciplinary analysis of gender. Recent examples include James Doyle and Michele Paludi's *Sex and Gender: The Human Experience* (1991), an overview of research perspectives and issues; Robert Connell's *Gender and Power* (1987), focusing particularly on social theory; Cynthia Fuchs Epstein's *Deceptive Distinctions* (1988), concentrating on the biological, sociological and psychological spheres; and Deborah Rhode's collection, *Theoretical Perspectives on Sexual Difference* (1990), which ranges between anthropology, biology, postmodern theory, history, ethics and legal studies. Indeed, such works may themselves be part of an interdisciplinary genre which can be traced to such earlier works as Viola Klein's *The Feminine Character* (1946; reissued 1989), and Simone de Beauvoir's 'feminist classic', *The Second Sex* (1949). Thus, interdisciplinary debates about the nature of gender, the causes of gender difference and its cultural expressions and social implications are not new and continue to develop.

It is clear that critical attention to gender is widespread across many discrete disciplines, and that a coherent overview demands a high degree of interdisciplinary integration. This very heterogeneity of theories of gender suggests that gender relations must necessarily be analysed as the product of many different dimensions and levels of human behaviour, from the realm of individual subjectivity, through relationships of cathexis and kinship, to the structural organization and institutions of the social order, and the historical, symbolic and philosophical foundations of any given culture. In addition, it is apparent that critical analysis of gender consistently challenges notions of a 'unicausal' or reductionist model. Rather, it would appear that the foundations of gender relations and gender identity are complex and multidimensional. Only an interdisciplinary perspective can adequately reflect this; and it reflects the extent to which gender is a ubiquitous phenomenon in culture and society; not simply a concern for 'women's role', but a central aspect of social relations, and thus of social theory.

The Influence of Feminist Theory and Practice

Much of the interest in gender as a category of human identity and social relations has been prompted by concern on the part of feminists to render women's lives and experiences more visible. I emphasized the necessity of seeing early post-war critical attention to gender as taking place in a wider social context in which, in everyday and institutional settings, the relationships and respective roles of women and men were changing, and 'second-wave' feminism was emerging as a movement for social and political change. This has involved critical attention to the ways in which 'patriarchal' society excludes and subordinates women; but also to the grounds upon which a specifically 'feminist' theory and practice might be articulated.

Feminist theory is not monochrome. Most commentators identify several distinct schools or perspectives within feminism, reflecting a diversity of analysis and practical strategy (Tong, 1989). The plurality of feminist *theory* may usefully be seen in the context of its dialectical relationship to feminist *politics*. Some of the earliest forms of modern feminism were 'liberal' feminism – based upon the analysis of Enlightenment liberalism in the eighteenth century – and 'socialist' feminism, inspired by the analysis and politics of Marxism and socialism in the nineteenth century. These fuelled the campaigns of so-called 'second-wave' feminism, which emerged in the 1960s and fought for a variety of equal opportunities measures. They can be seen as part of a project to end sexual discrimination by promoting the access of women to public life on equal terms with men.

Subsequently, from the early 1970s, the agenda of 'radical' or 'cultural' feminism became more apparent. It emanated from a clear articulation of the unique and distinctive nature of women. Its political and strategic goals were directed towards the creation and celebration of women's 'difference', often in opposition or contra-distinction to the qualities of what was regarded as an inherently pathological masculinity and patriarchal culture (Jaggar, 1983:106–16). More recently, forms of feminist theory have drawn upon critical movements (such as poststructuralism and psychoana-lysis) within cultural and literary studies, which have concentrated on the devices and representations by which prevailing notions of gender identity and gender relations are transmitted, and the links between cultural imagery and material politics (Tong, 1989:139–72, 217–33; Weedon, 1987).

Although to a certain extent all these varieties of feminist analysis and politics have co-existed and cross-fertilized, it is also possible to discern three distinct stages or movements within the overall deve-lopment of feminism which have particular bearing on its concep-tualization of gender. Deborah Rhode summarizes these various positions as follows:

> One strategy has been to deny the extent or essential nature of differences between men and women. A second approach has been to celebrate difference – to embrace characteristics historically asso-ciated with women and demand their equal social recognition. A third, more recent strategy attempts to dislodge difference – to challenge its centrality and its organizing premises and to recast the terms on which gender relations have traditionally been debated. (Rhode, 1990:7)

Thus, the diversity within feminism, as well as reflecting theoret-ical differences, may also be identified as existing in a tension between the perspectives of 'equality' and 'difference'. It concerns a diagnosis of gender identity which is either one of the intrinsic similarity and equality of women and men, or of the fundamental and innate bipolarity of human qualities. Pressure for equal oppor-tunities legislation was founded on an appeal to the qualities of human reason and self-determination as common to both women and men, and therefore as the bedrock of justice and freedom for all. Similarly, campaigns for equal pay and equal rights in the workplace reflected a vision of an equitable economic system in which women's work, at least in the public paid sphere, is given due reward. Certain kinds of categorical or essentialist feminism, by contrast, rest on a self-assertive naming of difference, especially the celebration of women's bodily experience as good rather than evil.

The diversity of feminist politics, and consequent proposals for change, therefore rest upon a range of diagnoses concerning the origins and mechanisms of gender difference. In scrutinizing the cultural prescriptions associated with 'femininity', identifying the social, economic and political manifestations of the subordination of women, or challenging the androcentric nature of the categories of science, knowledge and truth, feminism inevitably renders the notion of gender problematic, and invites further critical attention.

Critical Studies of Men and Masculinity

The critical study of men and masculinity has several roots. Much of the impetus has undoubtedly been prompted by the women's movement, as the changing context of women's lives prompts changes in men's self-understandings. Such responses may initially have come from male academics' exposure to academic feminist theory; but equally, they have also been prompted by men's own relationships and the changing attitudes and roles of women partners or colleagues (Morgan, 1992; Hearn, 1988).

Further interrogation of men's roles and gender identities has been stimulated by the various gay and lesbian campaigns and organizations that grew up in response to the 'Stonewall' riots in New York in 1969 (Weeks, 1977:185–206). Gay and lesbian activists and theoreticians problematized the conventional link between biological sex and sexual preference in the same way as the women's movement questioned the equation of reproductive function and gender role. Protagonists within the gay men's movements have also worked at re-examining and deconstructing 'straight' and 'gay' expressions of 'masculinity' in search of new identities and strategies (Butler, 1990; Segal, 1990:134–44).

There is a clear range of responses within the genre: as with feminism, masculinity studies diverge theoretically and politically (Ford and Hearn, 1988). Many voice distress and bewilderment at the achievements of feminism and the women's movement, arguing that women's self-discovery has left many men uncertain and dis-placed (Lyndon, 1992). Others, most notably Robert Bly, argue that, confronted by the shifting patterns and *mores* of gender transformation, men must rediscover an 'essential' masculine iden-tity, founded on the mythical powers of 'Iron John', a wild man of folklore (Bly, 1991).

As many commentators on the Iron John phenomenon have noted, it focuses its analysis on an appeal to an unreconstructed or romantic 'essence' of masculinity, arguing that men can transform their lives by retreating to the forest and 'getting in touch' with their inner 'wildness'. Critics have noted the problematic nature of such an approach, concerned that it represents a collapse back into reified notions of 'masculinity' and is, strategically speaking, purely indi-vidualistic and therapeutic, seeking personal healing, not social change. In this respect, it may be closer to solutions and strategies of androgyny, or even psychotherapy, than to a critical approach to men and masculinities operating at academic and/or political levels (Pryce, 1993; Segal, 1990).

However, most critical studies of men and masculinity take a social constructionist perspective, regarding gender identity as neither biologically nor mythologically innate, but also trying to move beyond the dualism of sex/gender distinctions. Thus, theorists show a marked tendency to refute notions of a constant or absolute category of 'men' or 'masculinity' (Segal, 1990; Morgan, 1992). The favoured perspective for the construction of gender identity there-fore attempts to integrate personal identity, power relations (men/women and men/men) and gender representation (especially the pressures and manifestations of 'being a man' in patriarchal society). There is increasing critical attention paid to the role of the male *body* in constructing and representing various manifestations of masculinity (Segal, 1990:83–103; Shilling, 1993:41–126; Nelson, 1992; Chap-man and Rutherford, 1988) and here, as we shall see in Part Two, critical studies of men and masculinity are contributing to an understanding of gender identity as necessarily a fusion of mind *and* body.

Methodological issues are to the fore in much of the material on men and masculinity: in particular, writers have emphasized the 'self-reflexive' nature of gendered experience. As Morgan (1992: 2, 37) comments, if men have been the powerful group responsible for

a particular patriarchal world-view, can they free themselves sufficiently of these hegemonic and exclusive values in order to establish
an adequate self-critique? How can men study themselves, and men
in relation to women? Perhaps significantly, much of the study of
men and masculinity is notably autobiographical, almost 'confessional' in nature (Morgan, 1992; Jackson, 1990), perhaps as an
experiment in dissolving the conventions of detached objective
'observer' of social phenomena towards an admission of writers' own
professional, personal, epistemological and political engagement
with gender issues.

Another feature of the study of men and masculinities has been
the emphasis on a plurality of masculinities: as characterized not just
by men's relationships with women, but men with men (in sexual,
institutional and inter-generational relationships), and 'criss-
crossed' by the dynamics of sexual orientation, social class, age, and
ethnicity. Lynne Segal was one of the first writers to examine in
detail the plurality of 'masculinities', insisting that no unidimensional or monolithic incarnation of masculinity was possible, given
that men's identities were always constructed within specific contexts of history, class, sexual orientation and economics
(1990:199–203). Connell advanced the notion of 'hegemonic masculinities', suggesting that masculinity is always imbued with degrees
of power and status, and that the adoption and representation of
certain forms of masculinity is never assumed independent of
relationships of power and difference to other groups – women or
other men (1987:202ff). Masculinity thus 'is something which in
part emerges out of and in part constitutes gendered encounters'
(Morgan, 1992:203).

Here, therefore, masculinity is not innate or fixed, but generated
through a pattern of social relations:

> Masculinity is not . . . the possession or non-possession of certain
> traits. It is to do with the maintenance of certain kinds of relation-
> ships, between men and women and between men. Homosociability
> is a collective name for an important set of relationships, referring not
> simply to the preference of men for each others' company, but for the
> location of these relationships in public or semi-public regions . . .
> and for the particular sets of exchanges and interdependencies that
> grow up between men. (Morgan, 1992:67)

A third aspect has been to require critical study of gender as
scrutiny of men and men's worlds rather than simply concentrating
on the status and destiny of women. By focusing on the problematic

nature of men's identity and roles, critical studies of masculinity refute the notion that men are 'normative' and 'neutral' beings, and women are the creatures who are uniquely sexual and gendered. Rather, the identity of men has also been associated with constructions and representations of 'masculinity' or 'maleness', family responsibilities or emotional lives in ways that invite more than a superficial glance. David Morgan's analysis of several sociological 'classics' for their characterization of men's relationships illustrates how even single-sex institutions are subtly 'gendered' and serve to construct particular expressions of masculinity.[1]

Much of the literature on men and masculinity emphasizes the fact that men, as well as women, are damaged and oppressed under patriarchy. The precepts of the work of Lyndon and Bly are very much of the 'wounded' male; and Mark Pryce (1993:3) articulates the conviction that men 'are distorted by sexism as well as women'. However, writers on men and masculinity generally refute the notion that the pressure of hegemonic masculinity on men is of the same proportions as women's oppression under patriarchy, a view Morgan rejects as a 'false parallelism' between the relative sufferings of women and men. Thus, perspectives of power and difference in the gendered experience of women and men may be discerned: men share with women a gendered identity, but the processes by which men inhabit and are shaped by the relations and demands of 'masculinity' will be of a different order.

The Influence of Postmodernism

Theorists of gender have turned increasingly to 'postmodern' strategies and analyses for critical tools to guide their enquiries. Like gender theory, postmodern perspectives render problematic the central issues of selfhood, social order and power, and the authority of knowledge, reason and truth. Postmodernism has aroused strong opinions, not least in what is seen by many as its nihilist and relativist tendencies, occasioned by the collapse of modernist conventions of aesthetic value and moral truth. Yet its supporters hail its effects in liberating thought and culture from a rigid conformity to scientific objectivity and the binary oppositional categories used to evaluate truth, beauty and reason. Many commentators have indeed characterized feminism as one form of postmodernism (Flax, 1987). Both movements function to challenge conventions concerning the constitution of human subjectivity, the grounds of reliable know-ledge and the foundations of social relations, language and culture – which are also the perennial themes of gender theory.

In the realm of individual subjectivity and selfhood, postmodern-ist critics have hailed what has been called 'the death of the subject'. The post-Enlightenment notion of the self as acting in full possession of the faculties of a unitary and rational consciousness has been refuted. In part, this has been due to the influence of psychoanalytic thought, based upon therapeutic strategies which disclosed the inchoate desires and drives of the pre-cultural self. Psychoanalysis claims to speak not only of the process by which 'eros' is sublimated into 'civilization'; but also of the impossibility of denying or silencing those elements of the former which are sup-planted into the unconscious.

Postmodern perspectives also challenge the categories by which we make sense of the world and which constitute the foundations of meaning and truth. The perspectives of poststructuralist criticism, especially in literary theory, semiotics and film and media studies, argue that the clarity of a text and the single, authoritative voice of the author belie a heterogeneity and fluidity of meanings (Lyotard, 1984; Weedon, 1987). This is because unified identity and definitive meaning are founded not on what Derrida termed 'the metaphysics of presence', but on 'speech-acts' validated only by cultural conven-tion (Derrida, 1978).

Post-Enlightenment notions of science and reason defend the superiority of their world-view as resting on a self-evident meta-physical truth; but postmodern epistemology denies any indepen-dent source of such a claim, apart from the conventions or 'narratives' recounted by these very authorities about themselves. The hegemony of reason and objectivity as the 'meta-narrative' which guides human affairs is revealed to rest on the contingency of story and subjectivity.

Thus, 'truth' is replaced by rhetoric and communication; and language systems have no external transcendent point to which the speaker or critic can withdraw, there to establish final and unambi-valent understanding. The self-referential nature of language implies that assertion of meaning also involves the suppression of non-meaning; but the latter remains, marginal and unvoiced, avail-able for retrieval via the 'deconstructive' attention of the reader.

Thus, deconstruction of the categories of gender identity and difference – masculinity/femininity, sex/gender, even man/woman –
emphasizes that such binary characterizations are not fixed in nature
but are the products of human discourse and culture, and are
potentially available to be recast in the service of alternative strategies (Weedon, 1987).

Post-Enlightenment faith in the powers of reason to guarantee
objective and authentic knowledge about the world is also exploded
by postmodern critics. In the work of Michel Foucault, for example,
all forms of social theory, therapy and scientific discourse are forged
from a Nietzschean 'will to power': knowledge is wielded specifically to control and coerce, representing an abuse of the pluralism of
meaning consistent with its deployment in the service of domination
and totalitarianism. It therefore follows that scientific and empirical
enquiry into aspects of gender difference, if subjected to postmodern deconstruction, will be revealed as 'ideological' forms of
knowledge, masquerading as neutral and authoritative, but effectively serving the political ends of the most powerful. However, the
extent to which such a conjunction of knowledge and power effectively relativizes *all* truth-claims has been identified as one of the
chief challenges of postmodernist thought (Tong, 1989:232–33;
Doherty, 1993:390–432).

Thus, critical attention to gender has developed since its emergence from the clinical and scientific testing of 'sex differences' to
encompass a much broader and theoretically-based set of disciplines
which seek to examine many of the most fundamental processes and
structures of Western culture and society. Many of the assumptions
and critiques outlined above are well established in academic disciplines, as well as being more widely disseminated in popular works of
feminism and men's studies. A glance in any serious bookshop, or at
publishers' catalogues for academic titles, will also reflect the extensive and sophisticated nature of 'gender studies' across the humanities and social sciences. However, it remains to be seen whether
academic theology and the Christian churches have shared in this
explosion of interest in gender issues. As I shall argue in Chapter
Two, although the churches have shared to as large a degree in
the reappraisal of gender roles and relationships as the rest of
Western society – indeed, any church debate or pronouncement on
anything to do with the rights of women, sexuality or gender
issues is guaranteed to ferment media headlines – the debate in

theological circles concerning gender identity, relations and representation has failed to engage with many of the trends and perspectives now well established in 'secular' circles.

Notes

1. For example, Morgan identifies themes in Max Weber's classic of historical sociology, *The Protestant Ethic and the Spirit of Capitalism* (1905) which exemplify the affinities between the rational accumulation of capital, individualism and Protestantism, and the construction of a particular variety of hegemonic masculinity. In *Street Corner Society* (1955), W.F. Whyte's 'classic' of ethnography, women are conspicuous by their absence; but what emerges is a study of masculinity as a study of struggle for power between men; Morgan terms it an investigation into 'homosociability' and the ways in which urban working-class masculinity is constructed through a complex and carefully-circumscribed network of relationships (Morgan, 1992:49–71).

2 · *Gender and the Churches*

'Is it a great day for feminism?' I asked a visiting Anglican priest from
Washington, DC, expectantly. 'It's a great day for the church,' she
beamed in return. (Baxter, 1994, on the ordination of the first women
priests in the Church of England, Bristol Cathedral, April 1994)

The extent to which some of the debates outlined in Chapter One are
reflected within the Christian churches and in theological debate is
the subject of this chapter. In many respects, theological engagement with gender issues mirrors many of the themes already identified in the human and social sciences. These include the debate over
whether gender is primarily a biological and ontological category, or
whether it is socially constructed; the value of the use of the terms
'masculine' and 'feminine'; appeals to a distinctive sphere of
'women's experience' and its putative origins; and questions of
power and difference in structural and political relations between
the genders. Although all these themes are present within gender
debates in the churches, many of their implications remain unex-
plored; and whilst it is clear that gender occupies a central place in
theological concerns, further debate is essential.

Many of the analyses of church and gender to emerge over the past
decade acknowledge and reveal the complexity of gender issues.
Jacqueline Field-Bibb has contributed a definitive study of debates
within the Church of England, and the Methodist and Roman
Catholic churches concerning the ordination of women (Field-Bibb,
1991). It reveals the convolution of the struggles, both on the part of
the supporters and opponents of ordination, and records in excellent
detail and with careful analysis some of the dynamics – psychological, institutional and ecclesiological – underlying the debates. It
serves as an illustration of the unconscious interplay of subjectivity,
power relations and representation in shaping attitudes and policies

of gender. Her historical analysis indicates that some of the reasons for institutional and individual resistance to the emergence of feminist theology and equality for women in the ministry are deeply entrenched in psychic, institutional and symbolic practices. The institutional churches have staked all on androcentric symbolism for humanity and God, as well as rendering appropriate subjectivity as masculine (Field-Bibb, 1991:290). No wonder that the various campaigns for greater inclusion of women should strike at the heart of such a 'father-identified' church.

However, few other studies have had the scope to examine the complexity of gender in such comprehensive detail. Nevertheless, gender as an issue emerges from a number of contemporary debates, and these will be reflected here. It is important to note that gender as an issue is intertwined with other issues: the nature of authority within the church, and whether it is possible for one denomination to institute such a radical change in church order and still remain part of a global 'catholic' church. However, complex and controversial though the issues may be, it is nevertheless instructive to examine the implicit assumptions about gender that have fuelled both the opponents and advocates of the ordination of women.

The question of the ordination of women to the priesthood, hotly debated by the churches within the Anglican Communion over the past twenty years, has aroused strong debate and is a notoriously complex issue. Another concern is that of the use of 'inclusive' language, both for the divine and for the worshipping community. The ingress of women into prominent positions of ministry raises questions about the distinctiveness or otherwise of a (gendered) pastoral presence; and many forms of emergent feminist theology also appeal to a previously silenced realm of 'women's experience' from which to build their knowledge-claims.

Priesthood as 'Male'

Opponents of the ordination of women have appealed to a particular understanding of human nature, arguing that women are biologically or ontologically unsuited for the priesthood. There are two main strands to this perspective: one concerns the nature of gender difference as functionally expressive of human sexual differentiation; and the other concerns the inability of women to embody or represent a Godhead understood as essentially 'male'.

One of the lines of dispute has been the question of whether women and men are innately or ontologically different beings, and therefore designed by nature to fulfil separate roles in church and society. Traditionalist interpretations tend to argue that men are intrinsically suited to priesthood in a way women are not. For those who subscribe to varieties of 'Natural Law', for example, priesthood expresses fundamental truths about the nature of God the creator that are essentially 'male': initiative, action, domination and, in the words of Thomas Aquinas, 'eminence'. Women are held to be tied to other qualities – passivity, reception and nurture – by virtue of their role in procreation, and therefore unsuited for leadership or priesthood. Thus, gender roles are believed to be ordained by God and sanctioned, amongst other ways, by the 'natural' created order of biology and procreation. In Stoller's terms, 'gender' is therefore effectively reduced to 'sex', and the respective roles and qualities of women and men express ontological and divinely-given orders of creation.

Thus, Graham Leonard identifies the functions of priesthood as taking the initiative, activity, creativity and innovation, which are, he believes, the 'essential' qualities of male human beings, exemplified in the sexual act; female traits being opposite but complementary: receptivity, passivity and nurturance (Leonard *et al.*, 1989). Although one might query whether his choice of qualities is the most appropriate for leadership and priesthood, Leonard's characterization of the respective roles of women and men confuses three discrete categories of human experience – biology, sexual orientation and gender identity – which in 'secular' gender studies have been analytically distinct. However, Leonard conflates them into the one essence of biological determinism: reproductive function (still bearing some rather Aristotelian vestiges of 'active' sperm and 'passive' ovum) dictating a particular form of normative heterosexual behaviour (of active husband and passive wife), which, in turn, can only lead to one pattern of gender roles (dominant masculinity and subordinate – if manipulative – femininity).

Another persistent argument in favour of an all-male priesthood is that women and men are 'equal but different', so that women can no more contemplate becoming priests than men can consider motherhood. Indeed, for many theologians, motherhood is the parallel and equivalent vocation for women. Gender difference and gender role are essentially connected; and the sexual division of labour is rooted in 'natural' and irrevocable functions.

> The vocation of every woman is to protect the world and men like a mother, as the new Eve, and to protect and purify life as the Virgin. Women must reconvert men to their essential function, which is priesthood. (P. Evdokimov, quoted in Oddie, 1984:70)

Thus, opponents of women's ordination tend to use arguments from nature to impute ontological difference; but in the process, they disregard models of gender development which emphasize a shared humanity and the importance of socialization in the adoption and assignation of gender roles.

Many of the debates about ordination have also focused on the question of representation: whether women can ever adequately represent Christ to the church at the celebration. Here, gender is intertwined with questions of eucharistic theology: whether the president is literally an icon of Christ or a representative of the worshipping community. Defenders of an all-male priesthood maintain that presidency at the eucharist is dependent on the celebrant embodying a male Christ. As God became incarnate in human form as a man – Jesus of Nazareth – then women can never be a full icon of the divine. Those who hold that maleness is essential to priesthood therefore proceed on the assumption that male gender is in some way privileged to represent the divine in a way that female gender is not.

> To speculate as to whether the Word could have become female human being is therefore not appropriate. And further, the fact that the Word became human as male is for us an essential aspect of the incarnation; to say otherwise is to negate God's revelation of himself. In the wisdom of God it was deemed fitting and right that the Son become male human being not female . . . However we may add that it does seem to be, from the human angle, more appropriate and fitting that the Second Person of the Trinity should be revealed in male rather than female form. (Leonard *et al.*, 1989:29)

The argument runs that the assumption of male gender by God in Jesus is a more fundamental aspect of the incarnation than Jesus' human nature, and that women's gender identity is subsumed by the male human incarnation. This does raise the question as to whether gender is an absolute and definitive aspect of a person's humanity in a way that ethnicity, culture, language and religion are not.

However, those who claim a shared humanity in the 'Imago Dei' are clearly arguing for the primacy of a shared human nature that may be conditioned by, but ultimately transcends, cultural or historical particularity. However, others argue that to see maleness as the primary condition of adopting human nature is inherently exclusive of women, and that Jesus' humanity and his message – and not his maleness – are the essential constituents of the incarnation. Jesus' Jewishness or Aramaic language are regarded as contingent aspects of his humanity in a way that his gender is not:

> To give a reason why the fact that Jesus was a male forbids the ordination of women is to show that the maleness of Jesus is not only something real about him, but something which is strictly constitutive for the fact that he is God-with-us. (Norris, 1984:75–76)

Others respond by saying that women as well as men are made in the divine image (Genesis 1:27) and therefore an inclusive priesthood is absolutely necessary in order fully to reflect the divine purpose in human affairs. However, those who pursue an 'ontological' view argue effectively that humanity as differentiated by gender is essential to personhood, and gender division is a universal aspect of the created order, and therefore expressive of eternal human realities.

Gender Representation and God

The debate on inclusive language is interpreted to denote the visibility or otherwise of women: to reflect 'feminine' terms more prominently within human experience. However, there may be a deeper issue, to do with the implicit assumptions buried within many other aspects of language: the appropriate activities and ambitions of women and men, the opportunities for women and men to speak directly from gendered experience, the imagery of God in relation to humanity, models of leadership and community in the church, and so on (Wren, 1989; Morley, 1984).

This is regarded as a matter of justice: a recognition that Christian tradition has become distorted in its denial of women's full humanity, and its exclusion of women from many aspects of its life. However, an alternative pattern may be recovered, of the Gospel affirmation of women's dignity and participation, and its proclamation and embodiment in the life and witness of the earliest Christians:

It is within this perennial challenge that the church must address some people's conviction that the feminine is suppressed in our liturgical language and that women are rendered invisible by the use of apparently male language to include women. (General Synod Liturgical Commission, 1989:6)

For many of the proponents of inclusive language, it serves either to reflect and perpetuate patterns of domination and exclusion, or to effect new visions of gender-inclusive relations. Such a perspective appears to acknowledge the 'political' nature of language and its power to shape as well as reflect gender relations and representations (General Synod Liturgical Commission, 1989; Morley, 1984:70).

However, the relationship between religious language and the gender of God has proved more controversial still. Here, gender becomes intertwined with theological questions to do with the function of human language in the representation of the Divine. Again, some proponents seem to be maintaining that the imagery of 'fatherhood' for the first person of the trinity is not merely accidental, but expresses something real and unchanging about the nature of God (Leonard *et al.*, 1989). Others insist that all human attempts to represent the divine are necessarily limited by the fact of their being human creations. Thus, divine imagery is always mediated by human, and gendered, experience; but this is merely metaphorical.

Brian Wren argues that resistance to inclusive language is a refusal to see language as part of a system of difference and power; to identify collusion with patterns of sexism and exclusion; to silence unfamiliar experiences or imagery, because they might challenge fixed identity and the certainty of the *status quo*. An insistence upon male generic is effectively still a refusal to admit women into full humanity: the male still represents the woman, linguistically and sacramentally, and male domination and privilege can remain. Leonard confuses the nature of divine revelation itself with the form of the human expression of that revelation: that inclusive language is attempting to overcome androcentricism in the name of its being merely a cultural convention and not a timeless truth.

Women are regarded as in some way more inherently 'sexual' and closer to nature, procreation and embodiment: all of which, according to the opponents, disqualify women from priesthood. This pattern recurs with great frequency, and, as we shall see later in this chapter, also characterizes debates about use of language and metaphor for God. A persistent underlying assumption is that language, imagery and characteristics associated with the 'feminine' or 'female' are inherently more carnal, closer to nature, procreation and embodiment, than those of the 'male'. Thus, to transpose inclusive or feminine language for humanity or the divine is in some way to 'sexualize' the object of that language. Clearly, the generically 'male' terms are not imputed as sexual in the same manner, and this essential difference disqualifies women from priesthood (Furlong, 1991:72–74). For Leonard, 'male' does not denote sexuality in the same way as 'female':

> God the Father is not a 'male' deity. In fact there is no hint of sexuality in God as God . . . There is in this Father divine characteristics which – at the human level – we would call feminine virtues or qualities. For example, compassion and patience which we believe to be in God but which we attribute more – in their human form – to women than men.
>
> So while God is presented as having (what we deem to be) the best female qualities, this God is nevertheless called Father and never Mother. (Leonard *et al.*, 1989:55–56)

The Social Construction of Gender

Supporters of a more egalitarian and inclusive church eschew such deterministic perspectives, however, preferring to adopt a perspective that, broadly, minimizes biological sex difference and sees gender as socially constructed. Many of the contemporary observers of gender in the churches adopt a straightforward 'socialization' model, in which upbringing, social and cultural expectations and media stereotyping all appear as strong factors influencing differential experience and affecting our life-chances.

> To put it bluntly, there is no biological connection between male gonads and the capacity to reason. Likewise, there is no biological connection between female sexual organs and the capacity to be intuitive, caring, or nurturing . . . There is no necessary (biological) connection between reproductive complementarity and either psychological or social role differentiation. These are the work of culture and socialization, not of 'nature'. (Ruether, 1992b:111)

The essential equality of women and men is often expressed, theologically, by reference to the unity of human persons as created in the image of God. For example, arguments from Scripture depict women and men as sharing a common humanity. Male (*Zakar*) and female (*Negebhah*) are 'seen as the crown and climax of God's creation but also because it is viewed as two sexes sharing the generic name, Adam. Both are made in the image of God' (Carey, 1983:1). Thus, women and men are distinguished by unity, equality and complementarity. Jesus, in his affirmation of the ministry and humanity of women, was only prevented by the cultural and social barriers of his day from fully appointing women as apostles. Within the early church, the universal and unconditional nature of salvation, of 'new life in Christ', was not restricted by class, race or gender (Galatians 3:28).

Rowan Williams (1984) reflects on the significance of gender and a greater awareness of steps needed to grant women a greater role in all aspects of church affairs. He expresses what is the general consensus within pro-ordination and anti-sexist opinion: that gender is socially constructed, and that biological sex difference is of uncertain and indeterminate status in its influence on human life. It is notable that in this area there is substantial 'agnosticism' concerning the nature and origins of gender difference, whereas those arguing for more 'traditional' gender roles seem more certain of the pervasive and direct effects of biological and reproductive function upon the social and ecclesial destinies of women and men.

Gender difference is therefore portrayed as a significant, but not deterministic, factor that colours all aspects of our lives. Stereotypes such as women being 'manipulative' are responses to women's lack of real autonomy, and nothing innate. Women's propensity to childcare is both biological and social, and though it may preoccupy them more than it does men, it is not a 'natural' trait.

Ruth Edwards adopts a conventionally 'social constructivist' position in distinguishing between biological and physiological difference, and intellectual, psychological and social factors. As I argued in Chapter One, however, this betrays a form of dualism and may therefore be problematic. However, Edwards does deploy the critical power of such an analysis when she argues that even the most 'obvious' sexual characteristics occur within a spectrum of behaviour and attributes. Sexual difference is much less bipolar than a series of gradations, with some individuals experiencing transsexualism. Sexual differences do not, she argues, generate a conclusive or absolute dualism in human behaviour, and cannot therefore determine cultural roles and relationships.

The common, though not universal, pattern of the male serving as provider and the female as home-maker, has led men and women to develop different characteristics of personality. Women are frequently more tender, compassionate, and skilled at the care of the weak and the young; men are often more assertive, more interested in public affairs, and more prone to cast themselves in the role of leaders . . .

But none of the qualities we have discussed are equally applicable to all men or all women. Some men are immensely tender and caring; some women sharp and aggressive. Many of the observable differences between the sexes are due to socialisation rather than inborn qualities. (Edwards, 1989:190)

Similarly, in quoting some of the surveys noted in Chapter One, Edwards concludes that evidence for intellectual or psychological difference cannot justify separate or unequal realms. No clear traits belong inherently to either gender; nor do they necessarily indicate suitability or otherwise for ordained ministry. Even if men were 'naturally' more aggressive, adventurous, strong and rational than women, would these traits necessarily be more valuable in the ordained ministry?

For the qualities needed by a Christian minister are not strong physique, high intelligence or any particular set of psychological traits, but rather spiritual and personal gifts – which can be found in women no less than men. Whether one stresses the differences between the sexes, or the overlap of their gifts and talents, on either view it is appropriate that both should be represented in the Church's leadership. (1989:190)

Edwards' arguments represent well the prevailing attitudes on the part of Christian writers who favour greater equality of women and men and who have spoken in support of women's ordained ministry by arguing that the variations between the genders give no conclusive grounds for excluding women from the priesthood. However, there does seem to be a form of dualism here: society may generate cultural differences, but the essential spiritual qualities remain, upon which 'external' cultural expectations or life-chances have no bearing. But is it quite so straightforward to insist that the reality of an individual's outlook or personality is not affected by gendered experience? Edwards' account displays some confusion: scientific differences are of questionable status; culture may influence our lives and shape us into gendered people with certain identifiable qualities and predilections; but ultimately, these do not affect the real, 'inner' person:

> It is theoretically conceivable that one day scientists might prove that women are intellectually inferior to men (or vice versa), or that men and women have inborn characteristics which make them radically different in important respects. But even if this were to happen, it would not upset this principle of the complementarity of the sexes, or show that women (or men) are unsuitable for ordination. (1989:190)

Thus, Edwards is effectively advocating a minimalist view of gender difference, and suggesting that gender actually has little or no effect on the qualities any one individual might bring as a person to the ordained ministry. She is insistent upon the equality of women for the functions of priesthood, therefore; but in the process she makes, it seems, little allowance for any distinctiveness of women's experience to be introduced anew into the life of the church. In her emphasis on complementarity – which, strangely, she seems to uphold regardless of whatever information might ever be adduced about gender at any stage in the future – Edwards loses sight of either the tension of women as subordinate, or as inhabiting discrete areas of life out of which they may conceivably minister differently to men.

Yet at the same time as advocates maintain that women are equivalent and equal to men, there are other people who campaign for women's ordination precisely because women may or will bring differential and novel experiences and qualities to the priesthood.

'Masculinity' and 'Femininity' in the Churches

The more prominent and equal participation of women in the churches and the pastoral ministry is, for many, an opportunity to affirm the 'feminine' in human experience, formerly occluded by androcentricism. 'Within every individual and every society there are masculine and feminine aspects which need to be integrated and balanced creatively' (Armstrong, 1993:228). Such a statement is an implicit commitment to a particular understanding of gender identity and gender relations, and is a very common sentiment. It is frequently claimed that a denial of 'the feminine' is psychologically damaging; pastorally, women possess qualities not fully recognized, but the inclusion of women in the ministry will offer the church a new fullness of 'feminine' sensibilities (Kelly, 1986).

Here is a typical example of an Anglican supporter of the ordination of women expounding the vision of a 'complementarity' that is assumed to be axiomatic, and will, it is believed, emerge spontaneously as a result of women's admission into the priesthood: 'Both sides would agree that God is calling us to a more balanced and fuller human partnership in which women have an equal share with men, and contribute their complementary gifts to the whole' (Baker, 1981:8). The notion of 'masculine' and 'feminine' as significant and tangible aspects of human experience is therefore equated with the need for a greater recognition of 'balance', 'complementarity' and 'inclusiveness'. Given that critical studies of gender have increasingly abandoned such concepts as cultural conventions and not empirical realities, however, it is instructive to probe theological usage of the terms. Close analysis of what theological writers mean by 'the feminine' tends to dissolve under scrutiny. According to Kelly, it is variously the telling of women's stories, gender-specific ways of knowing, and a form of moral reasoning (Kelly, 1986). He characterizes women as more prone to 'spiritual self-surrender' (1987:131) and a greater honesty about their need for self-affirmation (1987:133): but such dispositions may have been born more of women's subordination and lack of self-esteem, rather than any innate quality. Thus, qualities are regarded as innate that more properly have a social and cultural dimension. It is questionable whether the fruits of such self-abnegation should be thus lauded, and it is questionable whether the churches would benefit from internalizing patterns of behaviour constructed over millennia of oppressed experience, categorization and role assignation.

Some references to gender relations in theological literature make use of the theory of 'archetypes' propounded by C.G. Jung. Although a person's conscious self is either male or female, their unconscious will carry traces of a 'contrasexual' identity. This is adopted to characterize a version of gender complementarity, in which each individual can realize and affirm a 'shadow' gender archetype and attain wholeness (Ulanov, 1971). Femininity is represented in the unconscious by the 'anima', identified as 'tenderness, sensitivity, seduction, indefiniteness, feeling, receptivity, yielding and understanding' (1971:38) and the masculine 'animus' expresses the qualities of 'capacity to penetrate, take charge, initiate, create, to articulate and express meaning' (1971:42).

As Morgan (1992) argues, pastoral care between women and men is essentially an encounter between animus and anima; women should concentrate on developing the 'feminine' qualities of ministry. However, Jungian archetypes have been criticized for portraying culturally constructed patterns of behaviour as eternal verities, and for denying a social or historical context to human personality. Although Jungian archetype theory is influential in some branches of Christian pastoral care (Perry, 1991), it has also been heavily criticized (Goldenberg, 1993). It is instructive to note that secular psychological and psychoanalytic debates about gender give little serious consideration to analytical psychology, and that Christian pastoral psychology is exceptional in its continuing enthusiasm for Jung.

Michael Jacobs, a psychologist and pastoral theologian, challenges what he regards as the 'unconscious sexism' in psychological evocations of a distinctively 'feminine' set of qualities (1991:155–56). Too often this is derived from psychological perspectives that implicitly regard women as inferior to, and derivative of, androcentric human nature. Women occupy space designated as 'feminine' only because patriarchal prescription delineates a special role for them; but it is not autonomously derived. Instead, it is assembled from all the elements not appropriated by masculinity, or patriarchy's selection of the roles and characteristics appropriate to the dominant group.

Contemporary Roman Catholic anthropology has also drawn upon notions of the complementarity of women and men (Boff, 1987). Thus Pope John Paul II, in the Apostolic Letter *Mulieris Dignitatem* ('On the Dignity and Vocation of Women') in 1988, insisted upon the equality of women and men as 'created in the image and likeness of God', and speaks against the 'sin' of sexism. However, he still couches discussion of the true vocation of women in terms of complementarity drawn explicitly from Natural Law, in which the respective functions of male and female in procreation are extrapolated into social and cultural roles.

Rosemary Ruether argues that the anthropology of complementarity is not one of value-neutrality, equality and mutuality, because one dominant partner is still speaking on behalf of an essentially silenced and objectified group (Ruether, 1991:14–15). So long as 'femininity' is defined as the polar opposite and negation of dominant and normative 'masculinity', it is still founded on a pattern of gender traits that are fundamentally asymmetrical.

The notion of complementarity divides women and men into two ontological species, separate, superficially equal; but like other anthropologies of complementarity, it ignores the objectification of the female within such a symbolic representation. However, the complementarity of women to men derived originally from the Thomist notion of subordination and inferiority, rather than from an anthropology of equivalence and mutuality; the complementarity is therefore drawn from a notion of women's relationship to men as bound by the laws of nature, meaning that they were to be consigned to biologically circumscribed roles.

Thus, as Ruether identifies, contemporary thinking on the part of the *Magisterium* concerning human nature as male and female remains confused and trapped in a bygone era. Whilst Thomist notions of the essential inferiority of women are no longer explicitly entertained, no alternative theological anthropology is advanced, either to endorse modern thinking on the equality of the sexes, or to identify alternative Christian understandings of human nature. It still wants to draw its anthropology from Natural Law without realizing that historically this rested in faulty biology, or that contemporary scholarship on human gender eschews simplistic connections between reproductive difference and social roles.

Therefore, references to gender complementarity do not take account of the lack of mutuality with which such categories are defined, and do not pause to consider whether the idealized feminine contributions are any more than the recycled projections of patriarchal objectification.

Power and Difference

Daphne Hampson also advocates a model of masculine and feminine as cultural constructs, overlaying a biological difference. However, she introduces a sharper perspective into gender debates that questions notions of a fundamental complementarity and consensus between women and men:

> A patriarchal society has given rise to the concept that God is to be conceived as peculiarly male. God is seen as transcendent above

humankind in what is an ordered hierarchy. Since men also see themselves as above women, 'humanity' has been designated as 'feminine' in relation to God. We arrive then at a whole social construct, whereby men are seen as good and strong and more spiritual, in relation to women who tend to be seen as sinful, weak and closer to things of the earth . . . What female and the feminine stands for thus becomes locked into a whole interpretation of reality. And it should be noted that it is a hierarchical interpretation, in which woman and the feminine are conceived as inferior and often as sinful. (Hampson, 1990:97)

Hampson thus sees the creation and determination of gender roles and characteristics as a function of androcentricism: that is, they are more the result of coercion and objectification of the 'feminine' rather than an expression of gender complementarity. She thus voices a concern for the relationships of power and exclusion inherent within the formation and realization of gender difference.

Elsewhere, there is little overt discussion of discrimination or structural sexism in the churches. Yet patterns of power and difference do imbue gender relations. For example, the advent of women in professional and ordained ministry has not been a tale of equality and balance, but more one of resistance. The evidence from the Free Churches in Britain suggests that discrimination and stereotyping still exist; that equality of access has not ended resistance to women ministers by some in the churches, and that formal equality obscures more subtle forms of inequality. It would therefore indicate that despite formal ends to discrimination, church authorities and congregations do still make judgements about ministers on the basis of gender stereotyping (Ashton, 1990).

It may be tempting to regard gender as irrelevant and to prefer to regard relations between women and men as a matter of individual rights. Dowell and Williams seem to be suggesting something similar:

In ordaining people to the priesthood, there should be no talk of anyone's 'natural' fittingness, since the whole thing is a matter of God's grace. Nobody is born a priest; priests are made by a mixture of God's calling and human need. Far too much of the debate has centred upon the respective positions of 'women' and 'men' rather than the gifts of individuals, and whether the Church has need of their particular skills in the priesthood. (Dowell and Williams, 1994:35)

Dowell and Williams' assertion that we must be judged on individual characteristics alone represents a refreshing openness to all people regardless of the 'labels' of class, gender, race and so on; reflects Edwards' 'minimalist' perspective on gender difference; and verges on arguing that gender is irrelevant and immaterial to our understandings of ministry, community or identity. However, such an insouciance towards the deeper dynamics of gendered experience in human affairs may risk individualizing and fragmenting our experience, obscuring the influence of structural factors in the formation of personhood and identity.

The Distinctiveness of Women

Visions of the contribution of women to a more gender-inclusive church deploy the language of complementarity, but also speak of the distinctiveness of women's qualities and experiences. It is intriguing to note that a 'special' or 'distinctive' nature for women has been advanced by both traditionalists and feminists. This may reveal some of the implicit problems which straightforward unqualified evocations of 'difference' may encounter. Those holding an essentialist view of gender wish to confirm traditional roles for women, circumscribed by home, family and motherhood, and have appealed to women's innate capacity for such tasks by virtue of their reproductive and biological function. However, others have suggested that women have a particular contribution to make to public life, and to the life of the church in this instance, beyond their traditional roles, due also to their special nature. These distinctive qualities have long been suppressed because of women's exclusion from powerful and prominent positions; but it is argued that society will benefit from the recovery and reappraisal of such 'feminine' qualities, whether it be in new styles of leadership and decision-making, new models of ethical discourse, or renewed relationships to the realm of 'nature' through a heightened ecological awareness.

Peter Selby exposes the assumptions of those who celebrate the pastoral sensitivity of women by appealing to their supposedly 'natural' predisposition for nurture, empathy and selflessness, yet who fail to question the low level of material reward or even the lack of power associated with the caring role:

> We have all been told how good women are as carers, and that they are intrinsically possessed of selfless devotion . . . It is true that our

admiration for these skills has not been reflected in the pay scales they attract; but if the skills are supposed to come naturally (unlike those needed to run a company or fly an aeroplane) that is perhaps not surprising . . . The honour paid to the caring aptitudes of women may well be genuine, but honour does not get anyone through the supermarket checkout. (1991:125)

However, the equation of cultural expectations of women as carers with women's free and willing assumption of such roles is effectively a form of ideology: as many feminist critics have argued, social policies such as care in the community which depend upon the unpaid labour of women depend on a set of cultural expectations that designate women as 'naturally' fitted for childcare, domestic labour and interpersonal relations. It is, as Selby notes, 'a myth of origins', deriving the greater pastoral sensitivity of women and their position in the gender division of labour – the home, family and unpaid care – from their reproductive and biological functions. It gives women no choice – either to seek alternative domestic arrangements, or even to dissent from the prevailing stereotype of women as gentle, intuitive, and caring:

> To root a person's vocation in her biology is in itself an act of oppression, and to declare the vocation a high one is not so much a consolation prize, as simply a way of compounding the offence.
> The linking of pastoral gifts to the sex of a person is a sophisticated form of palmistry. The theory says in effect that you can tell that a person is predisposed to caring, if not by the lines on their hands then at least by the evidence of the missing Y-chromosome. (1991:126)

Selby is right to query the spurious link between maternal or reproductive function (which, as we shall see in Part Two, may be more subject to cultural intervention than is often supposed) and pastoral aptitude. In this respect, the discourse of women as more naturally and innately 'pastoral' betrays the confusion and determinism of many in the churches about the origins and nature of gender difference. However, in resisting the simplistic link between women as carers and women's admission into pastoral roles – and in the process challenging the collusion of this with the lack of proper recognition afforded, not because such tasks are natural but because they are performed by subordinate groups in the domestic and marginalized realm – Selby risks not granting any space for the alternative path of exploration, which is precisely to explore what differences women do and might bring into the church's ministry. If every sphere of pastoral ministry is open to women and men alike by virtue of their ability to do it all equally competently, then here is a clear appeal to gender equality and equivalence.

From his own experience of struggling against sexism, both in men-only and mixed groups, Selby concludes that patterns of conditioning create the 'differences'; implicitly he may be suggesting also that such gendered traits are not so much the properties of individuals, but collective characteristics, generated not by genetic or innate predispositions, but structural and cultural expectations and experiences:

> I am sure now that the pastoral growth which comes from the struggle against sexism does not come from the fact that women are biological females and men are biological males; in this as in so many other areas, our struggle is not against flesh and blood. Our struggle is not with our biology but with our history. (1991:130)

Thus gender relations work to separate women and men by the structural dynamics of sexism and exclusion; women's distinctiveness has emerged strategically, rather than ontologically, from a need to develop new ways of knowing and mutual solidarity in order to survive and resist. This, for Selby, rather than any 'mysterious biological reason', is the source of women's differential experience and pastoral expertise. Yet the question still remains: how will women minister from their own experiences of marginalization to develop their own authentic counter-cultural voice (Dowell and Williams, 1994:78); and will it be appropriate to consider gender difference as in any way a factor in this new pastoral presence?

One of the most outstanding features of feminist theology is its claim to articulate the perspectives, aspirations and values of a group formerly excluded from theological discourse. Whereas classical theology has traditionally claimed to speak for all human experience, feminist theologians have founded their most fundamental and primary critiques of that tradition by exposing its 'androcentric' nature. Thus, theology's claim to represent a universal human experience is countered with the claim of feminist theology to have identified and articulated, for the first time, the category of '*women's experience*', which promises to transform the partial and ideological perspectives of patriarchal theology into a more inclusive and universal vision.

Traditionally, the nature of the being of God and accounts of what it meant to be human were cast in exclusively androcentric terms: maleness as normative and superior, femaleness by implication 'misbegotten' or deficient. However, with the rise of modernity, and the greater access by women to higher education and theological study, such definitions have been challenged and exposed as linguistic practices by which social relationships of visibility, subordination, domination and power are effected. Whereas classical theology is founded on a notion of maleness as the norm of full humanity, feminist theology proceeds in the belief that women now claim a right to full humanity for themselves. Ruether argues therefore that although feminist theology identifies *women's experience* as a primary resource, it is also insisting that all elements of theology are codified human experience:

> The uniqueness of feminist theology lies not in its use of the criterion of experience but rather in its use of *women's experience*, which has been almost entirely shut out of theological reflection in the past. The use of women's experience in feminist theology, therefore, explodes as a critical force, exposing classical theology, including its codified traditions, as based on *male* experience rather than on universal human experience. (1992b:13)

Thus, feminist theology derives its critical and reconstructive power from representing women's experience as a legitimate resource for theological discourse. ' "Experience" includes experience of the divine, experience of oneself, and experience of the community and the world, in an interesting dialectic' (Ruether, 1992b:12). This commitment to rendering women's experience visible and valid constitutes a major ethical and epistemological principle:

> The critical principle of feminist theology is the promotion of the full humanity of women. Whatever denies, diminishes, or distorts the full humanity of women is, therefore, appraised as not redemptive. (Ruether, 1992b:18)

However, there is an awareness that no experience is unmediated or independent of culture. Much of the emergent work in Third World feminist theology characterizes the distinctiveness of women's perspectives as a combination of biological and cultural experience. There is a greater emphasis on the formative nature of economic and social factors upon women: of economic marginalization (as in, for example, the phenomenon of the 'feminization of poverty' (Fabella and Oduyoye, 1988)); sexual stereotyping and objectification (the prevalence of 'machismo' in Latin American culture (Tamez, 1989)); or the snares of the 'sex industry' selling women and girls into prostitution for tourists from the West and Japan in many parts of South-East Asia and the Pacific (Chung, 1991); as well as the political solidarity of many of the women's groups raised up in resistance.

Thus, women's position in society, and their unique self-understanding, is regarded as historically conditioned and socially constructed. The identity of women in third world countries is also recognized as conditioned by the interplay of class, race and gender (King, 1994). However, there are also occasional but clear references to women's 'special' and 'unique' reality to which unequivocal appeal as a source of alternative world-views is made. Often, as in this testimony from a group of feminist theologians in India, such appeal to innate qualities is juxtaposed with a critique of gender roles as formed by media images, economic inequality and sexist culture:

> Women's respect for life and their potential for motherhood give them a special sensitivity to ecological and environmental issues, and suggest the possibility of a special female contribution in this area. (Indian Theological Association in King, 1994:61)

Appeal to 'women's experience' is therefore a critical concept in feminist theology. However, as a category it has received very little critical attention, although some challenging voices are beginning to be advanced. Some of these, as in the work of Susan Brooks Thistlethwaite, echo concerns that the voices of white middle-class feminists have obscured the differential perspectives of working-class feminists, 'womanists' (Afro-American feminists) or 'mujer-ista' (Hispanic-American feminists) (Thistlethwaite, 1990). As we shall see, challenges to a single univocal category of 'women' are a major feature of contemporary feminist theory. From the perspective of theories of gender, however, the question of whether there is a unitary or fragmented 'women's experience' is related to the question of the influence of class, region and ethnicity on the structural nature of gender.

The work of Pamela Dickey Young represents the most sustained critical attention to the idea of 'women's experience' in feminist theology. She admits that the term is used more liberally than it is defined. She divides it into five subcategories: bodily; 'socialized' (culturally constructed); 'feminist' (politically orientated); historical; and individual. She avers that no experience is ever unmediated or free of cultural definition. Young identifies the complexity of these experiences, and some of the problems of interpretation involved. However, if there is unlikely to be one 'women's experience' that is not contradictory and ambivalent, there is still a key difficulty in how we can decide whether some aspects of 'women's experience' are more authentic than others, and how we gain access to them in our theological formulation. Young appears to conclude that women's 'feminist' experience guarantees such authenticity, but still fails to identify the sources and dynamics of such a process:

> Women's feminist experience is the experience of questioning all that we have been told about being women. It is the experience of refusing to take at face value anyone's definition of what it means to be a woman. It is the experience of redefining what 'woman' means by redefining whose experience counts as valuable. (Young, 1990:55)

Here, therefore, is an issue of politics and epistemology: if there is an authentic 'women's experience' attainable through critical and transformative strategies of feminism, by what criteria – of authentic or valid knowing – are such feminist definitions to be recognized? Given the complexity of women's experience, is it still a reliable or usable category upon which to base an alternative theological perspective?

Conclusion

A brief survey of some debates reveals many unanswered questions about the fundamental categories of gender identity, gender relations and representations. A major question still for many Christians – focused on ordination but present in many issues of leadership and gender roles – is whether differences between women and men are simply a matter of cultural conditioning and historical and social context, or whether there is something essential and endemic that differentiates women from men, thus suiting them for separate functions and roles in church and society.

Whilst 'essentialist' accounts of gender identity abound, the social construction of gender – and the heuristic distinction between sex and gender – has been absorbed in many other theological circles.

However, such a perspective risks anachronism at a time when secular gender debates move towards a greater theoretical and interdisciplinary sophistication. Thus, there is a need for more detailed analysis of the actual processes of cultural acquisition of gender, and whether any gender traits – such as bodily or psychic difference, or emotional and interpersonal qualities – are immutable or innate.

In terms of implicit models of gender relations within theological literature, there is also a tendency to dwell on individualistic aspects of gender identity at the expense of considering how structures and institutions – of language, symbolic representation and the sociology of knowledge – also create a gendered culture. This leads to a tendency to regard gender as an individualistic or psychological phenomenon, rather than something more deeply embedded in our culture as a whole. Similarly, the language of 'gender complementarity' betrays vestiges of a confusion between the mutual interaction of reproductive function and wider cultural roles and relations, and belies some of the secular perspectives which emphasize the disparities of power inherent in gender relations.

Another question to emerge is whether the symbolism of gender representation is associated with timeless qualities of women and men that transcend cultural conditioning; or of contingent categories of human construction. Here, we have seen in the theological literature a tendency to use the language of 'masculine' and 'feminine' to express eternal realities, in the face of criticisms which identify the latter as the negation and derivative of the former.

However, it remains to be seen whether those qualities of gender are deemed unchanging and essential to human nature, and whether they adequately reflect the complex and multidimensional nature of gender identity, relations and representation. Just how eternal are the categories of 'masculine' and 'feminine', and whether they provide helpful and authentic ways of talking about our experience, is therefore a moot point for theological discourse about gender.

In terms of theological language, the question is whether the language for God is a portrayal of actual essential qualities that are the properties of the divine, or provisional metaphors that speak of ultimate concerns in the limited and temporal tones of human experience: whether 'God [is] revealed historically, *through* Abba/ Father-Son-Spirit language, or timelessly, *as* Abba/Father-Son-Spirit' (Wren, 1991:139).

Once more, therefore, gender as an essential and immutable dimension of the nature of God – a tangible and unchanging quality that goes beyond the vagaries of human interaction – is contrasted by the notion of gender as a metaphor for human characteristics that may be helpful in drawing analogies between divine action and human behaviour. Is gender a human artefact or do the qualities of maleness and femaleness exist beyond culture and outside human agency? Can they be applied to language about God?

Finally, the churches and theology may be confronted by questions about the ethical and political implications of a time of changing gender roles. Elaine Storkey (1988:56–57) argues that if cultural roles are human creations and not natural imperatives, they need to be guided by self-conscious values. This takes us beyond simple facts about gender into questions about the values deemed fundamental to Christian relations between women and men, and the practical steps adopted to make them a reality. Given that the vision of a 'community of women and men in the church' cannot simply be derived from 'naturalistic' arguments, the challenge is to articulate and implement normative principles upon which gender roles and relations might be founded.

What strategies can we adopt as women and men to explore the possibility of difference without appropriating such traits as subordinate or deterministic; of speaking of distinctive gender experiences without doing so through the categories of power and subordination? Is it possible to talk about distinctive gender experience without using the language of otherness, inferiority and polarization? Can women and men speak from gendered vantage points without recourse to strategies of power and difference? What new ways of talking about being human can be drawn from culture and theories of gender that offer a more authentic and less distorted account than the inherited models?

The problem of the relationship of sexual and reproductive difference to Christian practice and theological ethics remains, as does that of how the church might resolve issues of gender roles. Are there alternative models of human nature founded on principles other than those of dualism and hierarchy – which informed the ancient classical accounts inherited by Christian theology – that give an account of human nature as gendered that is consistent both with available cultural evidence and orthodox Christian anthropologies?

Part II
Gender Disciplines

3 · Anthropology: Gender, Nature and Culture

Men and women are, of course, different. But they are not as different as day and night, earth and sky, yin and yang, life and death. In fact, from the standpoint of nature, men and women are closer to each other than either is to anything else – for instance, mountains, kangaroos, or coconut palms. *Far from being an expression of natural differences, exclusive gender identity is the suppression of natural similarities.* (Rubin, 1975:179–80)

The purpose of this chapter is not primarily to offer a substantive overview of accounts of gender roles within various cultures, or of the differential treatment and life-chances of women and men. The discussion will concentrate instead on the significance of debates about the cultural representations and conceptualizations of gender, and whether or not universal and causal patterns can be discerned, both in the symbolic and material destinies of women and men.

The influence of feminist scholarship in anthropology has enabled questions of gender relations to achieve a remarkable degree of prominence (MacCormack, 1981). Strathern voices the feminist anthropologists' insistence that 'what happens to women cannot be comprehended unless we look at what happens to men and women, and that what happens in that realm cannot be comprehended without attention to the overall social system' (Strathern, 1987): a valuable insight, by which gender issues in anthropological enquiry are seen as indicative of, and thoroughly integrated into, questions of social, symbolic and economic structure and practice. Strathern's article highlights some of the resistance to feminist anthropology, which whilst acknowledging the presence of the 'woman question', still marginalizes it into a separate category of gender analysis. None the less, the concept of gender is seen as central to the anthropological analysis of many institutions and customs: marriage, kinship, the family, incest taboos, reproduction and subsistence. Contemporary anthropologists are acknowledging that no social institution or practice can be studied without some consideration of gender relations therein. Anthropological studies of gender reflect the more general trends identified in Chapter One: from the earlier projects to expose androcentricism in scholarship and to refute naturalistic and polarized accounts of gender difference, more recent studies in the 'anthropology of women' focus on sexual differentiation in primate behaviour, gender roles and division of labour in early hunting-gathering societies, and the plausibility of matriarchal cultures prior to the development of private property and large-scale agrarian society. Feminist anthropologists have also attempted to redress the invisibility and marginalization of women's lives in many ethnographic studies by recording their perspectives and activities in such areas as the division of labour, kinship, power relations and religion (Di Leonardo, 1991; Mascia-Lees *et al.*, 1989).

Is Gender Universal?

Anthropologists seem to be agreed about the universal nature of gender categories within all known cultures, past and present. Salvatore Cucchiari maintains that gender is 'one of the most fundamental, and unquestionably universal, characteristics of human cultures . . . genderless human organization cannot be observed in either present or historical ethnography' (Cucchiari, 1981:31). However, this unequivocal affirmation of the universality of gender systems occurs within the context of a piece of historical hypothesizing about the origins of gender, and specifically of gender hierarchy and the subordination of women. Thus Cucchiari separates the universality of gender differentiation and stratification from any suggestion of its naturalism:

> That human beings are thought to come in two distinct varieties is primarily a cultural fact; this system of meanings is related to other meanings in the realm of culture. This does not mean, however, that the gender system is unrelated to biology. But how is it related? One is tempted to see the obvious connection between the two gender categories, man/woman, and the two biological categories, male/female. The obvious in this case, however, is misleading: Our notion of the biological or sexual dichotomy is more a product of our gender ideology than the reverse. (Cucchiari, 1981:33)

Cucchiari further emphasizes the constructed, cultural character of gender, sustained by human agency, via his discussion of the concept of the gender system:

> A gender system is a symbolic or meaning system that consists of two complementary yet mutually exclusive categories into which all human beings are placed . . . Associated with each category is a wide range of activities, attitudes, values, objects, symbols, and expectations. Although the categories – man and woman – are universal, the content of the categories varies from culture to culture, and the variation is truly impressive. (Cucchiari, 1981:32)

Anthropologists from Margaret Mead onwards have emphasized the extent to which cross-cultural data on Cucchiari's 'activities, attitudes, values, objects, symbols, and expectations' serve to challenge many of the taken-for-granted assumptions about the gender systems of the West, because they show a vast range and diversity of male/female roles. The work of Margaret Mead is regarded as the classic testimony to the cultural relativism of gender roles, at least in content and substance (Mead, 1935). The variations in cultural characterizations of the sexual division of labour and the meaning of 'masculinity' and 'femininity' between the Arapesh, Mundugamor and Tchambuli in northeastern New Guinea have been quoted extensively ever since to challenge the 'naturalism' of gender stereotypes and divisions.

Mead's reputation and research findings have been challenged, as for example in the work of Derek Freeman, who accuses Mead of falsifying substantial elements of her research evidence (Freeman, 1983). Despite these criticisms, however, Mead's general principles remain intact, and her legacy, of deploying cross-cultural evidence to illustrate the diversity and plasticity of 'human nature', continues to inform critical studies of gender (Oakley, 1972; Archer and Lloyd, 1985; Doyle and Paludi, 1991:Chapter 6). However, whilst the substantive nature of actual gender relations may vary – and indeed manifest themselves in many and various forms – it seems that along with universal gender dualism goes the ubiquity of female subordination and gender hierarchy.

Cucchiari states that few cultures have gender systems built upon more than two genders. Evidence of exceptions does exist, such as the Navajo Indians, who recognize a third gender, the *nadle*, characterized as possessing ambiguous genitals and other sexual features.

They are reported to be at liberty to wear women's clothing when engaged in women's work, and to dress as men when undertaking men's activities. However, it is by no means clear from the ethnographic evidence whether the *nadle* mediate between the other two genders specifically to reinforce the distinction, thus serving as a derivative and secondary category, rather than as a true third gender which dismantles binary opposition altogether.

The *berdache* also feature in anthropological studies of the Native Americans of North America. No physiological ambivalence was apparent, the intermediate role and identity being entirely assumed as a distinct gender in its own right (Doyle and Paludi, 1991:163–65). Amongst the Mohave Native Americans, two other gender roles existed: the *alyha* and the *hwame*, who were respectively men living as women and women living as men.

Such anthropological evidence suggests that gender identity can transcend or subvert straightforward biological functions, with cultures recognizing that gender may be adopted, changed or assumed in certain circumstances.

An important emphasis within anthropology is to link gender dualism with other cultural expressions. Despite the exceptions noted above, the majority of cultures seem to fit their notions of gender difference into a broader conceptualization which sees much of reality as existing in bipolar oppositions. Thus, nature/culture, raw/cooked, domestic/public, altruism/self-interest, gathering/hunting, female/male, seem to be dichotomies which occur throughout human culture. Inevitably, also, the first element of the pair is considered inferior or secondary to the second.

A theoretical perspective on such a human tendency to order the world into binary oppositions is provided by the structuralism of Claude Lévi-Strauss (1969). According to Lévi-Strauss, what characterizes us as human is our ability to interpret, to create worlds of meaning from our simplest observations of, and interactions with, the created order around us. The distinctive feature of structuralist thought is the claim that this interpretative process occurs via the operation of binary categories which serve as ordering principles for the human mind. The fundamental vehicle of communication which forms the basis for culture is the medium of exchange – often, the exchange of women through marriage. The whole of a culture can be decoded or translated like a language (much of Lévi-Strauss' work is drawn from the linguistic analysis of Ferdinand de Saussure), and will always reveal the essential and underlying binary structure to the observer.

The fundamental binary opposition is that of self and other, and is the foundation for the establishment of personality. This is developed on a societal or tribal basis as people construct rules for interaction, sexual conduct and trade. Thus the incest taboo is a fundamental law concerning sexual intercourse and marriage which establishes the boundaries and principles upon which humans may and may not marry, establish links of kinship and trade, and produce the next generation.

Gayle Rubin offered an early account of gender relations which utilized Lévi-Strauss' analysis of kinship structures as underpinning all social systems (Rubin, 1975). Kinship, she argues, depends upon the subordination of women, because it is the organized and controlled exchange of women by men. This requires the regulation of sexual behaviour, and in particular the imposition of heterosexuality, a gendered division of labour and female subordination. This analysis led Rubin to define what she called the 'sex/gender system', seeking to differentiate between biological difference and social organization. Through kinship systems and the resulting division of labour, she argues, women's reproductive capacities are reified and regulated – largely through the family – to bolster patriarchal domination. Gender is thus a product of social relations in which 'natural' differences are accentuated, and similarities between women and men repressed.

Thus, consideration of systems of land distribution, political institutions, cultural practices, customs and technological developments cannot be complete without attention to the role of women, marriage and sexuality. However, as many critics have noted, the actual connections between material and commodity exchange and the 'traffic in women' still remains theoretically and practically problematic (Mitchell, 1971; Connell, 1987:92ff).

Structuralism therefore posits a link between gender relations and a whole system of binary and oppositional pairs within culture as a whole. The low social and symbolic status of women is due to their association with that which is characterized as 'Other': that half of a dichotomy deemed inferior, secondary and derivative. To place the relationship of man/woman in this general cultural pattern, therefore, is to ask how such dualisms achieve and maintain their material and metaphorical significance: the processes by which human agency, both material and mental, acts upon its natural surroundings to produce a cultural and social order which is characterized by categories of domination and subordination. In the face of 'natural' evidence, therefore, cultural renditions of gender emphasize dichotomy and difference at the expense of similarity:

> Our notion of the biological or sexual dichotomy is more a product of our gender ideology than the reverse . . . If gender runs counter to biology – even moulds it to its own image – what are the constraints on the gender system that produce its universally dual character? (Cucchiari, 1981:33)

Gender, Nature and Culture

The line of argument relating women's subordination to polarizations between nature and culture is developed in detail in Sherry Ortner's article, 'Is female to male as nature is to culture?' (1974), in which she attempts to offer a causal analysis of such a universal phenomenon. Biological facts do not explain the degree of sexual divisions; gender asymmetry is accorded significance via cultural systems of value and prestige. Women are subordinate to men because societies construct women as closer to devalued and appropriated nature. Men are regarded as the beings who can transcend nature and create culture, whereas women are required to remain tied to the reproductive and domestic sphere.

It is thus the way in which biology is rendered culturally significant which is of interest to Ortner, who is searching for a connecting factor between the biological facts and the social system. She sees gender dichotomy and hierarchy as a metaphorical transformation of the universal and innate bifurcation of nature and culture. She therefore argues that human culture acts upon physical difference to construct a cultural and evaluative hierarchy of being. Women are associated with the 'lower' aspects of human endeavour, namely nature, because of their proximity to childbirth, their necessary confinement to the domestic sphere during childrearing, and the perception of their psychic state as being more orientated towards relationality, subjectivity and nurturing.

Ortner is not arguing that any of these qualities are innate; instead, she is claiming that the universal human condition of experiencing ourselves as simultaneously rooted in a physical body and part of an abstract, psycho-cultural world made up of other individuals and inherited traditions will lead to a division of reality into rival categories of nature and culture. In that sense, she adopts the structuralist orthodoxy of binary division as constitutive of culture. Ortner argues that every human society is the outcome of the struggle to negotiate between the given order of non-human creation (nature) and the constructed, transformed world (culture). Every culture sees itself to be the product of a human attempt to 'transcend' nature, and thus as a superior category. As one sex is believed to have a greater affinity to nature than the other, so gender differentiation is mapped onto the pre-existing binary opposition of nature and culture:

> Woman's physiology, more involved more of the time with 'species of life'; woman's association with the structurally subordinate domestic context, charged with the crucial function of transforming animal-like infants into cultured beings; 'woman's psyche', appropriately moulded to mothering functions by her own socialisation and tending towards greater personalism and less mediated modes of relating – all these factors make woman appear to be rooted more directly and deeply in nature. (Ortner, 1974:84)

An extensive debate in response to Ortner's paper has since ensued. Michelle Rosaldo's article, 'Women, culture and society', also published in 1974, has been accused of following the same analytical lines as Ortner, via her (Rosaldo's) delineation of gender as organized around a cultural division between the 'domestic' and the 'public'. Rosaldo has gone some way to revise her position since then in 'The use and abuse of anthropology' (1980). The 'practice theory' of Pierre Bourdieu has also been identified as characterizing the differential spheres of women and men through a binary structuralism derivative of Durkheim's distinction between the 'sacred' and the 'profane'. All these analyses may be similarly vulnerable, like that of Lévi-Strauss, to a failure to distinguish between 'natural' and 'constructed' phenomenologies.

By way of critique of such perspectives, Brown and Jordanova set out to question the broad assumption of the universality of the nature/culture distinction, arguing that it falls prey to an essentialist understanding of gender difference, namely that differences between women and men can be derived from and reduced to biological distinctions. There is nothing inherent in the biology of women which links them to nature, nor is there an automatic

connection between nature/culture distinctions and evaluative concepts, much less systems of power and subordination. As a result,
'masculinity' and 'femininity' become fixed properties attached to
biological persons, rather than, as Brown and Jordanova wish to
suggest, being socially constructed in different ways according to
historical, economic and scientific influences:

> Women and men are products of social relations, if we change the
> social relations we change the categories 'woman' and 'man'. On both
> political and intellectual grounds we would argue that to put it at its
> bluntest, social relations determine sex differences rather than bio-
> logical sex producing social divisions between the sexes. (Brown and
> Jordanova, 1982:393)

Ortner clearly states that the boundaries between nature and
culture are culturally determined, not self-evident; but, drawing on
the work of MacCormack and Strathern, Brown and Jordanova go
further to say that the very categories themselves are not fixed, nor is
one necessarily universally valued over the other:

> Recent accounts show that nature and culture are *not* universal native
> categories, at least not in the form in which they are conceptualised in
> our society. The notion of culture as superior to and dominant over
> nature is not universal. Nor in societies which do have such concepts,
> is there necessarily a simple or consistent relationship with male and
> female. In both empirical and theoretical critiques of the debate,
> there is an implicit denial of the value of a rationalist discourse.
> Nature and culture are relativised concepts, their meaning derives
> from their place within a particular metaphysics: neither has a unique
> meaning either within Western thought or cross-culturally. (Brown
> and Jordanova, 1982:392)

MacCormack sets out to answer the dilemma posed by critiques of
Ortner, namely whether there is any logical or inevitable connection
between women and nature, and men and culture. Even within a
structuralist perspective, which claims that human mental processes
impose a binary structure on interpretations of reality, it is possible
to argue that such bipolarization is itself a cultural construct.
Pointing to a certain ambiguity in the work of Lévi-Strauss on this
account, MacCormack argues that such binary structures must not
be regarded as in some way 'innate' to human thinking. This opens
the way to an understanding of the two halves of any binary pair as
the products of certain social relations, and not pre-existent in

nature. Yet, argues MacCormack, it is not sufficient for structuralists simply to concentrate on the form or structure of binary contrasts, for they must also explore the meanings and contexts attributed to such constructs:

> Thus, although Lévi-Strauss has attempted to cast the nature-culture contrast in a timeless, value-free model concerned with the working of the human mind, ideas about nature and culture are not value-free. The 'myth' of nature is a system of arbitrary signs which relies on a social consensus for meaning. Neither the concept of nature nor that of culture is 'given', and they cannot be free from the biases of the culture in which the concepts were constructed . . . Our minds structure myth, and in a feedback loop myth instructs our perceptions of the phenomenological universe. (MacCormack, 1980:6)

Thus, the familiar metaphors of nature/culture, raw/cooked, wild/domestic, female/male cannot be taken to represent a universal human cognate structure: they are products of a cultural process which is more complex than a simple superimposition of 'meaning' upon an uncultured pre-given reality. Indeed, concludes MacCormack, there is plenty of anthropological evidence to show that nature/culture is not a universal human dichotomy; instead, we need to study the various transformative practices in which human beings engage via structures of kinship and marriage, economic activity and the division of labour in order to understand the pressures which determine cultural categories: 'The attributes we assign to gender categories are based upon our perceptions of what men and women do' (MacCormack, 1980:13).

Attention to the methods of anthropological enquiry has itself emphasized the importance of a self-critical understanding for researchers concerned with the fundamental organizing categories of any culture. It has been argued that one of the central tasks of anthropology is to question the status of the taken-for-granted categories by which any culture is ordered, and to identify the dynamics of dominant/other which inform such axiomatic dichotomies as human/non-human, civilized/primitive, culture/nature, masculine/feminine. Strathern's case study of the 'Hagen' people offers an example of a gender system not founded on a 'nature/culture' dichotomy. Instead, the organizing categories are 'rubbish' and 'prestige' respectively. Women represent anti-social, individualistic and unpredictable aspects of human endeavour, and men appear as the initiators of human activity, and as the locus of importance. The categories by which gender is characterized are not related to evocations of nature, although social hierarchy is still related to the sexual division of labour (Strathern:1980).

Similarly, Mathieu accuses anthropological accounts of gender relations of themselves frequently resting upon unexamined assumptions about the fixity of the categories of man/woman, culture/nature, and the connections between them. She challenges Edwin Ardener's thesis that women are silent and invisible in many anthropological and ethnographical writings, because women do not inhabit the public and cultural arena, which is often the only realm accessible to the anthropologist (Mathieu, 1978). Women are thus rendered inarticulate by virtue of their being enclosed in the domestic and natural world, whereas men inhabit the public, visible and authoritative field. Mathieu argues that Ardener regards women's exclusion from public view and cultural agency as something biologically derived: women are innately natural, men essentially cultural. This essentializes sexual difference and implies that biology determines social segregation and status. However, it is this very ideological expression of the fixity of gender roles in a biological 'given' which should be exposed, not endorsed, by a critical observer:

> To think of sex more or less implicitly as reified categories, complete in themselves, and to refuse to see that in each instance they are defined in a system of social relations, leads . . . to these attributes and contents becoming set *differences*, or even opposites, between the sexes. The reification is based on the model of *biological differences*: men and women have 'naturally' different behaviour, reasoning, and views of themselves and of the world. (Mathieu, 1978:59)

Such a view fails to acknowledge the impact women have on the cultural realm, and the extent to which they are active agents, and not inarticulate objects, within the shared social world of women and men. Many anthropological studies from Margaret Mead onwards portray reliable and authoritative accounts of their cultures by women, and often emphasize strategies by which women subvert or negotiate the circumscriptions of power and other cultural conventions (Mead, 1943; Di Leonardo, 1991). A more recent survey of anthropological writing on gender echoes this critique, and supports the contention that 'nature' and 'culture' are social products, rather than self-evident categories. Yanagisako and Collier argue that, unwittingly, analyses like Ortner's, and Michelle Rosaldo's domestic/public distinction, import notions of biological fixity and inevitability. The sphere of reproduction – characterized as nature, private, domestic or profane – is regarded as in some way 'essentially' that of women. Women are excluded or subordinated from the primary spheres of society because, by definition, they are tied into the functions which automatically characterize procreative roles. In a sense, 'gender' is too closely dependent on unexamined notions of 'sex', in this case reproductive and heterosexual functioning; but Yanagisako and Collier argue that such a perspective never asks 'how has our culture come to focus on coitus and parturition as the moments that above all others constitute maleness, femaleness, and human reproduction?' (1990:140).

Of course, Yanagisako and Collier ask this as members of a culture that has learned to control its birth rate, where couples can exercise choice over the timing of children, and women have an expectation that there will be significant periods of their adult life when they are not pregnant or nursing babies. However, this in itself is not a cultural or historical universal, although it does enable us to challenge the assumption that reproductive necessity is itself an immutable human imperative.

However, so long as the demands of coition and parturition are afforded primacy in the allocation of separate gender domains, gender analysis will continue to reflect the unexamined assumption that sexual reproduction determines cultural difference. Yet biology itself, as will be indicated in a later chapter, is socially constructed and liable to reflect patriarchal ideologies. The notion that 'sex' and 'biology' are in some way outside culture is a flawed understanding; but in assigning women at the point of reproduction to the extracultural sphere, anthropologists simply replicate the assumptions of their subjects, and block any further analysis of how the realm of nature is constituted. Furthermore, such a perspective runs counter to Strathern's claim that gender relations are derivative of the whole of the social order, and not simply confined to the 'domestic' or procreative sphere.

> We do not doubt that men and women are different any more than we doubt that individuals differ, generations differ, and societies differ. But we question whether the difference in reproductive function that our culture defines as the universal basis of the relations between males and females constitutes the structural basis of gender relations

in other societies and even in our own. Like kinship studies, gender studies have foundered on the unquestioned assumption that the biological difference in the functions of females and males in human sexual reproduction lies at the core of the cultural organization of women's and men's relations. Only by calling this assumption into question can we discover how cultures construct the relations between women and men . . . In dismantling the notion that sex is to gender as biology is to culture, we enlarge our analytical project to encompass the symbolic and social processes by which sex as a system of difference is itself culturally constructed. (Yanagisako and Collier, 1990:141)

The association of women:nature/men:culture in anthropological analysis represents a replication of the qualities and relationships which actually require critical deconstruction. It fails to give a satisfactory account of the hierarchy of culture over nature (or the public over the domestic, and the symbolic over the practical), beyond an assumption that the human attempt to transcend nature also presupposes a relationship of dominance. However, as I shall argue in Chapter Five, the domination of nature is itself an expression of particular forms of social organization. Thus, the categories of 'nature' and 'culture' are themselves neither reified nor stable, but depend on the contingencies of historical and cultural categorization. It is within the productive and generative processes of human agency, not in metaphysics, that the dichotomy between the two spheres, so influential in forging the metaphors and differentials of gender, has its origins.

The Origins of Gender Hierarchy

The necessity of regarding the genealogy of gender divisions as historical rather than natural has resulted in growing interest in tracing the origins of gender hierarchy, and in particular by attempting to trace the historical emergence of 'patriarchy'. Much of this analysis presupposes an earlier 'golden age' of matriarchy and goddess-worship, as in, for example, Bachofen's notion of 'Mutterrecht' or 'mother-rule', which is overturned by the gradual development of male domination (Bachofen, 1967; Lerner, 1986:22ff). This approach is criticized by Rosaldo as misguided. It represents an understandable attempt to interrogate the past in order better to interpret the present, but in its over-generalized and speculative treatment of anthropological data, it implicitly appeals to an ahistorical model of human nature:

> By using anthropology as precedent for modern arguments and claims, the 'primitive' emerges in accounts like these as the bearer of primordial human need. Women elsewhere are, it seems, the image of ourselves undressed, and the historical specificity of their lives and of our own becomes obscured. Their strengths prove that we can be strong. But ironically, and at the same time that we fight to see ourselves as cultural beings who lead socially determined lives, the movement back in evolutionary time brings inevitable appeal to biological givens and the determining impact of such 'crude' facts as demography and technology. (Rosaldo, 1980:392)

The link between 'universal' and timeless, essential human nature and existing gender systems, now and in ages past, is severed by positing the origins of gender divisions in historically changing social relationships. As Rosaldo argues, 'even universal facts are not reducible to biology' (Rosaldo, 1980:397); and the search for the temporal origins of gender is a necessary corrective to universalizing and generalizing tendencies. Such a historical enquiry needs to concentrate on the wider context of relationships between women and men, and not on concerns or activities specific to women alone:

> Thus, without denying that biological facts like reproduction leave their mark on women's lives, I would insist that facts of this sort do not themselves explain or help us to describe sexual hierarchies in relation to either domestic or public life . . . In every case, the shapes that gender takes – and so, the possibilities and implications of a sexual politics – are things to be interpreted in political and social terms, that speak initially of the relationships and opportunities men and women may enjoy, in order then to comprehend how they may come to be opposed in terms of interests, images, or styles. (Rosaldo, 1980:416)

Thus, work by anthropologists and primatologists has shifted emphasis away from earlier focus on 'man the hunter' as the primary agent of human evolution and civilization, to be superseded by greater attention to women's contribution to early hominoid development. The domestication of plants and animals – the 'gathering' mode – was always a crucial factor in the survival of early human societies; women's restricted mobility due to childcare may have influenced the initial division of labour in this direction. However, other studies of hunter-gatherer tribes suggest greater integration and equality of function. Certainly, studies of primate groups suggest a wider diversity of roles, resulting from considerable negotiation between males and females, rather than a rigid sexual division of labour (Epstein, 1988:60-71).

The quest for the origins of gender and the genesis of patriarchy has therefore attained increasing importance within anthropology. Cucchiari argues that the key concepts of anthropology – like kinship and incest taboos (defined here as any social sanctions on sexual behaviour, be that exclusive heterosexuality, possible marriage partners and so on) – are unthinkable without rigid gender definitions and distinctions. Although many kinship structures include relationships of nurture that do not depend on procreative ties, a system which failed to set any boundaries around categories like 'parent', 'child', 'sibling' and 'spouse' would have no language around which to construct the essential connections of consanguinity, procreation and inheritance which are the substance of kinship. Thus kinship is dependent on strict dichotomous gender definitions for its structure; and, as Yanagisako and Collier argue, the binary nature of gender safeguards the 'naturalism' of heterosexual desire.

Two historical analyses have been well-received in their accounts of the historical roots of patriarchy: Gerda Lerner's *The Creation of Patriarchy* (1986), and Peggy Reeves Sanday's *Female Power and Male Dominance* (1981). Both recognize that the history of gender needs to understand that gender constructs and systems are themselves historically contingent, and that history itself, in the sense of recorded data concerning the relations of women and men, is also the product of differential power relationships between the genders. Both are also concerned to trace why, at particular stages in human history, under certain economic and social processes, specific gender systems developed, embodying particular gender relations. Sanday places emphasis on schools of symbolic interactionism and anthropology which discuss the notion of 'cultural selection': why, given the infinity of cultural configurations open to women and men, should a specific system gain pre-eminence at a particular point in history?

Lerner's analysis draws upon Frederick Engels' *The Origins of the Family, Private Property and the State* in linking gender relations and the subordinate status of women with the organization of economic relations and the ensuing social order. However, she effectively 'turns Engels on his head', by speculating that the regulation and appropriation by men of women occurred prior to and as a precondition, and not a result, of private property and class. This is derived from the work of Lévi-Strauss and Meillasoux, which sees the foundation of society as resting upon the 'exchange of women', a practice whereby women's reproductive capacity is reified and exploited. However, this needs to be seen as taking place within the context of social relations, and not as the inevitable outcome of psychological or physiological qualities. Lerner therefore dismisses simplistic and unicausal explanations.

The state was modelled on the patriarchal family, and early codifications of laws relating to the public regulation of women's sexuality in the Ancient Near East (*c.* 3100–600 BCE) reveal a gradual transfer of such control from the family to the state. Symbolic representations of women in religion, and their cultic participation, are also gradually subsumed into androcentric expressions. By the time of Aristotle (384–322 BCE) the symbolic, legal and material conditions of the subordination of women were complete.

A distinguishing feature of Lerner's analysis is its clear insistence that this historical process is the product of human mediation, and rests as much in action and interpretation as in social structure or economic determinism. Even the initial phases of the enslavement of women, argues Lerner, should not be seen as evidence of some innate 'masculine' need to dominate: although one contributory factor is women's ability to bear children, and their greater physical vulnerability as a result, this is not to be understood as biologically determinant. It may be a necessary, but not a sufficient or singular, cause:

> The story of civilization is the story of men and women struggling up from necessity, from their helpless dependence on nature, to freedom and their partial mastery over nature. In this struggle women were longer confined to species-essential activities than men and were therefore more vulnerable to being disadvantaged. My argument sharply distinguishes between biological necessity, to which both men and women submitted and adapted, and culturally constructed customs and institutions, which forced women into subordinate roles. I have tried to show how it might have come to pass that women

agreed to a sexual division of labor, which would eventually disadvantage them, without having been able to foresee the later consequences. (Lerner, 1986:52)

The central concern of Sanday's work is to establish that the changing symbolic and religious representations of gender provide the most reliable source of information about its origins. Sanday thus follows Ortner and Whitehead in characterizing gender as a 'symbolic construct': gender, sexuality and reproduction are treated as created systems of meaning, rooted in social and cultural contexts, rather than self-evident realities. The role of religious belief and practice assumes some importance in providing a public, systematic set of symbols which express, perhaps in mythological form, some of the most fundamental dilemmas of the human condition. It is culture – symbols, religion and language – which makes us human and social; thus this particular genre within historical anthropology emphasizes the symbolic 'universe' of a particular culture as the key to interpreting and explaining the wider social order. It is not to be understood, however, as suggesting that the social order can be reduced to ideas alone; nor do such symbols derive from innate or essential features of human nature:

> Sex-role plans are cultural and not biological. This means that they do not derive from human genetics but from the historical and political circumstances in which people find themselves when they are forced to come to terms with their environment and themselves as a social unit. If sex-role plans were derived from the human biological structure, we would not find the variety of plans that do exist. (Sanday, 1981:15–16)

Each society therefore has its own 'script' for gender roles: ideas about what it means to be male and female and how they inter-relate, which depend upon the organization of subsistence, and human perceptions of their relationship to their environment. It is in this respect that Sanday's analysis may need to be questioned, as she posits two different kinds of orientation to the environment: an 'inner' orientation, stressing harmony and partnership with nature, emphasizing female power; and an alternative, 'outer' orientation, elevating male dominance in hunting and killing. There is, however, no suggestion on Sanday's part as to whether these distinctions are innate, or whether they derive from a process of the division of labour.

Further criticisms might also be made of Sanday's portrayal of a culture 'choosing' a particular sex-role script to accord with their material 'needs'. This smacks of theories of structural-functionalism, in that particular roles are only of use when they exhibit a certain congruence with the needs of society as a whole. Such a model underestimates the autonomy of the symbolic sphere, when Sanday has been at pains to stress the importance of such representations in their own right. Such a model is also problematic when it comes to the question of consensus or conflict over the choice or perpetuation of a particular sex-role script. In attempting to encompass a broad range of symbolic representations (relationship to environment, to sources of creative power in the universe as they form the 'sex-role script'), Sanday sacrifices questions about the complexity of historical sources, as well as failing to recognize that 'inner-outer' orientations still need to be explained as constructions of gender identity, and not as self-evident. Although Sanday discusses the sexual division of labour (Chapter 4), she appears to suggest that the division of labour is derivative of inner-outer orientation, and has little material impact in shaping conceptual patterns.

In conclusion, therefore, there is a strong emphasis within anthropology upon theories of gender relations and origins that are non-naturalistic. Cultural representations and categorizations of gender serve to enhance and polarize the differences between women and men; such symbolic dichotomies serve to construct and prescribe gender differences, rather than merely describe them:

> In other words I would see ideological intention . . . in the desire to produce a dichotomy (nature vs. culture) out of a set of combinations (all the meanings that nature and culture have in our culture, rich in semantic ambiguity). *It is the same logic which creates 'opposition' out of 'difference'*. (Strathern, 1980:179, my emphasis)

Many analyses attempting to explain the subordination of women have drawn upon binary systems of demarcation between nature and culture, profane and sacred, or domestic and public. However, by assigning women and men to respectively separate spheres, such analysis obscures the fact that such binary divisions are not pre-existent or axiomatic; nor do they inhabit human mentality in some 'innate' sense. This can be demonstrated by reference to other cultures which may have binary oppositions underpinning their symbolic representations of the world they inhabit, but do not follow some universal pattern regarding content. Similarly, universal symbolic systems do not adequately account for the historical variations and differential material manifestations of sexual subordination.

Much of the literature suggests a pattern for further interpretation which sees the key process as human transformation – effectively via different processes of applying human labour to the environment and engaging in a kind of dialectical relationship with its surroundings. Such an analysis enables us to avoid placing women and men in separate ontological spheres; instead, the relationship is one of negotiation, transcendence and transformation; a constant interplay between practical labour, symbolic construction and social structure. Lerner's historical account comes closest to this: female subordination may be universal, but it is possible to provide a coherent account of the mechanisms of this which rests in actual human *practice*.

4 · Biology: Sex, Gender and Science

> In our critique of biology, one thing becomes clear: not only must we
> not believe that biology is our destiny: we must re-examine whether it
> is even our biology. (Hubbard, 1981:217)

Biological arguments have long been used to justify gender inequalities. Appeals to the immutability and incontrovertibility of human behaviour as biologically programmed provide a perfect rationale for male domination and female subordination. The biological foundation of differences between women and men – and thus an implicit assumption that certain arrangements and roles will be more 'natural' than others – is a central issue to the study of gender. In referring to human behaviour and attributes as grounded in our 'biology', debates assume that biological facts are incontrovertible in shaping social differences and individual traits. Biological science – the study of physiological, genetic, hormonal and chromosomal features of human development – is therefore a key discipline in the debate about gender ontogeny, formation and identity. In developing a critique of much biological orthodoxy about gender, feminists have questioned its empirical accuracy.

However, critics have also advanced a model of such 'biological facts' themselves as socially constructed; and thereby begun to explore wider questions of the nature of scientific objectivity. In particular, they have theorized a link between scientific knowledge and practice (and the social context of science), and economic relations, power structures and ideology. This in turn fuels questions about the relationship of the cognitive, the conceptual and the political: how 'scientific' enquiry into sexual difference is shaped by wider cultural understandings of notions of the masculine and the feminine, and of power relations between men and women.

Biological Essentialism

The biological basis of perceived differences between women and men has been a crucial area of contention since the Scientific Revolution. In the nineteenth century, Darwinian biology was regarded as providing a scientific and objective account of human nature, and commentators on the appropriate role of women in society based many of their opinions on the principles of natural selection. Ever since, as we shall see, 'arguments from nature' from Darwin to the sociobiologists to popularizers of the 'human animal' have served as a particular kind of apologia for regarding human behaviour – including and especially gender relations – as rooted in and driven by the 'laws of nature'. In terms of sex differences, such biological essentialism maintains that the social categories 'man' and 'woman' can be defined purely in terms of biological characteristics. For many, the theory of evolution provides a model by which sexual differentiation – in morphology and reproductive specialization – is functionally necessary to ensure the survival and development of the human species.

The dissemination of Darwinism coincided with the first signs of the 'first-wave' women's movement in the 1870s. The deployment of the precepts of natural selection to resist and refute the claims of women's education, legal and political enfranchisement thus illustrates how science is often linked with cultural ideology. A popular thesis, derived from the natural sciences, of nature driven by a 'vital force', and the nervous system as governed by the circulation of finite natural energies, was first propounded by Edward Clarke, in his book *Sex in Education*, published in 1873. He argued that given the finite amount of vital energy in any human system, effort expended in one area would always be at the expense of some other function within the body. Thus, women who developed their intellectual capabilities by pursuing higher education ran the risk of impoverishing, even atrophying, their reproductive organs (Fausto-Sterling, 1985; Ehrenreich and English, 1979:113–20).[1]

Darwin himself was not interested in applying the principles of natural selection to human social organization, although many later social scientists did adopt his general theory of evolution by transposing evidence from animal and plant species into Victorian society. Effectively, they were using the language of biological science to 'naturalize' social inequalities; and projecting cultural or political metaphors back into nature, but appealing to this politicized portrayal of animal life as the model for what is natural for human beings. In particular, Social Darwinists such as Herbert Spencer speculated that because males were called to more specialized tasks than females, they were more highly evolved and were concerned to ensure a greater degree of sexual selection in order to maintain their genetic superiority. However, as Ruth Hubbard notes, the qualities deemed preferential for evolutionary progress bore a marked resemblance to the virtues of the nascent Victorian capitalist and imperialist (Hubbard, 1981:221–25).

The force of such arguments rested on what became known as 'biological essentialism': that the forces and imperatives of biology were natural and unchanging, and that gender and social behaviour were definitively and absolutely biologically determined. Thus, the conclusion was that social relations between women and men should mirror 'natural' functions; male dominance and aggression and female subordination and passivity were therefore deemed to be inevitable features of human social organization.

In the 1960s and 1970s, as the women's movement grew more prominent, research into the nature of biological sexual difference grew more critical of the simple logic of biological essentialism. A number of points were emphasized. Firstly, in developmental terms, human beings display biological bisexuality, not dimorphism, in the first stages of fetal development; the fetus only begins to exhibit physiological and genetic differentiation after six or seven weeks (Baker, 1980; Fausto-Sterling, 1985; Lambert, 1978). The process of sexual differentiation is complex, involving the respective development and interaction of many different factors. Biologically, 'sex' is shaped by a complex interplay of genetic and hormonal mechanisms. The primary and fundamental difference is genetic, depending upon differential chromosomal patterns: the two sex chromosomes of a human male are XY, those of a human female XX. However, this pair of chromosomes accounts for little more than 2 per cent of our genetic material, and the number of non-sex specific chromosomes totals 44. Genetic composition may indicate a predisposition towards certain patterns of development, but is by no means the sole factor in determining any human characteristic.

As the fetus matures, further sexual differentiation is triggered by means of the secretion of hormones; exposure to androgens determines whether the fetus will develop male characteristics. 'Biological' difference will thereafter be apparent in the following characteristics: gonadal development (ovaries and testes); pre- and post-natal hormonal elements (androgens and testosterones) and anatomical structure (internal and external sexual organs, musculature, height, body hair) (Baker, 1980; Fausto-Sterling, 1985; Archer and Lloyd, 1985:67–75). Although biological scientists tended to refer to sexual 'dimorphism' (two bodies, or two forms), in terms of physiological and behavioural differences tests revealed as much statistical variation within any single-sex sample as existed between groups of males and females (Lambert, 1978).

Evidence pertaining to dimorphism of the brain is more complicated, focusing on the extent to which neurological functions – and therefore, potentially, cognitive and psychological capability – reflect pre-natal physiological differentiation, in a process sometimes referred to as 'lateralization' of the brain. Norman Geschwind is regarded as the leading proponent of sexual differences in the brain (Epstein, 1988:52–56), although this field has had its popularizers too (Durden-Smith and de Simone, 1983). However, critics have disputed the findings of such research. It is doubtful whether the functioning of the brain is affected by differential exposure to the 'sex' hormones of testosterone or oestrogen, for example; nor is there any conclusive evidence to confirm Geschwind's thesis that the brains of males and females develop asymmetrically, and that this accounts for measured differences in linguistic or mathematical ability. Experiments reveal no significant grounds for claiming that the brains of males and females are more or less lateralized (Rogers, 1988). Indeed, there is evidence to suggest a greater variation between right-handed and left-handed groups of people than between any group of women and men! Given the complexity of the development of the brain and its relationship to other hormonal, biochemical and physiological developments, therefore, it is impossible to isolate 'brain differences' as a deterministic cause of gender-related characteristics or behaviour (Fausto-Sterling, 1985).

Critical studies of gender also quoted evidence from a range of clinical studies conducted during the 1970s on so-called 'intersexed' individuals (Bem, 1993:23–29; Archer and Lloyd, 1985:76–84). These were children who had experienced 'discordant' patterns of chromosomal or hormonal development, usually due to particular clinical syndromes.[2] As a result, they were born with various abnormalities in primary and secondary sexual characteristics; and their biological sex and reproductive status was often ambiguous due to such disorders. However, clinical tests on the psychological and physical development of such children (Money and Ehrhardt, 1972; Imperato-McGinley *et al.*, 1979) have provided the opportunity to study more closely the precise connections between biological sex and social roles.

Given the ambiguity of such children's 'sexual' identity, or absence of any straightforward connection between biological sex and social gender, it was believed that observation of the children's progress towards maturity would reveal the decisive factors in determining adult gender. The evidence pointed towards upbringing and environment as being more definitive causes than biological constituents. Although some studies emphasized that biological and morphological differences were significant in affecting behaviour (Imperato-McGinley *et al.*, 1979), it was concluded that the precise scope of such biological factors was impossible to evaluate. Thus, although physical and hormonal factors could not be discounted, ultimately gender identity seemed more decisively shaped by 'nurture' than 'nature'; however, studies tended to concur on the fixing and consolidation of gender identity as occurring in most children somewhere between the ages of two and three years (Baker, 1980; Bem, 1993).

Developmentally, therefore, males and females were most accurately represented as sharing a common physiological origin; when 'biological sex difference' was evoked, it was therefore more appropriately thought of as a continuum within which individuals may display a diversity of hormonal, physiological, neurological and reproductive features. Furthermore, the suggestion from such studies was that strong elements of learned behaviour, cultural influences and upbringing were present in gender roles. By the mid-1970s, therefore, the view of gender was that although it may have a biological basis, it was subject to significant cultural elaboration (Oakley, 1972).

Studies of psychological and cognitive traits also produced evidence which refuted notions of 'sex' as a strictly dichotomous phenomenon. Maccoby and Jacklin's review of these studies identified only four areas in which there were some discernible differences between boys and girls: girls having greater verbal ability, and boys displaying superior visual-spatial and mathematical ability, and greater degrees of aggression than girls. However, later comment-ators have challenged the conclusiveness even of these areas, and argued that these 'innate' differences in psychology may still be due to differences in upbringing (Doyle and Paludi, 1991:96–121). Anne Fausto-Sterling suggests that some of the skills may even be improved by intensive training, and that different cultures display diverse aptitudes in visual-spatial ability, depending upon their natural environment. She also challenges the statistical viability of Maccoby and Jacklin's findings, arguing that the differences are much less significant than they claim. In particular, she argues that differences in spatial skills still do not account for occupational inequalities. The ratio of males to females with above average aptitude in spatial tests is approximately 2:1; but in professions calling for such abilities, women are still disproportionately under-represented: as less than 1 per cent of chartered engineers in the USA, for example.

Other critiques of testing for psychological sex differences argue that such measurements cannot generate a 'pure' and objective record of innate differences; social contexts and the conduct of the experiments themselves will have an influence on the outcome. In particular, they focus on the dynamics of male experimenter and female subject, where a lack of assertiveness on the part of the latter may influence the rigour with which she performs (Fausto-Sterling, 1985:148ff). Thus, critics have begun to challenge the 'objectivity' of empirical scientific tests for sex differences; and enquiries into the empirical basis for gender divisions have increasingly embraced epistemological and philosophical issues relating to the construction and verification of scientific knowledge.

Sociobiology and Ideology

Since the mid-1970s, contemporary forms of Darwinian appeals to 'natural selection' have re-emerged, both in academic and popular science. Chief among these protagonists are the sociobiologists, who draw upon Darwinian concepts of natural selection to argue that differential gender roles and characteristics are determined by male and female reproductive strategies designed to ensure the optimal survival of the species. Male aggression and dominance, and female passivity and nurturance, are the means by which genetic continuity is guaranteed. Implicitly they tend to minimize cultural factors in human behaviour, and dismiss theories of socialization (Wilson, 1975, 1978; Barash, 1981; Dawkins, 1976). Much of this evidence has been central to the advancement of the 'counter-revolution' to feminism. Such movements aim to illustrate the futility of measures such as equal opportunities strategies or positive discrimination designed to improve women's life-chances, by seeking to re-establish the 'naturalism' and inevitability of gender stratification and polarity. The discipline also has its popularizers, notably the writer and television presenter Desmond Morris. Another recent contribution to this genre resurrected the studies of brain lateralization, aiming to 'prove' that there are indeed 'scientific and clinically demonstrable differences between male and female brains' (Moir and Jessel, 1989). This was serialized, amidst much publicity, in the *Daily Mail* in October 1989. However, one review advanced the opinion that its reasoning rested at the level of 'saloon-bar cliché' (Mantel, 1989).

On empirical and methodological grounds, the claims of sociobiology can be refuted with comparative ease. Given the relative marginalization of sociobiology within the scientific community, it is perhaps surprising that even relatively recent surveys of scholarship pertaining to gender should afford such prominence to the claims of the discipline, and expend considerable effort in its refutation (Lowe, 1978; Lewontin *et al.*, 1984; Sayers, 1982; Fausto-Sterling, 1985; Birke, 1986; Epstein, 1988; Doyle and Paludi, 1991). The amount of energy expended to refute sociobiology over the past fifteen years probably equals the output of the original writers. However, much of the importance of sociobiology rests in its political and epistemological significance. As Janet Sayers argues, debates about the 'scientific' foundation of sex differences tend to resurface at times of challenges by women to male enclaves of education, employment and politics (Sayers, 1982:84ff). As with the Victorians' deployment of Darwinian biology to defend a particular social order against external threats, appeals to biological data serve a useful role in offering scientific credibility and weight to the theories which support the social interests of particular groups. Marian Lowe summarizes this phenomenon when she says, 'We do not have to treat sociobiology seriously as a scientific theory of human behavior. Unfortunately, we do have to take it seriously as a political theory' (Lowe, 1978:123).

However, there is a more general sense in which many of the presuppositions of sociobiology reflect wider tendencies within more 'mainstream' science, which is regarded by some feminists as similarly inimical to critical studies of gender. Scientific studies of 'sex differences' present themselves as politically neutral and objective, whilst providing theoretical and experimental rationalizations of patriarchal values. Bias both in biological and psychological studies has been exposed, particularly in underestimating the degree to which the experimenter's own actions or presumptions influenced the final outcome, or the extent to which an unwarranted weight has been attributed to statistical differences between males and females, often at the expense of significant similarities (Doyle and Paludi, 1991; Archer and Lloyd, 1985).

In this respect, it is arguable that certain epistemological aspects of sociobiology are simply extreme expressions of tendencies within other areas of biological science.[3] One is the assumption that society is in some way a 'mirror' of the natural order. As Donna Haraway points out, concepts of the 'body politic' date back to the ancient Greeks: 'To see the structure of human groups as a mirror of natural forms has remained imaginatively and intellectually powerful' (Haraway, 1991:7). As has already been argued, much of social theory in the nineteenth century evoked the connection between social and economic development and natural – and after Darwin, evolutionary – forces. What Haraway calls 'the union of the political and the physiological' is therefore significant in identifying how so much of the discourse about culture being 'rooted' in nature, and the power of the ability to make an appeal to nature, permeates discussions about gender.

The search for biological foundations to gender differences represents an attempt to set tangible and unchanging patterns of causation, and thus to preclude programmes of change, in the name of a fixed human nature. However, many critics of such a tendency argue that the relationship between culture and nature, politics and physiology, should be reversed, so that the constructs of human *culture* may be seen as defining our concepts of '*nature*', and not the other way around (Cucchiari,1981:2).

No respected scholar argues that sexual or other biological factors are not relevant to human behaviour, but . . . the problem is how to distinguish between biological determinism, a theory of limits, and biology viewed as a range of capacities, a theory of 'biological potentiality'. We must also ask why men and women are classified in the social order in ways unrelated to their biological differences and biological functioning – that is, by their intellectual, moral, and emotional makeup. We also should identify the ways in which only the female sex is identified in terms of biology while members of the male sex are regarded as social beings. (Epstein, 1988:6)

Determinism and Reductionism

Lynda Birke identifies two further tendencies in schools of thought like sociobiology, which serve to bolster the claim that the facts of the natural world are primary and prescriptive for contemporary society (Birke, 1986:56–82). The first is the syndrome of determinism, and the second is reductionism; these may effectively be regarded as mirror images of one another. In such spheres as sexual behaviour and orientation, patterns of work and the desirability or otherwise of aggression, violence and competition in society, sociobiologists are convinced that societal outcomes are the inevitable and immutable result of our biological programming. Human biology itself is undeniable, and exercises an inexorable monopoly on the social and political order.

Deterministic theories assume that every individual possesses 'fixed' amounts of masculinity or femininity, and that these are discrete and absolute qualities which pertain to individuals, rather than being aspects of social organization. Human beings are assumed to have an innate sexuality or sex drive, and this is the sufficient and sole cause of all manifestations of behaviour. If men display aggressive sexual behaviour, like rape, that is simply the 'natural' expression of their masculinity which is proved to be functional and healthy. Women bear responsibility for triggering such urges and must modify their behaviour, dress or travel arrangements to avoid 'provoking' the male response. The double standard of such logic has been attacked as a rationalization and universalization of particular manifestations of male sexual behaviour and aggression. It removes and abstracts sexuality from the critical scrutiny of the social and political, and attempts to render gender relations immutable and amoral. Feminist resistance to sociobiology centres upon the latter's attempts to reassert such an inevitable logic and to emphasize the primacy of the biological realm over all else (Hubbard, 1981).

Reductionism also assumes the primacy of biology in human affairs by reinforcing the categories by which we classify the world around us. It assumes that levels of explanation and analysis for one level of being are adequate for other levels. So gender differences are reduced to the biological dichotomy of male and female, which is an adequate framework for understanding sexual reproduction, but resembles life less satisfactorily the further we try to extend the analysis into gender roles and characteristics.

Critics of reductionism emphasize evidence, surveyed above, that only a tiny fragment of the Y chromosome can be held to 'determine' sex by stimulating a protein which in turn sets off a chain of events diverting the fetus from female patterns of development into male ones (Fausto-Sterling, 1985; Baker, 1980). This is quite different from a reading of gender development which posits 'male' and 'female' hormones as belonging uniquely to one side or the other, and which determine an exclusive gender identity. This reflects the influence of prior conceptual and political commitments to a rigid gender dichotomy which are then projected back onto the scientific evidence, subsequently presented as irrefutable proof that simple biological polarities do exist. Other sources record the extent to which cognitive interpretation of biological evidence is coloured by interpretative frameworks. Similarly, evidence suggesting as much physiological variation within one sex group as there is between males and females presents a picture of bimodal distribution with significant overlap, rather than ontologically or biologically separate species (Birke, 1986:72). Thus it may be just as appropriate to think of a continuum in many matters of biological difference; yet gender characteristics are assumed to depend upon, and derive from, a set of primary 'facts' of sexual bipolarity.

Biological determinism and reductionism are both modes of analysis which attempt to discover one single point of origin, or one source of causation, to any phenomenon, be it sex differences in behaviour, or racial differences in intelligence. Alternatives to the primacy of causation in biology alone have been developed, which attempt to shift explanation away from exclusive concentration upon the biological, and begin to introduce some kind of social or environmental factors.

One theory posits what might be called an 'additive' model, by which 'raw' biological facts are overlaid by cultural interpretations. Janet Sayers calls this the *'social constructionist'* model: 'biology determines sexual divisions in society primarily via the way it is socially constructed within that society' (Sayers, 1982:107). This model succeeds in separating culture from nature, and therefore offers an alternative model to a simple biological determinism by severing the link between biological fact and social reality. It is implicit in the classic definition of the distinction between 'sex' and 'gender' by Robert Stoller, and in much of liberal feminism, and represents a very discrete separation between the body, which is given and sexed, and the person, who is rational, social and gendered.

This model thus posits a 'core' human being, over which environmental factors are superimposed. As Birke points out, such a view betrays its origins in liberal individualism, which maintains that human rationality is somehow pre-social, and exists in a raw state which only requires some kind of environmental vessel, the shape of which is effectively irrelevant. Thus, it operates ultimately to deny the importance of bodily needs and material contexts in the formation of human identity. In their attempts to break the stranglehold of biological determinism, the additive theorists seem to surrender hostages to fortune in a kind of 'biological agnosticism': bodies and minds are separate, what matters is the essential rational person. It posits a form of philosophical idealism as the solution.

Yet the experience of many women would attest to the significance of bodily needs and representations as in fact highly crucial to the formation and mediation of gender relations and identities. As feminist critics of biotechnology have argued, medical control of women's bodies is a powerful tool of the existing gender system. Shulamith Firestone's (1971) advocacy of a non-patriarchal future in which women were allowed to transcend their physiology by technological advances has not come to pass. Donna Haraway, responding to Firestone's vision, argues that this sort of feminism represents an effective denial of the body (Haraway, 1991:10). Our physiology is not so much transcended as ignored completely. Such a view of liberation, that it can take place independent of physical bodies, therefore still assumes a profound dualism.

Sayers argues that social constructionism can also serve to obscure the real needs of women, by underplaying the reality and impact of physical experiences like menstruation. For many women, menstruation is physically and mentally stressful; but practical responses – for example in offering better facilities at the workplace – need to be undertaken, which acknowledge such discomfort without 'enclosing' women in their difference (de Beauvoir in Simons and Benjamin, 1979, quoted in Sayers, 1982:118). This suggests that what is required is not an abandonment of the connection between bodily experience and personal identity – even gender identity – but a severing of bodiliness from an association with ontological inferiority and gender polarity.

Critics of social constructionism therefore contribute the important insight that it is important not to dismiss the link between ideas and material circumstances, even though it is necessary to reject any deterministic or reductionist accounts of the relationship between biological sex and social and cultural gender. One criticism of both sets of theories is that by locating the prime and exclusive generation of gender in either the body or society, they do not enable these factors to engage in any kind of interaction. Neither biological essentialism nor social constructionism – both forms of deterministic, unicausal thinking – are therefore adequate or satisfactory.

Writers in the 1960s and 1970s therefore began to develop a perspective which attempted to synthesize the alternatives of sole biological agency and the total denial of physicality altogether. Such theories may be characterized as 'interactionist', and they attempt to bridge the gulf between the two poles of body and society, or 'nature' and 'nurture'. In an essay assessing the debate about the status of biological influences in determining sex differences, published in 1978, Helen Lambert opts for an analysis within which biology and social factors combine to contribute elements of an individual's traits and attributes:

> The composite result may be a biological difference, in the sense of having a basis in neural organisation but not in the sense of being determined entirely by intrinsic factors specific to women . . . It seems likely that complex, multiple causation is the rule for this and many other behavioral sex differences. *Social environment multiplies and magnifies, in many ways, an average kernel of intrinsic predisposition.* (Lambert, 1978:113, my emphasis)

Interactionism has been exposed to criticism on a number of grounds. Birke argues that implicit within the notion of interaction is the assumption that nature and environment are still discrete factors. This then leaves open the possibility for claims to be made that at least some of a given behaviour is due to universal biological characteristics whose features remain unchanged in the process of interaction. Such a process is, for some critics, no less unsatisfactory than the additive model; it is seen implicitly to privilege a foundational and unitary human nature which, whilst acting within a cultural context, is not fundamentally constituted by social factors, or absolutely dependent upon an entry into culture to be considered fully human:

> Although the problem of correctly describing human behaviour is a serious one, the deeper issue lies with the very notion of human essence – not with the idea that there is a human nature, but with the thought that there is a *particular* human nature, visible when all culture and learning is stripped away . . . The notion of a naked human essence is meaningless because human behavior acquires significance only in a particular social context. (Fausto-Sterling, 1985:196)

The vulnerability of interactionism was further exposed by the debate which ensued after the publication in 1977 of a paper by Alice Rossi, 'A biosocial perspective on parenting'. Although critics acknowledged the legitimacy of her insistence that feminist theory should reflect women's experiences and activities of childbearing, concern focused on her use of the term 'innate' to describe a greater intrinsic predisposition of mothers over fathers in their readiness and aptitude to care for and bond with their child. Commentators argued that Rossi's perspective, whilst acknowledging the influence of environmental and social factors, nonetheless posited given biological proclivities as definitive and primary:

> In the biosocial perspective, biological factors are treated as a starting point for human choice. The formal model of the biosocial perspective proposes interdependence and interaction between genetic, hormonal, and environmental factors. Social factors – psychological and sociological – are included in the list . . . In practice, however, biological factors are given precedence. Our ability to create culture is excluded from our mammalian heritage. Hence, culture stands apart, suspect as something that may inadvertently distort our biology. (Nona Glazer in Gross *et al.*, 1979:701)

However, so long as the category of biology remains unqualified and unreconstructed, any attempt to retain the legitimacy of reproductive or somatic experience will be vulnerable to charges of essentialism or reductionism. Dissatisfaction with an interactionist model has therefore led some theorists to propose a further model, which sees the interplay within biology and environment in terms of a *dialectical* relationship. For example, Emily Martin illustrates the latest 'integrated' perspective by using the analogy of a cake to emphasize the complex inter-relation of a number of factors in human gender development. Quite clearly, cakes are different from cake ingredients and mixtures; so this model emphasizes a view of causation which identifies how a finished product – be it a chocolate cake or a woman – is made through the combination of different elements, but takes on an independent and transformed character which is ultimately unique and distinctive. The cake analogy gains even more significance, says Martin, if we are told that it was:

> . . . chocolate, baked by a 64-year-old widow on the occasion of her only daughter's departure for an extended residence abroad. Adding these complexities, we would be hard pressed to say how much the bittersweet taste of the finished cake was due to the chocolate and how much was due to the social significance of the occasion. (Martin, 1989:12)

This reflects Martin's argument that material factors alone cannot tell the entire story, and that human subjectivity must be integrated into any account of gender formation. Clearly, the kind of meanings we attach to all human experience, but perhaps especially to bodily experiences, cast doubt on some of the mechanistic, unicausal accounts to be found in other more deterministic theories. Yet, as Martin argues, many scientific and medical accounts of women assume such a mechanistic air, treating menstruation, childbirth and menopause as functional events, unrelated to the minds and lives of real women. Such perspectives call into question the extent to which minds and bodies can in real human experience be separated, but also suggest that such a dichotomy may be ideological in sustaining women's passivity in the face of the scientific and medical establishment.

It may be possible to think of many aspects of human history and culture in which our 'biology' has been significantly transformed by social evolution and human agency. Innovations in medical science and technology have transformed the potential of scientific and technological intervention: for example, surgery which ranges from alterations to physical appearances for cosmetic reasons, to full 'sex-change' treatment. However, there are less dramatic, although no less controversial, areas: the control or modification of physical and mental conditions through the use of drug treatments, preventive health care such as inoculation and public health measures, or radiological or pharmacological treatments of cancer and other diseases. Arguably, the reliability of modern methods of contraception has given women unprecedented control over their own fertility, and this may actually constitute the most significant causal factor in the changing expectations of women and the transformation of gender relations that has taken place this century. Medical science can now manipulate the very genetic basis of life itself; using new reproductive technologies children are born to parents for whom 'natural' processes offered only infertility. The fact is, the human brain has conjured myriad possibilities for manipulating and transcending 'nature'. This has not removed humanity from nature, but merely placed us in ever new and complex relationships with nature, albeit mediated by new technologies:

> Of course, there would be no birth without wombs or sight without eyes or intelligence without brains. But humans can decide to have twenty children or none, to be myopic or to see far into other galaxies, to become informed or to burn books. As humans are ordered by nature, so too do they order it. (Epstein, 1988:71)

Such a dialectical account of gender therefore sees a complex and multidimensioned relationship between biology, social conditioning and individual consciousness. So intertwined, indeed, are the various components, that it becomes difficult to make any meaningful differentiation between biology and culture, or nature and nurture. This model begins to undermine any notion of fixity and stability in such categories, along with the utility, indeed the veracity, of the polarity of categories such as 'nature' and 'culture'. It may be convenient to talk about 'biological' and 'environmental' factors, but it is also necessary to recognize that these appear as a result of processes of enquiry, that they are effectively artefacts of science, and not naturally occurring, universal features of reality. Human biology is not static and unchanging, a foundation upon which society constructs itself; it too, can be part of a wider dialectic between what we broadly call 'nature' and 'culture':

> There is no way to tease apart genetic and environmental factors in human development or to know where genetic effects end and environmental ones begin; in fact, this is a meaningless way to view the problem since from conception the relationships between the gene's protein synthesizing activity and the fetus' maternal environment are interdependent. As Lappé has said, 'Genes and environments do not simply "add up" to produce a whole. The manner in which nature and nurture interact to cause biological organisms to flourish or decline is an extraordinarily complex problem'. (Bleier, 1984:43)

Such a view of gender, as a process, constantly in a state of being reconstructed, renegotiated or reinforced, rather than as the fixed property of an individual, or the inexorable outcome of an immutable determinism, offers much potential for a renewed understanding of human personality and behaviour. For example, it suggests that gender identity may be affected, but not in a deterministic fashion, by bodily changes at puberty, pregnancy and old age; and that major surgery, such as mastectomy, could profoundly affect gender identity. These are not simple mechanistic changes which set off a predictable train of behavioural consequences; they are only available to us via interpretation and social context. What is more, such changes may be biologically imposed (by the passage of time and physical maturation), but may also be chosen, as in changes in body shape, metabolism and capability through exercise. Many biological functions, such as body size, strength, hormone levels and brain development, can actually be affected by changes in environment, be that nutrition, lifestyle or other physical surroundings. Ruth Hubbard argues that such an interplay of biology and environment is practically axiomatic when we consider the differential upbringing of boys and girls in our society:

> If a society puts half its children into short skirts and warns them not to move in ways that reveal their panties, while putting the other half into jeans and overalls and encouraging them to climb trees, play ball, and participate in other vigorous outdoor games; if later, during adolescence, the children who have been wearing trousers are urged to 'eat like growing boys', while the children in skirts are warned to watch their weight and not get fat; if the half in jeans runs around in sneakers and boots, while the half in skirts totters about on spike

heels, then these two groups of people will be biologically as well as socially different. Their muscles will be different, as will their reflexes, posture, arms, legs and feet, hand-eye coordination, and so on . . . There is no way to sort the biological and social components that produce these differences. (Hubbard, 1990:69)

What is more, such 'natural' changes are events which we actively interpret; bodily phenomena are thus never independent of human interpretation within a wider social context. Thus Bleier argues as follows:

Human behaviours are the products of our brains-minds-bodies responding to their environments; . . . the brain-mind itself, like the rest of our body, has evolved genetically *and* in dynamic interaction with its environment; . . . all developments and behavior must be seen as the product of continuous interactions between biological and environmental influences from the time of conception; and . . . the capacity of the brain to be modified by environment and experience, to *learn*, to acquire language, and to *invent* has freed human behaviors from stereotypical or pre-determined responses to biological factors, though not, unfortunately, to cultural forces . . . Biology can be said to define possibilities but not determine them; it is never irrelevant but it is also not determinant. (Bleier, 1984:52)

The danger of such a perspective is that we begin to see gender as something more plastic and less binding than it really is. From seeing gender as determined by the fact of an individual's being born into one biological sex or another, we are in danger of going to the opposite extreme: of regarding gender as a mere psychological attribute, a function of personal choice: private, individualized and existential. This bears some comparison to the voluntaristic perspective of androgyny as ultimately discrete from social and biological influences or from power relations. By way of analogy, it may be noted that sociologists of medicine, whilst receptive to notions of personal agency and subjectivity, resist notions that 'health' may be regarded as entirely a question of personal lifestyle or propensity to germs. However, certain forms of behaviour can increase chances of good or bad morbidity and mortality, but we must not allow the 'cult of choice' to blinker us to the economic and environmental contributions to health and sickness (Townsend and Davidson, 1982).

As with health, so with gender: a dialectical understanding of gender which allows for some freedom from physiological reductionism must also avoid an individualistic and voluntaristic agenda which over-privileges personal subjectivity. Clearly, although it is social convention which binds us to particular experiences of ourselves, the power with which these conventions govern us, even to the point of collusion, should not be underestimated. More specifically, power relations which constrain personal freedom to negotiate between biology and culture will affect women differently from men, as Ruth Hubbard's example illustrates.

Indeed, the intersection between subjectivity or consciousness, social structure and ideology, has proved a fruitful area for gender theorists. A number of issues can be identified as occupying their attention. Firstly, although the rhetoric may characterize human nature as multivalent and complex and the causative processes of gender identity as dialectical and anti-deterministic, the reality is that we live in worlds which appear to mirror the natural order, and experience ourselves as unable to transform or transcend physiological destiny. Bleier echoes much writing in psychoanalysis and social theory when she articulates this problem from the biosocial scientist's perspective: 'we have the paradox of a brain, structurally and functionally capable of permitting a nearly limitless variety of behavioral responses, being constrained in the full range of its possible expression by the cultures it has itself produced' (Bleier, 1984:52).

Secondly, definitions of scientific objectivity need to be examined more closely. The argument is advanced that biology is itself part of the ideology of gender inequality, rather than an independent authority which can offer neutral arbitration on the 'facts': 'Popular ideas about sex differences in biology are . . . not necessarily based on actual knowledge and understanding of biological data, but are, rather, rooted in the ideology of women's place in Nature' (Bartels, 1982:254).

Thus feminists writing in this area have attempted to articulate theories of gender which retain attention to physiological factors, but which see scientific interpretations of them as inextricably bound up with the gender relations which they attempt to describe and explain. Thus we return to the political significance and function of theories like sociobiology, and the realization that biology is not a value-neutral, objective set of facts about women, bodies or gender differences. In Part Three, I shall be reviewing in more detail some of the debates within feminist philosophies of science which attempt to expose the androcentric bias of much research, and which aim to generate the conditions – and the epistemology – appropriate for a feminist 'successor science'. For the time being, however, it is clear that one implication of a critique of science as value-free, reflecting a physical or natural reality immune from ideological distortion, is that science itself – and notions of objectivity and value-freedom – must be seen as a human creation, existing within conventions of language, cultural imagery and gender divisions:

> It is apparent that the importance attached to biological explanations of sex, race or class differences in ability, behavior, or social role comes from the political context of the theories rather than from their scientific merit. If race, sex and class were not politically and eco-nomically significant categories, it is likely that no one would care very much about biological differences between members of these groups. To pay attention to the study of sex differences would be rather peculiar in a society where their political importance was small. Biological determinant theories, which pretend to explain why the world is the way it is, are built on the myth that social structures are determined by the biological nature of human beings. (Lowe, 1978:55)

On the contrary, feminist critics of the 'givenness' of biological facts argue that the categories presented as objective and unassail-able must be seen as products of androcentric discourse. In particu-lar, what biology claims to discover and observe as 'natural facts' and as truthful reflections of an external reality must be challenged. Furthermore, feminist biological scientists are questioning the relia-bility of the very distinctions between 'biology' and 'environment', thereby reflecting similar opinions in anthropology which cast doubt on the self-evidence and universality of the distinction between categories of 'nature' and 'culture'.

Critics of theories which support sex or race difference usually emphasize the extent to which such claims are supported by 'bad' science. This is generally supposed to mean that the 'facts' about human nature have been distorted by politically biased and irrespons-ible scientists – such as sociobiologists – who have not been telling the 'truth' (Bleier, 1984:Chapters 1, 2 and 8). 'Bad' science is assumed to be a poor approximation to the (objective) truth, but this obscures the social context and ideological aspect of scientific dis-course. Also, such an account of the distorting offences committed by a few ideologues against an innocent, value-free science is further challenged by this alternative reading of the relationship between scientific 'facts' and the social context which produces them.

It is therefore necessary to begin to construct plausible theories which trace alternative patterns of causation. Part of the scientific 'mystique' of biology is the assumption that it does refer to a real world of nature: but what happens when that is exposed, when it is asserted that our accounts of the supposedly pre-given, essential parts of human nature are simply products of our own construction? Many feminist accounts of such issues are using the analytical and explanatory tools of postmodernism to assist them in these explorations.

Donna Haraway argues that the relationship between scientific representations of – in most instances – women's nature and wider social relations is always open to reinterpretation. There is no objective truth, because such facts cannot exist independent of the framework established to tell the story (Haraway, 1987). She rejects Janet Sayers' attempts to acknowledge women's actual experiences of their own bodies as unsatisfactory because of their subtle Idealism and dualism. Sayers confuses reality with representation, and mistakes historical and cultural constructions of nature and bodies for actual physical experience:

> The word *biology* is a stand-in for the body itself. 'Biology' is repeatedly claimed to do or not to do this or that: biology here is a thing, itself without history, not a socially constructed discourse with highly mediated connections to what I will call our bodies. For Sayers, biology is a social text, not a body. But her apparent firm materialism seems finally rooted in a curious idealism that mistakes the discourse for the body. (Haraway, 1987:63)

Haraway therefore refutes even the 'dialectical' model, because all such dichotomies protect us, wrongly in Haraway's opinion, from seeing the ideological appropriation behind the division between Idealism and materialism, between a 'thing' and the way we talk about it. Any connection between the signified – human bodily experience and the natural order – and the traditional signifier, 'biology', which has been assumed to grant us unbiased access to the world of real nature, is purely contingent. Nature and bodies do not exist in some pre-ordered state, independent of, or external to, language. Such a perspective represents a considerable challenge to, and potential for, our analysis. Part of the answer to this is to understand that we are heirs to historical cultural products which have classified nature in certain ways for particular reasons.

In a recent survey article, Ruth Hubbard summarizes the main characteristics of the 'additive', 'interactive' and 'dialectical' models of biology and culture; but, reflecting the postmodern turn in such accounts, she adds a fourth model, which she names *complementarity* (Hubbard, 1990:68ff). Its characteristics draw upon the qualities of quantum physics, which states that the basic constitution of matter – light, for example – is not essential but contingent, being simultaneously wave-like and particle-like. Whichever description is used or deemed appropriate is a function of the process of observation, not a fundamental property of light itself. This position, says Hubbard, establishes clearly that the very categories of 'biology' and 'environment' are themselves the products of the *practice* of scientific enquiry. The distinctions between any element of human behaviour and identity are therefore socially – or scientifically – constructed, and not part of the natural order, because 'nature' itself cannot be understood to exist apart from human discourse. This in turn, for Hubbard, challenges theories – like sociobiology – which rely on an *a priori* human nature to support their claims. In that sense, she argues, there is no such thing as an abstract or essential human nature; all we have is human agency and activity: 'It is questionable whether the concept of human nature means anything. People's "nature" can be described only by looking at the things we do' (Hubbard, 1990:70).

Just as the fixity and discreteness of the categories of 'biological', 'environmental' and 'social' have to be questioned, so do straightforward models of causation which isolate one genetic or hormonal factor as the 'master key' to gender. The challenge is to develop new models of gender development which do not place biology as the sole agent of causation, but allow a number of factors to interact. However, a necessary aspect of such an enquiry must also embrace critical questions into the very nature of scientific practice itself. Feminists have exposed the 'objective' claims of scientific knowledge; in particular, as here shown, within the biological and natural sciences, as reflecting the social and cultural biases of their creators. It has been strongly suggested that science itself is 'gendered', in that standards of enquiry, procedure and verification in some way reflect androcentric values which operate to support and rationalize the structures of patriarchy.

However, some of the difficulties inherent in certain kinds of feminist claims to an alternative type of knowledge, some kind of 'woman-centred' epistemology, will be developed further in Chapter Nine. For the moment, it is necessary to note that considerations of theories of gender in biological science serve to problematize questions of what we know and how we interpret, what is counted as knowledge and how we can evaluate knowledge as objective and valid. As the unfolding hypotheses within the biological and natural sciences about the nature of gender reveal, enquiry into gender difference leads us into questions about knowledge, rationality and objectivity, and the necessity of analysing how claims to know and report upon 'natural facts' actually have their roots in social relations and human practice.

Notes

1. Unfortunately for the opponents of women's emancipation, the women who were granted opportunities to enter the male worlds of education and public life appeared to thrive, physically and intellectually. However, there may still be vestiges of this attitude in stereotypes of powerful women as risking their femininity, and of the 'masculinizing' effects of power and status (Sayers, 1982:Chapter 2).

2. 'Abnormalities' in chromosomal development include 'Turner's Syndrome' in which a female has no second X chromosome, resulting in malformation of the ovaries; 'Klinefelter's Syndrome', an excess of chromosomes in males; 'Double-Y Syndrome', in which the sex chromosomes are YY rather than XY in males. There are also a number of pre-natal hormonal disorders: 'andreno-genital syndrome', or 'fetally masculinized girls' with an excesss of androgens in chromosomally-XX fetuses (Money and Ehrhardt, 1972); and 'pre-natally-feminized boys' with a deficiency of pre-natal testosterone (Imperato-McGinley *et al.*, 1979).

3. However, it is important to note that many biological scientists adopt evolutionary perspectives without falling prey to biological essentialism. See the work of Stephen Jay Gould, who holds to the general notion of natural selection whilst arguing that patterns of selection are often complex, wayward and capricious; and of the primatologist Sandra Blaffer Hrdy who argues that some aspects of primate and human behaviour can be explained in terms of the maximization of genetic fitness, but concludes that this requires strategies of collaboration, not competition (Gould, 1984a/b, 1991; Hrdy, 1981).

5 · *Psychoanalysis: Gender, Subjectivity and Knowledge*

No contemporary writer offers a theory of the human self matching the scope or complexity of Freud's. Although he fails to carry out his project, Freud specifies compelling criteria for an adequate account of a human being. Any such concept would have to include and account for a being that is simultaneously embodied, desiring, rational, speaking, historical, social, gendered, subject to laws both 'immutable' and unconscious and temporal, and capable of autonomy from social and biological determinants. Psychoanalysis as a discursive practice incorporates and transcends the boundaries between biology, politics, history, anthropology, philosophy and linguistics. It includes a theory of mind, psychosexual development, gender, knowledge, and politics as well as a therapeutic practice and method of training. The scope and depth of Freud's work are part of its continuing appeal . . . (Flax, 1990:49)

Classical psychoanalysis occupies an especially influential place in theories of gender. Its analysis of the development of the infant into socialized adult affords the acquisition of gendered traits and characteristics a crucial significance. As a discipline it debates the core questions of human 'subjectivity' (identity, motivation and consciousness), and the relative significance of individual psyche, early experience and social norms in the formation of adult, gendered personality.

Freudian ('classical') psychoanalysis has proved controversial since its emergence, as have subsequent generations of followers and interpreters. More recently, second-wave feminists have been divided on the terms of their engagement with, and support for, the various schools of psychoanalysis. Many feminists see in Freud a valuable and distinctive account of the formation of feminine personality under patriarchy, which offers the language from which a feminist psychoanalysis can function. Others see it as a major source of women's oppression, a quasi-scientific body of knowledge which theorizes and practises restrictive and sexist models of 'femininity'.

However, psychoanalytic theory is a complex and diffuse discipline. Freud himself revised his thought several times during his long career, and communicated many of his theories in the form of lectures rather than systematic expositions (Brown, 1961). As I shall argue, attempts to reclaim and reinterpret Freud's theories are a central factor in the encounter between feminist theory and psychoanalysis, and provide a key to a particular understanding of the relationship between theory and practice and the epistemological status of psychoanalytic discourse.

As well as being characterized by theoretical pluralism, psychoanalysis can be said to be distinguished by a diversity of disciplinary dimensions. Firstly, it can be understood as a general theory of developmental psychology, advancing various hypotheses about the human journey from infancy to adulthood. Psychoanalysis focuses especially upon the development of the adult psyche in connection with the acquisition of socially-sanctioned sexual orientations and gender roles and attributes. Secondly, psychoanalysis stands as a specific form of psychotherapeutic practice; a clinical discipline, helping people to recover long-suppressed memories and thus begin a process of self-revelation and healing. Thirdly, psychoanalytic theories provide analytical frameworks for the interpretation of wider aspects of human culture: themes in art, religion, literature and politics.

The founder of psychoanalysis was Sigmund Freud (1856–1939). Although he developed many of his early theories in conjunction with other colleagues, it is upon his work that the parameters of the early discipline were based, and he remained at the centre of the discipline until his death.[1]

In seeking to treat and understand patients with various forms of anxiety, sexual problems and psychosomatic ailments, Freud developed a perspective on their complaints which explained their conscious, physical or presenting problems as the observable manifestation of deeper psychological symptoms. Apparently 'irrational' or meaningless actions or psychoses were all tangible clues to the sources of a particular individual's distress; Freud talks about the process which draws patients into analysis as beginning with increasingly unfamiliar and bizarre behaviour, resulting in a feeling that they have become strangers even to themselves. However, such neuroses and complaints were also crucial in revealing the deeper psychosexual dynamics of all human personality and the underlying psychic forces common to everyone. This 'continuum' of normality and deviance points towards a fundamental tenet of psychoanalysis, that of the insufficiency of the superficial conscious mind in constituting human identity.

Freud posited that human behaviour is motivated by a strongly physical and biologically-rooted force, whose end lies in the satisfaction of its sexual and sensual desires. Contrary to prevailing models of child development, Freud argued that the infant's earliest impulses are directed by certain basic 'drives' which shape our desires, needs and wants. Freud called the inherent force '*das Trieb*', sometimes translated as 'instinct' but better rendered as 'drive' or 'libido'. Freud considered *das Trieb* to be primarily biologically-derived and organic, as an innate property of the nervous system; however, he also argued that sexual instincts could not exist independently of their psychic (and object-related) manifestations. Drives therefore lie 'on the frontier between the mental and the somatic' ('Instincts and their vicissitudes', in Freud, 1986:201).

Chief amongst these desires are two competing impulses, which Freud termed the 'life' and 'death' drives: respectively, an instinct towards self-preservation, love, intimacy and co-operation with others, and an opposing instinct of self-destructiveness, self-hatred, aggression and competition. These drives are powerful and chaotic; so the mind has to find some way of resolving the tension between them and of retaining some kind of equilibrium.

The imperative which demands such containment is derived from another dichotomy, that between the 'pleasure' and 'reality' principles: the necessity of the primitive drives to be contained in the name of civilization and social order. In anthropological terms, this requirement is expressed via the incest taboo: the custom which requires a group to resist introversion and practise exogamy in order to survive. The powerful sanctions against incest therefore impel the developing individual to direct and sublimate his/her chaotic desires, and provide a paradigm for the path from unsocialized infant id to cultured, adult ego.

Freud argued that the key to the development of an adult personality able to negotiate between the demands of its own drives and the

requirements of public culture lies in the child's earliest relationships. The child experiences the early relationship with its parents as
highly sensual; in this respect, it is experiencing the fulfilment of the
drives associated with pleasure, life and sexuality. Freud talked
about the infant as knowing only 'polymorphous pleasure' in the
initial stages of its life: being fed, washed, nursed and held are all for
the child profoundly sensual, and in a very implicit and undirected
fashion, sexual pleasures (Freud, 1986:277–394).[2]

However, in order to enter the adult world, where such polymorphous pleasure is unacceptable, the child passes through stages of
development which teach it to channel and focus that sexual drive
into socially acceptable forms. Freud theorized four different stages,
corresponding to different stages of maturity: oral, anal, phallic and
genital. The stabilization of desire thus takes place via the concentration of sexuality to a genital heterosexuality; but it also has a
psychological dimension, in terms of a realignment of the objects of
polyverse attachment. Freud's hypothesis is that children must
resolve the forbiddenness of their desire for their parents, and
redirect the focus of cathexis. This occurs via two related psychosexual 'crises': the Oedipus and castration complexes. These give
accounts of the differential responses of male and female children to
a prohibition on unsocialized desire, and are the linchpin of gender
formation for classical psychoanalysis. The complexes represent an
inspired fusion of the psychic and the somatic, a dynamic theory
involving sense of body, perception of self and relationships with
significant others.

For Freud, gender identity and difference is the result of a process
of sexual maturation; and because biology and anatomy are differentiated, boys and girls will experience this transition in contrasting
fashion. This is the crux of the Freudian aphorism, 'biology is
destiny' (1986:402–11). The process begins with the child's awareness of bodily, genital difference, but occurs in the context of the
child's early attachment to parents. The boy's attachment to his
mother as primary love object inspires him to cultivate a desire to
dispose of his father in order to replace him as the mother's sexual
partner. However, his realization that he possesses a penis and
women do not leads him to assume that his mother has been
castrated by another, more powerful creature, namely his father.
The boy fears the possibility of the loss of his own penis by some
corresponding punishment; for him, this can only be for the crime of

attempting to replace his father in his mother's affections. He therefore has a choice to identify with his mother, and thereby risk castration; or to abandon his attachment to his mother and identify with his father, thus protecting his manhood. Thus desire for the mother is repressed, and the authority of the father is internalized into the 'superego': the social conscience which sanctions that which is culturally normative and acceptable. The search for a mother-substitute impels the boy into heterosexual desire.

The ego and superego therefore develop in response to the pressures of the instincts of self-preservation and gratification of basic needs. The ego is the location of reason, representing the emergence of a conscious, thinking self, aware of the contrast between pure instinct (the id) and the social presentation of self. The superego develops in response to the internalization of the authority of the father after the Oedipal crisis; the father is the personification of the ethical demands of culture. Through this identification with father and renunciation of mother, the boy acquires a 'masculine' identity: a sense of his proper social role, a conscience, an expectation of his place in a (gendered) adult world. However, the id remains unaffected, a psychic substratum in each person's unconscious.

The girl child's first attachment is also to the mother. Her transition also occurs at the point of realization of anatomical difference. The recognition of her own lack of a penis, and the comparative inferiority of the corresponding sexual organ, the clitoris, brings about the crisis of the castration complex. She develops what Freud termed 'penis envy', and blames her mother for her deficient state. In resentment, she abandons the mother's affection and turns to the father, whose evident superiority, symbolized by his sexual organ, she desires. Thus she seeks, in compensation, to become the object of her father's love and to displace her mother; but, in turn, this desire gives way to the wish for a baby as a penis-substitute and to the more socially-acceptable aspirations of the 'feminine' identity.

A later interpreter, Karen Horney, developed a theory of masculine envy of women's reproductive power ('womb envy') in an attempt to posit an equal and countervailing 'feminine identity' which did not merely assume that a girl's clitoris was a lesser masculine organ. However, other commentators, especially Mitchell, argue that this misappropriates Freud by positing two, rather than one, distinct biological natures for women and men prior to the entry into culture and gender roles (Mitchell, 1974:129).

According to Freud, therefore, it is the castration complex – involving a psychic response to anatomical difference – which proves decisive in the formation of a stable gender identity and the adoption of culture and its values. The conscious self emerges as a socialized, heterosexual adult, the infantile desires and wishes repressed into the unconscious residuum of the id. Women, argued Freud, possess a weaker superego due to the lesser identification with the father and the less pronounced fear of castration. The achievement of stable feminine identity is deemed more problematic because the girl has to shift attachment from the pre-Oedipal mother to the father, and to sublimate clitoral desire in favour of vaginal sexuality, thus suppressing the active 'masculine' nature of her libido. The boy simply has to defer his desire away from his mother towards a future wife. The pre-Oedipal phase is more crucial for the girl, because the attachment to the mother is more intense. It would therefore appear that the connection between the development of femininity and its propensity to neurosis rests in the stress of adjusting to the expectations of the feminine role, rather than any inherent weakness (Freud, 1977:143–44).

However, the fact that femininity only emerges as the result of submission to cultural conformity serves to illustrate the extent to which femininity is a problematic and indeterminate concept for Freud. It also indicates one of the primary sites of critical engagement between classical psychoanalysis and feminist theories of gender development. A girl is, to Freud, initially a 'little man'; her proto-masculinity must be suppressed in order for her femininity to develop. Thus, although the sexes do not follow identical or symmetrical pathways towards psychic adulthood, it is questionable whether within classical psychoanalysis 'the feminine' is anything other than repressed masculinity. The same applies to the status of bisexuality, the initial pleasure-seeking stage. Is this a genuinely polyverse orientation, out of which either homosexuality or heterosexuality could evolve, or is it simply a raw, pre-social masculinity? Freud noted the confusion and imprecision of the term; comments to this effect may be seen in his 1915 footnote on 'The differentiation between men and women' in 'The transformations of puberty' (1905) in *Three Essays on the Theory of Sexuality* (Freud, 1977:355).

He appears to have abandoned bisexuality as a primary concept altogether by 1920.

Psychoanalysis contributes some very important perspectives to theories of gender; but these are highly problematic, and have attracted fierce criticism and debate. Critics such as Simone de Beauvoir, Viola Klein, Betty Friedan and Kate Millett have emphasized the implicitly prescriptive tone of psychoanalysis, whether this is endemic to Freud's work or simply a later conservative revision of successive generations of practitioners (de Beauvoir, 1988:69–84; Klein, 1989:71–90; Millett, 1970:109; Friedan, 1963:93–95).

Feminist opposition to Freudian psychoanalysis has focused on his representation of the feminine personality as problematic, and his assumption that the attainment of adult heterosexual masculinity is normative. According to Freud, girls who do not adjust to a feminine and maternal role have a 'masculinity complex' and are adjudged to be abnormal. Women's discontent is thus firmly secured in their refusal or inability to embrace a biological role, rather than dissatisfaction with the social and cultural prospects of femininity. Furthermore, the depiction of femininity as 'lack' of penis, the clitoris as an 'immature' equivalent, and a concentration on vaginal desire within adult feminine sexuality, are regarded as prescriptions for penetrative heterosexual activity and women's reproductive destiny. In contrast to the active, inherently 'masculine' auto-eroticism of the pre-Oedipal infant, femininity is a denial or reversal of earliest sexual desire. Such a reading of psychoanalysis presents 'penis envy' as something inevitable, decisively distorting psychosexual development at an immature stage. The girl must accept her lack and move on to an adult sexuality (motherhood); if not, she is deemed not to have properly resolved the Oedipus experience, and risks neurotic rejection of her proper role in life. Psychoanalysis therefore portrays women as passive, limited in intellect, naturally unstable and neurotic, with no justification for a dissatisfaction with their 'natural' maternal and domestic role.

Certainly, Freud is perplexed and bemused by 'the feminine', and perhaps his later revision of his theories to afford greater emphasis to the castration complex reflects his dissatisfaction with the concept. However, it is clear that what he was trying to convey was that the pre-Oedipal child has yet to acquire the traits and psychic patterns of relationship which serve to differentiate the genders. However, whether this is the inevitable working out of biological predisposi-tion, or the surrender to the contingencies of the patriarchal family and of social expectations of adult women and men, is still open to question (Mitchell, 1974, 58–60).

However, accusations of biological determinism misjudge the model of human development within Freud's thought, which, whilst conceptualizing the biological as a blind, instinctive force, regards the psychic adjustment to anatomical difference as crucial:

> One could argue that Freud's 'anatomy is destiny' is not only part of his rejection of irrational responses to notions concerning women . . . but also his attempts to ground future discussions of masculine and feminine characteristics in the body's presentation of itself in the social world . . . His concern with the unconscious was to add another layer of truth to the question of one's being, to see how one's social personality is a consequence of one's biology. Freud's views . . . have to be understood within this framework of grounding an understanding of character and personality in the interplay of bio-logical and psychic factors. (Farganis, 1986:14–15)

Freud's overall work may therefore be read as an insistence that gendered subjectivity is contingent upon the entry into culture. However, as Chris Weedon notes, Freud's use and understanding of the term 'culture' is very generalized and ahistorical; although there may be scope to see gender as socially constructed in a theoretical sense, those who see this as a resource for a radical critique of present gender systems should recognize that this still precludes any real sense of change or human agency:

> At one level Freudian theory marks a radical break with biological determinism by making the structures of psychic development the foundations of *social* organization. This occurs in the context of the nuclear family and, in normal development, leads to the acquisition by children of heterosexual gendered identity. Yet the degree to which structures of psycho-sexual development, which have a uni-versal status in Freudian theory, can be seen as fully social is open to question, since they are neither historically nor culturally specific . . . However, in its claims to provide a universal theory, psychoanalysis reduces gender to an effect of pre-given, psycho-sexual processes and closes off gender identity from history. (Weedon, 1987:46)

Flanagan also argues that Freud's evocation of cultural factors is superficial and ultimately rhetorical in the face of a more over-whelming biologism:

It is the child's inevitable observation of the biologically-determined genitals . . . which is *the* decisive factor in all subsequent psycho-sexual development . . . Freud gives little attention to 'nurture', and makes virtually no mention of any unique environmental *input* that might occur in any particular child's life, e.g., the child might lack a same or opposite sex parent or might never see the genitalia of the opposite sex . . . Freud theorizes as if the Oedipal drama operates in a closed system, and in an inevitable and universally repetitive fashion, immune from outside influences once put in motion by the child's biological sex. All boys fear, all girls envy; all boys love their mother, all girls love their father; all girls feel wounded, all boys feel superior. (Flanagan, 1982:67)

Despite its inconsistencies and limitations, it is perhaps the degree to which classical psychoanalysis has problematized notions of selfhood and identity that attracts gender theorists to regard Freudian psychoanalysis as worthy of critical analysis and reappraisal. A clear theme within classical psychoanalysis is that of the fragmentation of the self, a subversion of post-Enlightenment portrayals of rational, controlled and unitary personhood, where the unconscious threatens to 'destabilize' the conscious self. Freud's case studies reveal profound disquiet on the past of analysands whose self-understanding was shaken by unbidden dreams, desires and fantasies. ('A question of lay analysis', 1926, in Freud, 1986:7–11). Psychoanalysis denies the possibility of an unambiguous ego not in some way subtended by the desires and drives of the instincts. Thus, the boundary between rational and non-rational is not certain; nor is the subject a fixed self, but contingent upon old memories, repressed fears or distress which may displace the self-controlled conscious 'I'.

This in itself is significantly anti-biologistic, as it portrays gender identity as the result of psychosexual struggle in early life, and therefore an attained, rather than an innate, human trait. To many critics, therefore, psychoanalysis offers an account of human identity in its 'natural' potential as being more diverse, plastic and uninhibited than our 'cultural' expressions. Terry Lovell argues that psychoanalysis offers a more satisfactory alternative both to biologically-derived accounts of gender and to sociological theories of 'sex roles' and socialization because it is able to take account of the strongly internalized nature of gender roles:

Biological explanations, spurious as they are, remain persuasive . . . out of a widely felt conviction that only something as fundamental as biology is commensurable with the taken-for-granted experience of gender as an essential and not an accidental component of personal identity. The acid test of feminist theories of gender is not their ability to refute biological arguments, but rather the capacity to put something as plausible in their place. What is needed is a theory which acknowledges and accounts for the depth and ubiquity of gender divisions, while yet powerfully revealing them as socially constructed and open to change. The attraction of psychoanalysis was its promise with respect to this important task. (Lovell, 1990:189)

Later Interpreters of Freud

Despite the ambivalence of classical psychoanalysis towards femininity, a number of Freud's most successful disciples were women: Karen Horney, Helene Deutsch, and Anna Freud, his daughter. These writers, and others of Freud's circle, expressed scepticism or dissidence concerning Freud's characterization of femininity; but active debate on female subjecitivity and sexuality has only emerged fully in the past twenty years. One particular school of thought, that of 'object-relations' psychoanalysis, after D.W. Winnicott, Melanie Klein and W.R.D. Fairbairn, has proved a popular and fertile source for further debates about gender identity. Many commentators sympathetic to the women's movement regard it as a more adequate account of the formation of gender identity. Whereas Freud posited the imperatives of the instinctual drives as fundamental to human motivation, object-relations theorists identify the roots of subjectivity in the search for, and gratification of, a need for relationship and bonding with others. Thus, the emphasis is upon 'intersubjectivity': human psychic development as emerging from interaction with others, and the outworking of 'inner' drives and dilemmas as necessarily expressed in so-called 'transitional relationships'.

The infant's early intense relationship with a parent, exemplified by the mother/child dyad, is seen as a central focus for early psychological and emotional development. It is also held to be the key to the formation of a differential gender identity, founded less on abstract drives and anatomical difference as upon responses to intersubjectivity (Chodorow, 1978; Gilligan, 1982; Dinnerstein, 1987).

The power of the mother as initial care-giver is an essential aspect of object-relations theory. As the primal, all-encompassing source of pre-social cathexis for the infant, she possesses the licence to give or withhold pleasure, causing the child to experience the primal relationship as a source both of security and of fear and vulnerability. The male child experiences a contradiction between the cultural expectations of masculinity – strength and autonomy – and his overwhelming dependence on his mother. The process of separation is therefore as critical to object-relations theorists as to Freud; but with the former, it is more of a question of internalizing cultural stereotypes and resolving ambivalent feelings of attachment and control, rather than conforming to biological necessity. Masculinity is problematic for object-relations theorists: it is created out of the repression of all qualities associated with the maternal and nurturant, constructing a psychosexual identity founded on control, objectification and detachment.

Object-relations theory thus turns the Freudian characterization of femininity as 'lack' and frailty on its head, to evoke an image of masculinity as fragile, insecure and unresolved. It is implied that female gender identity is more easily attained and consolidated, whereas a coherent sense of self on the part of the male child is less stable on account of the continuing identification with the mother. Yet there may be an unexamined contradiction here, between a brittle and threatened male subjectivity and a dominant, hegemonic cultural construction of masculinity: can object-relations theory give an adequate account for the institutionalization of what Chodorow terms an 'arelational masculinity'?

By contrast, the girl is able to continue her early intimacy with the mother, as the transition to adulthood via separation is not dependent on the fracturing of the bond, as with the development of male subjectivity. For the girl, the transfer of affection to the father is always incomplete: the mother is both the rival of the daughter and the irreplaceable role model. Thus, the girl achieves normative gender identity which retains capacity for relatedness and nurturance. 'Because women themselves are mothered by women, they grow up with the relational capacities and needs, and psychological definition of self-in-relationship, which commits them to mothering' (Chodorow, 1978:209).

Many feminists see in object-relations psychoanalysis a plausible account of patriarchal masculinity, as well as a greater attention to the benefits, as well as the deficiencies, of 'feminine' qualities and the importance of social relations in the constitution of selfhood. It also provides insights into women's experiences of gender identity as ambivalent. Although it posits women's maternal instinct as the result of the attainment of adult gender identity, rather than an innate capacity, it does also suggest that there are emotional needs fulfilled by mother-daughter bonds that overcome some of the flaws of motherhood as an institution. It allows for gender identity to be both deep-seated and simultaneously constructed and achieved; but it regards the process of gender development as a psychic response to early self/other relationships rather than the assimilation of problematic genital awareness. 'Femininity' is thus not an innate or deterministic entity, but a cultural role, emerging from patterns of intersubjectivity and relationships, reinforced by psychic and cultural processes.

However, although this offers a framework within which many of the qualities of conventional femininity can be valued, as well as offering a critique of established models of parenting, it is debatable whether it extrapolates particular Western structures of mothering into psychic universals, and whether its evocation of feminine gender identity as still founded upon lack, and upon incomplete achievement of autonomous subjectivity, leaves cultural conformity to patriarchal masculinity unquestioned. Whilst it identifies the sources of differential gender identity in varying patterns of inter-subjectivity, it does not adequately explain the origins and dynamics of the detached and emotionally repressed masculinity to which male children must conform.

Despite the engagement with object-relations psychoanalysis, however, many other feminist critics have chosen to engage directly with Freud himself, believing that only a wholesale reappraisal of his thought would enable psychoanalytic theory to become the friend, and not the foe, of Western women in their pursuit of greater autonomy and self-definition.

Juliet Mitchell and the Rehabilitation of Freud

Mitchell came to psychoanalysis through a desire for a framework of analysis which combined the material roots of gender relations with an account of women's internalization of patriarchal norms. She differentiated between Freud and many of his later interpreters, arguing that a reconstruction of the central themes of classical psychoanalysis would result in 'a return to Freud' – an interpretation of his work as a critical account of the formation of feminine identity under patriarchy. Freud's characterization of the post-Oedipal feminine personality as inherently unstable, criticized by feminists as a mark of his misogyny, is for Mitchell an illustration of the coercive and imposed status of feminine gender traits; and Mitchell uses the work of the neo-Freudian Jacques Lacan to emphasize the importance of the penis (the Phallus) as symbolic, not of mere anatomical difference, but of male privilege under patriarchy (Mitchell, 1974:384–98). Thus psychoanalysis helps feminists understand how women's identities are constructed and learned, and how entry into a culture founded upon the 'Law of the Father' results in female masochism, submissiveness and instability. Deeply ingrained though these traits may be, they are nevertheless socially constructed as a requirement of a particular form of social relations.

Mitchell is right to defend classical psychoanalysis against charges of simplistic biologism, but perhaps underestimates the extent to which her own analysis can lapse into abstraction. Her rendition of Freudian psychoanalysis offers a helpful account of the individual's psychic adaptation to, and internalization of, dominant gender roles and relations, but that still leaves questions unanswered as to the real nature of an external, gendered world which is maintained and ordered in such a way as to leave the child in no doubt as to its place in the order of things. The dynamics of the Oedipal and castration complexes are identified as symbolic, rooted in the universal structures of the cultural exchange of women (1974:370–76). However, by emphasizing such an essentially structuralist – and therefore ahistorical – interpretation of social relations, Mitchell misses the opportunity to root the formation of the psychosexual identity in the actual realm of cultural practice.

Similarly, by attempting to resolve the ambiguities in Freud's understanding of the feminine and its psychosexual origins, she may be accused of glossing over Freud's own ambivalences. He never fully resolved the extent to which the girl/woman's resignation to her feminine fate is the functional and inevitable resolution of her assumption of social norms, or a potentially subversive and contradictory struggle which simultaneously explains women's compliance with the expectations of patriarchy while offering the potential for resistance and change. Mitchell's interpretation of that may be a valuable correction to Freud's understanding of femininity, but it cannot be authentically described as the 'return' which she claims for her work.

Mitchell's work thus raises questions about the acceptability and plausibility of 'reclaiming' major theorists, regardless of later interpretations, for (in this case) feminist ends. Mitchell's solution is clear: her purposes are to rescue the real Freud from his (conservative and sexist) followers, and returning to the pure origins of his theories, to make him accessible and available to a new audience, previously repelled by his seeming sexism and biological determinism.

> In violently rejecting a Freud who is not Freud, I would argue that the only important possibilities for understanding the psychology of women that we have to date have been lost, and that in misconceiving and repudiating psychoanalysis a crucial science for understanding ideological and psychological aspects of oppression has been thrown away. Neither Freud's contribution on femininity nor the science of psychoanalysis are anywhere near unflawed or complete – but a return to these would seem to be the way forward. (Mitchell, 1974:301–302)

The logic of this argument is that, beneath the patriarchal veneer, the generations of misinterpretation and appropriation, lies a pristine and authentic theory upon which a more favourable canon can be rebuilt. By going back, we can then go forward; feminist opponents have misunderstood or taken out of context the basic, liberatory tenets of the 'faith'.

However, other schools of thought argue that this is not possible: to strip away the layers of interpretation to reveal a single original source is a hermeneutical impossibility. Contemporary interpreters cannot divorce themselves from the generations of practice which go to making a body of knowledge what it is. Freud himself may be an honorary feminist, but Mitchell herself acknowledges that psychoanalysis and its practitioners have stifled women's protests against their lot. Thus, if feminism, or any theory of gender, is to re-encounter psychoanalysis, it must recognize that theories become ideologies via their use, and that it is social and operational contexts which render bodies of knowledge oppressive or liberatory.

One difficulty with Freudian theory is that although it is often presented as a theory of developmental psychology (starting at the beginning of a child's life and reading forwards), it originated as a form of therapy which interpreted retrospectively (looking for clues to present behaviour in the relationships and dynamics of the past). Various interpreters of Freud have therefore argued that classical psychoanalysis does not refer to chronological events, any more than it claims to be revealing real events of seduction or desire: instead, it must be read as a particular kind of narrative on the often simultaneously existing layers of human un/consciousness. It is more appropriately an interpretative or hermeneutical discipline: the 'talking cure' which brings to speech those silenced aspects of the psyche. Mitchell herself contends that the elements which structure the unconscious are the residues of the historical past, but that the work of reclamation is only significant insofar as it enables an illumination of the patient's present condition:

> The snag with Freud's presentation of his discoveries and, therefore, of any attempted simplification and re-presentation of them, is that a description *reverses* the analytic procedure. Freud was listening to the *recollected* history of his patients, he reconstructed infantile life from the fragmentary stories the patients told in which time past and time present are one. He read the history of the person *backwards* – as it is always essential to do; but in retelling it, he describes it as a march forwards, a process of development where it is in fact a multi-level effort of reconstruction . . . Again, what can be forgotten is that at every moment of a person's existence he is living and telling in word, deed or symptom the story of his life . . . (Mitchell, 1974:14)

Critical appropriation of major theoretical perspectives such as classical psychoanalysis cannot therefore remain immune from considering the operationalization of their knowledge-claims, and the extent to which, for better or worse, many of those claims developed through therapeutic practice. In this respect, the context within which such a relationship is conducted – especially the differentials of power and gender between analyst and client – and the ends to which such therapy is pursued become of paramount importance. The concern of Freud's critics about the ideological impact and social applications of psychoanalysis, particularly in sanctioning traditional gender roles and heterosexual conformity, underlines the inseparability of theory and practice in assessing the significance of psychoanalysis.

Jane Flax's critique of psychoanalysis adopts this perspective, which allows her to reappropriate a Freud who is interpreted in his own context. Like Mitchell, Flax sees in Freudian psychoanalysis much that is helpful in articulating problems of the self, gender and knowledge. However, Flax's reappropriation entails a critical dialogue with Freudian theory and practice, rather than an attempt to retrieve the 'truth' of his work in some original form. In this sense, her hermeneutical approach to Freud differs from Mitchell's, in that she is concerned to exploit the silences and ambivalences of Freud's thought. The key to this for her is the tension within psychoanalysis concerning its own knowledge-claims. Freud himself never resolved the question of the fundamental epistemological identity of psychoanalysis: was it to be a 'science of the mind', an extension of his neurological training; or, given its location and origins in the therapeutic relationship, and its commitment to the fragmentary, non-rational model of self, a discipline that explodes the notion of the objective, mechanistic and value-free nature of analysis, transference and therapy (Flax, 1990:66–67)?

Influenced by deconstructionist theories of knowledge, Flax argues that Freud's work is full of unresolved dichotomies. It is only possible to grasp the significance of that ambivalence if we appreciate Freud as a creature of his own culture, rather than attempting to sever the essence of his thought from the context which generates such knowledge.

The critique of classical psychoanalysis earlier in this section has already identified many tensions and ambiguities in Freud's work. He may have successfully posed a hypothesis of human identity that is anti-dualistic by uniting body and mind in the fundamental impulses of *das Trieb*; but in other ways he still characterized much of his thinking in dualistic terms. The conflict between desire and civilization (pleasure principle versus reality principle); the unresolved confusion over whether instinct or object-relations governs early infant sexuality; the status of bisexual desire, and the true balance of masculine/feminine sexuality in the individual; and the status of psychoanalysis as empirical, rational science or interpersonal, affective therapy all reveal the dualistic character of psychoanalytic discourse. Furthermore, these dichotomies are part of a culture in which such bipolar categories are imbued with the evaluative categories of gender hierarchy.

> The process of acculturation is simultaneously and necessarily a process in which people are gendered . . . The polymorphous perverse infant becomes . . . the heterosexual, genitally oriented male or female adult. In this process part of 'natural' sexuality is sacrificed

. . . Family ties must be sacrificed to demands of the larger group. The incest taboo is both the culmination of this process and its symbol. Women represent the family and its 'natural ties'. Their demands begin to oppose those of culture, just as the son's 'natural' desire for the mother conflicts with the demands of the father/culture . . . In associating women and what they do with nature, Freud transforms a concrete product of social activity into an inevitable consequence of the evolution of civilization, as inescapable as 'modernity' itself. (Flax, 1990:77–78)

A discipline such as psychoanalysis which seeks to transcend the categories of human culture in its accounts of the acquisition of selfhood cannot avoid using categories which themselves deploy the dominant thought-patterns of a gendered world. Flax's argument is that psychoanalysis must not seek to withdraw from this tension in a misguided pursuit of certainty and objectivity. Freud's genius lay in his recognition of the power of the unconscious, the fusion of body and mind in the drives and the fragmented and heterogeneous self: in the inherent ambiguity and self-reflexivity of human consciousness and agency. Such categories refuse to be collapsed into simple dichotomies, rendering differentiation and autonomy as an ultimate separation and repression of the 'Other'. Instead, Flax sees in the psychoanalytic method a valuable means of understanding and transforming gender relations, because it embodies in its own praxis a fusion of oppositional values and a blurring of dichotomous hierarchies of science/therapy, mind/body, self/other (Flax, 1990:84).

Freud recognizes that selfhood, experience and difference are the results of complex processes, rather than the static essences contained within simple binary opposites; but he fears the implications for his own professional authority and self-possession (Flax, 1990:85). He wishes simultaneously to undermine and transcend these tensions, but he cannot avoid ultimately privileging one half of the relationship, the one which reflects patriarchal values. None the less, the 'repressed' part of the dichotomy remains, and can be restored as part of a renewed critique of Freud's theories, which must be read as complex and multivalent. The transcendence of dualism is therefore thwarted by Freud's own retreat into values associated with patriarchal science, and results in the privileging of libido over object-relations, biology over culture, active over passive and science over relational therapy. It also explains his inability to differentiate between the descriptive and prescriptive account of the child's entry into culture and the desirability or mutability of the adoption of cultural norms of gender identity.[3]

Flax is also concerned to identify the potential of psychoanalytic theory and method for subverting the so-called 'Enlightenment project' of the rational, transparent individual. In this respect, she argues that psychoanalysis is, with feminism, a postmodern discipline. The use of reason as self-evidently leading to self-knowledge, truth and emancipation is countered by psychoanalysis, which undermines the notion that the rational individual possesses all that is necessary to perceive truth, self-understanding and enlightenment, and is thus able to act decisively and in a goal-oriented fashion to realize their intentions. According to Freud, the conscious ego is not 'master in its own house', but often acts to defend itself against the uncomfortable and unbidden promptings of the unconscious. Transcendence of the consciousness is necessary in order to hear the testimony of the repressed unconscious and is, for practising psychoanalysts and their clients, the more authentic path to self-discovery.

Psychoanalytic theories of mind also contradict and challenge many contemporary epistemologies. Both the rationalist's faith in the powers of reason and the empiricist's belief in the reliability of sense perception and observation are grounded in and depend upon assumptions about the mind. It must have the capacity to be at least partially undetermined by the effects of the body, passions, and social authority or convention. However, psychoanalysis throws into doubt all epistemologies that rely on the possibility of accurate self-observation and direct, reliable access to and control over the mind and its activities (Flax, 1993:53).

For these reasons, Flax is adamant that psychoanalysis is not, and never can be, a science in the objective sense. Rather, the whole psychoanalytic process contributes new and exciting perspectives to accounts of epistemology, philosophies of mind and human development as well as theories of gender. Although psychoanalysis has colluded with the maintenance of conformity, it can also assist in subverting unitary or hegemonic standards of sexual preference, human development and family relations.

Estelle Roith and Philip Rieff, both engaging in critical yet supportive appreciations of Freud's work, add further dimensions to Flax's critique (Roith, 1987; Rieff, 1959). Both claim that there are contradictions within Freud's work which can only be explained by exploring Freud's own psychic and social background, to explain why certain biases are present. In Roith's case, she believes that Freud's theory of female sexuality is unconsciously influenced by rabbinic views on sexuality, and that Freud resisted clinical evidence when it did not correspond with the implicit assumptions of his own background.

For Rieff, Freud's thinking, for all its radicalism, is still rooted in nineteenth-century Western thought, which displays incipient gender dualism. Despite liberating discourse about women from a Victorian sentimentality, Freud still saw women as representative of nature, men of culture, reflecting a Romantic tradition which perceived women as sensual and the enemies of the intellect and of culture. Freud claimed to be promoting a science of psychoanalysis in his therapy, but was, as Rieff claims, unconsciously endorsing a power relationship between therapist and client which betrayed the values of the wider culture. In his condescension to his female patients, Freud lets slip the mask of value-freedom and scientific objectivity which conceals the inherent biases of theories which are actually portraying specific, gendered worlds whilst pleading for a universal human condition:

> By insisting that the emotions generated in an analysis are part of the analytic *situation*, and arise without regard to the individual personalities of either patient or physician, Freud seems to say that it does not matter who is involved: certain characteristic erotic responses will occur. Yet it made a great difference to Freud, as therapist, who was being analyzed – whether male or female. Not so much in his case histories as in his theoretical remarks, Freud shows condescension towards his female patients . . . Not only does Freud aver that girls *feel* biologically at a disadvantage, inferior, because they do not possess a penis; he affirms that they *are* in the greatest sense something less than boys. (Rieff, 1959:173–74)

The conclusion may therefore be drawn that Freud's theory *and* practice was submerged in a gender hierarchy of which he was unaware, and his clinical and theoretical explorations into what constituted *human* nature were preoccupied with the question of gender difference. Perhaps, when, late in life, he returned to redraft earlier work on the central conundrum of the nature of 'the feminine' it was out of a recognition that human subjectivity could not be anything other than gendered, and that it was in the very enigma of femininity that the key to his theories lay. Indeed, Juliet Mitchell argues a very similar point in her more recent evaluation of Freud (Mitchell, 1984). Freudian psychoanalysis, therefore, is a testimony to the prevalence and self-reflexivity of gender systems, imbuing not only the forces which shape our consciousness, but the structures of thought – myths, sciences, therapeutic techniques – we summon in order to analyse that same consciousness. As a body of knowledge, psychoanalysis cannot be codified or simplified into an abstract theory of patriarchy or a science of the mind, any more than it can merely be regarded as a pragmatic form of therapy innocent of cultural values and norms of implementation. Instead, it must be regarded as a 'discursive practice' which deliberately transcends the boundaries of theory and practice, mirroring its own commitment to a model of human agency, selfhood and knowledge as simultaneously embodied and transcendent, desiring and rational; as the creators *and* products of a gendered culture.

Notes

1. Freud developed psychoanalytic techniques whilst studying hypnotherapy in Paris in 1885. He published *Studies in Hysteria* with Joseph Breuer in 1893 and continued developing and revising his theories until his death. A chronology of his work and publications follows:

   1893 *Studies in Hysteria*;
   1894–1900 developing theories of unconscious, repression, neurosis;
   1900–10 revising work on repression and theories of infant sexuality: hypotheses of Oedipus and castration complexes;
   1900 *The Interpretation of Dreams*;
   1901 *The Psychopathology of Everyday Life*;
   1902 first psychoanalysis seminars in Vienna;
   1920–38 further revisions: life and death instincts, ego, id and superego;
   1922 *Beyond the Pleasure Principle*, *The Ego and the Id*;
   1933 *New Introductory Lectures in Psychoanalysis*.

2. A contemporary controversy concerns whether Freud's accounts of child sexuality, and especially accounts of seduction and incest, were actual events in the lives of his patients or merely sublimated fantasies. Intrepreters such as Jeffrey Masson claim that Freud refuted early claims for such events' factual status for fear of the scandal it would cause. This debate does raise an important issue associated with the epistemological and scientific status of psychoanalysis, namely whether it is a therapeutic discipline concerned with the excavation of repressed events of child abuse, or an abstract form of social theory about the co-option of the individual into patriarchal culture (Masson, 1985; Crews, 1993).

3. It is also possible that Freud's own position as a Jew in bourgeois pre-Anschluss Vienna (and thus as an outsider) contributed to his own professional ambivalence between seeking acceptance for psychoanalysis as a derivative of neurology's 'science of the brain' and as a novel and innovative critique of bourgeois family structures (see A. Freud in Freud, 1986:271). Certainly, this is part of the sub-text to Masson's work; that the discovery of actual instances of child abuse in Freud's clinical work were too controversial to expose, and so Freud preferred to amend his findings by positing such events as 'fantasies' of childhood seduction by adults. The greater sympathy with which accounts of child sexual abuse are now received has sharpened contemporary awareness of this phenomenon; but if Freud did repress such important evidence, I would contend that his own ambivalent position in the Viennese medical establishment may have had something to do with it (Masson, 1985; Crews, 1993).

Part III
Gender Themes

6 · *Bodies: History, Epistemology and Practice*

> The demand to acknowledge women's bodily integrity is not an essentialist demand. There is a critical difference between arguing that biology creates particular kinds of persons, such as nurturant women or violent men, and recognising that bodies do not exist outside of political structures. (Bacchi, 1990: 223–24)

Part Two indicated how gender studies in anthropology, the biological sciences and psychoanalysis are challenging the political and epistemological nature of appeals to 'biology' and 'nature' as self-evident objective realities, arguing that they must instead be seen as social products and the result of already gendered processes of enquiry, language and categorization. One of the results of this has been a revision of the analytical adequacy of many of the conventional analyses of gender which have tended to draw a definitive distinction between the fixed and immutable categories of 'nature' or 'biology' and the constructed and plastic products of 'culture' or 'environment'. One of the most enduring forms of analysis, the distinction between 'sex' and 'gender', has been subject to such critical reappraisal (see Chapter One).

Val Plumwood (1989) uses the 'female body suit' on the cover of Germaine Greer's *The Female Eunuch* to illustrate the tendency in conventional accounts of the sex/gender distinction to regard gender as a social uniform or learned role which can be adopted or discarded at will, leaving a 'core' biological identity that remains outside culture, and unaffected by experience of any kind. However, scientific accounts of biology as a discourse shaped by social conventions, and psychoanalytic accounts of subjectivity that refuse to render the body inert in the acquisition of identity, serve to remind us of the extent to which 'sex' is already gendered. A supposedly pre-social sex has been given meaning and status (differential between men and women) by a society in which gender relations already operate. A theory which presupposes that bodies are passive objects of gender, and that bodily difference is incidental to gendered identity and experience, thus obscures the way in which bodily difference has itself emerged from culture.

> In its feminist senses, gender cannot mean simply the cultural appropriation of biological sexual difference. Sexual difference is itself a fundamental – and scientifically contested – construction. Both 'sex' and 'gender' are woven of multiple, asymmetrical strands of difference, charged with multifaceted dramatic narratives of domination and struggle. (Haraway, 1990:140)

In attempting to avoid biological determinism, the sex/gender distinction therefore risks a corresponding form of social 'categoricalism' by seeing learning, social roles and externally-imposed norms as the sole constituents of gender identity. Yet this obscures the body as an agent in the formation of gender altogether, with two consequences. Firstly, gender is perceived as a matter of behaviour and consciousness, presupposing disembodied minds as the primary and determinant sites of gender: a perpetuation of, rather than a challenge to, Cartesian dualism. Secondly, the privileging of consciousness universalizes and abstracts the material and historical aspects of 'lived experience'. Such a theory of gender thereby posits a rationalist, ahistorical account involving neutral, passive bodies:

> What I wish to take to task in implicit and explicit investigations of gender theory is the unreasoned, unargued assumption that both the body and the psyche are a post-natally passive *tabula rasa*. That is, for theorists of gender, the mind, of either sex, is a neutral, passive entity, a blank state, on which is inscribed various social 'lessons'. The body, on their account, is the passive mediator of these inscriptions. The result of their analyses is the simplistic solution to female oppression: a programme of re-education, the unlearning of patriarchy's arbitrary and oppressive codes, and the relearning of politically correct and equitable behaviours and traits, leading to the whole person: the androgyn. It is precisely this alleged *neutrality* of the body; the postulated *arbitrary* connection between femininity and the female body; masculinity and the male body; and the apparent simplicity of the ahistorical and theoretically naive solution, viz.

resocialization, that this paper proposes to challenge. (Gatens, 1991:140)

The polarized impasse of biological essentialism and sociological categoricalism is undermined by a reintroduction of the body, albeit as socially mediated, as a key actor in the drama of gender. Moira Gatens argues that a social theory of gender which incorporates embodied, lived and enacted experience is able to resist what she calls the 'forced containment' (1991:141) of a false disjunction between essentialism and environmentalism.

For Gatens, the subject (body/mind in unity, active in constructing its own subjective sense of self) must also always be a sexed subject. Her insistence upon this springs from her commitment to a subject who is already embodied, but cannot experience a gendered self independent of a cultured sex. The psychoanalytic concept of the 'imaginary body' influences her: an internalized perception inherited from culture about the significance and meaning of certain bodily functions or organs. This imaginary body is specific through language, the shared privileging of certain organs or parts of the body, and institutional practices, and becomes constitutive of the subjective self. Gender identity is a strategic response to this internalized imaginary body, and is reproduced physically in the outworkings of the unconscious.

Other gender theorists affirm Gatens' concern that to deny critical access to the body as a primary constituent of gender is to occlude questioning of the power relations surrounding use and abuse of practices in the biological sciences, medicine and the social management of sexuality. As Connell – echoing Gatens – argues, gender theory has challenged biological determinism only to fall prey to the categoricalism of social construction or sex-role theory, and the resulting neglect of the body. This disqualifies a whole range of bodily experiences which are central to our lived knowledge of a gendered world: 'pleasure, pain, body-image, arousal, youth and ageing, bodily contact, childbirth and suckling' (Connell, 1987:74).

Symbolically, 'nature' may be opposed to 'culture', the body (fixed) opposed to history (moving). But in the reality of practice the body is never outside history, and history never free of bodily presence and effects on the body. The traditional dichotomies underlying reductionism now have to be replaced by a more adequate and complex account of the social relations in which this incorporation and interplay occur. (Connell, 1987:87)

Attention has therefore turned to the role of 'The Body' in theories of gender: how it is signified historically, and how representations of the body go beyond the merely morphological to reflect entire cosmologies; bodies as sites of coercion and manipulation, via regimes of practice and ideology, for example, reproductive technology, medicine and prescribed forms of sexual and familial expression and lifestyle; and bodies as bearers and creators of meaning and cultural significance, as well as being the sources of subversive and transformative practice.

History of the Body: Changing Practices and Definitions

One area of study has been that of enquiries which serve to emphasize the extent to which the Body has a history – or, more accurately, a set of histories; that the human body has been so enmeshed in other aspects of culture that only by thoroughly contextualizing examinations of bodily representations and practices can it be possible to grasp its full significance. Such histories of the Body seem to fall into two categories: the grand theories, attempting explorations of how meanings and uses of the Body have changed over time; and the tentative and specific, which rely more on the dissonance between the present day and the past, with exotic, often incredible means of harnessing and representing bodily experience.

As an example of the first, Laqueur undertakes a panoramic survey of understandings of sex differences 'from the Greeks to Freud' (Laqueur, 1990). His intention is to juxtapose periods of history when, for whatever reason, aspects of the body and gender relations were in transition or dispute. His thesis is that, inevitably, such debates are both reflections and generators of wider social, epistemological and political shifts. In particular, the relationship between two different models of sexual difference, and the factors which led to the abandonment of one in favour of the other, can be seen as reflections of changes in the history of ideas concerning differences between women and men, the nature of scientific enquiry and their bearing upon wider sociopolitical realities. A strong emphasis of his study is the extent to which anatomical renderings of the human body – in this case, especially human genitalia and the reproductive system – continued to conceptualize on a 'one-sex' model despite the development of clear evidence to the contrary from empirical dissection methods. However, Laqueur's argument is that the 'ideological' framework served to override the clinical evidence, so that bodies are never true or unambiguous speakers about themselves, but have to be seen as bearers of 'texts' which have been inscribed on them. However, they can also, within certain limits, be redrafted:

> No one was much interested in looking for evidence of two distinct sexes, at the anatomical and concrete physiological differences between men and women, until such differences became politically important . . . And when differences were discovered they were already, in the very form of their representation, deeply marked by the power politics of gender.
>
> I have no interest in denying the reality of sex or of sexual dimorphism as an evolutionary process. But I want to show on the basis of historical evidence that almost everything one wants to *say* about sex – however sex is understood – already has in it a claim about gender. Sex . . . is explicable only within the context of battles over gender and power. (1990:10–11)

In an important respect, therefore, Laqueur picks up a favourite theme of Michel Foucault: an exposure, as ideological, of the dictum that our bodies (for Foucault, it is sexual bodies) express and – literally – embody the truth about ourselves, transparently and absolutely. Although we are in a very fundamental sense our bodies, bodily identity has already been enscribed and demarcated for us, although not in an essentialist or deterministic sense. Modern times see bodies as fixed, and culture as imposed, changeable and alien; and it is this tendency that the sex/gender distinction reflects. Yet Laqueur's evidence suggests that previous ages held a contrary perspective of sex as the epiphenomenon, and culture as the primary reality which suffuses all else with its meanings.

According to ancient, mediaeval and renaissance accounts, physical bodies could experience profound and miraculous transformations. They saw social sex (gender) as foundational, and biological sex as mutable; thus the notion of an 'essential' maleness or femaleness resting in the body was foreign to them. Only when political and scientific changes displaced a fixed ordering of social and gender classes did it become expedient to root explanations of the social order in appeals to nature, thus paving the way for a 'two-sex' model which located 'difference' in biology, and rendered sex as primary and bipolar.

Laqueur's book has been severely criticized in some quarters (Jordanova, 1991; Mason, 1990). Certainly, his representation of the 'ideological' nature of the body lacks detail and has the effect of presenting human bodies as strangely cipher-like, merely passive objects of social processes. The basic claims of his thesis still stand, however, as his critics admit. He has simply attempted too ambitious a historical survey. The problem in such an exercise is that as yet scholars seem unable to combine consistency and unity of analysis with specificity and detail of historical and ethnographic examples. The story of how we live our bodies in and against historical and cultural contexts, where meanings are contested by a variety of discourses – medicine, religion and politics, as well as whatever constitutes our sense of those categories we call selfhood, subjectivity and experience – is immensely complex.

Other historical surveys by Winkler and Halperin develop explorations of the ways in which sexual activity and sexual desire are shaped historically, even though there are often points at which subversion can take place (Winkler, 1990; Halperin, 1990; Nussbaum, 1990). Similarly, Ludmilla Jordanova's work in the history of medicine, and collections like *Body/Politics*, have traced in some close and specific detail how particular practices, symbolic and material, reflect particular constructions of gender (Jordanova, 1989; Jacobus *et al.*, 1990).

By engaging closely with the changing language and symbolism of scientific practice and medical technology, it is possible to trace the connections to wider manifestations of gender inequality. The treatment of bodies, especially the feminine body, speaks also of other political structures as well as gender, because gender relations, and gendered bodies, are infused with cultural meanings.

From 'The Body' to 'Our Bodies'

Attention to specific circumstances of the treatment and conceptualization of bodies stands in contrast to Laqueur's broadly-based approach. For Feher, the history of the Body is necessarily a complex and tentative hermeneutic, carrying contradictions and oppositions as well as clear meanings (Feher *et al.*, 1989). The essays in his collection are truly no more than 'fragments', or snapshots of specific instances. Feher's own editorial article is brief, and attempts no systematization beyond the rationale behind the organization of each volume; but this is intentional, aiming to emphasize the essentially provisional nature of the writing of such a history. The overall mood of the collection is that, once confronted with cultures and historical periods different from our own, we can see how various are the interpretations and understandings of the Body, and how even our own flesh and blood is meshed into other kinds of networks of meaning. Bodies are therefore reflections of political orders and social contracts; sexual relations are expressions of civic hierarchies; anatomy a concern with the shape of the cosmos as much as with the human form. Thus emerges a diversity of metaphysical systems of the relationship between mind and body, human and divine, male and female.

Not all the essays are about gender identity or relations; but there is an implicit recognition throughout that bodies are both sexed and gendered; conversely, that 'gender' as a category is interconnected with institutions and relations of power, religion, art, cosmology and medicine. In this respect, the essays witness to the impossibility of building an account of the Body which posits a pristine, phenomenologically discrete and immutable form independent of, and only acted upon by, history, culture and language:

> The history of the human body is not so much the history of its representations as of its modes of construction. For the history of its representations always refers to a real body considered to be 'without history' – whether this be the organism observed by the natural sciences, the body proper as perceived by phenomenology, or the instinctual, repressed body on which psychoanalysis is based – whereas the history of its modes of construction can, since it avoids the overly massive opposition of science and ideology or of authenticity and alienation, turn the body into a thoroughly historicized and completely problematic issue. (Feher *et al.*, 1989:11)

What constitutes 'the Body' – which is actually always ourselves *as bodies*, in a particular place at a particular time – is instead a continuous process of remaking under the influence of factors which, as Frank argues, serve as a collection of hermeneutical boundaries: body and mind; male and female; interior/exterior; the state/civil relations and reproduction, kinship and filiation. We produce ourselves through the medium of the body, which has already been charted and loaded with cultural significance; yet, as many of the articles indicate, there is often room for renegotiation, even subversion, of given conventions and understandings.

Such historical enquiries reinstate bodily difference as the site of gender ideology, fold the nature/culture distinction into itself and argue for the re-emergence of the body as central to gender studies, albeit accompanied by critical scrutiny of the way in which 'powerful prior notions of difference or sameness determine what one sees and reports about the body' (Laqueur, 1990:21). The emphasis on the specific, lived experience affirms the importance of human practice and interpretation, and begins to dismantle notions of a universal theory of 'the Body' seen as axiomatic and constant for all time. Feher establishes the primacy of context, language and situation for any theory of the body; as Frank comments, 'The government of the body is never more than a provisional ordering' (1991:47).

The study of the Body has also re-emerged in social theory (Turner, 1984; Shilling, 1993). Bryan Turner argues for the centrality of critical study of the body to sociological theory, which for too long has privileged a view of the individual as a rational, disembodied agent, thus marginalizing questions of human embodiment. Social theory, however, has to take account of how bodies are controlled and represented, and how populations are restrained and disciplined. The development of industrial society can be read through the stories of changing regimes of bodily order, encompassing practices, conventions and institutions as various as sexuality, marriage, reproduction, the control of urban masses, sanitation, illness and medicine, health, diet and fitness, asceticism and religion. Bodies are the locations of these very material practices through which all social relations, but most especially gender relations, are formed. Any sociological theory, therefore, must consider the reproduction of individual bodies and populations. There is a close connection between the management of bodies and social philosophy concerning order, control, reproduction and the nature of community.

The criteria for a sociology of the Body, therefore, concern the centrality of human agency; the intervention of a dichotomy between nature and culture that transcends and redefines mere biology; and a view of bodies as social, not atomistic or individual, so that the ontology of the body always pre-exists individual consciousness and reflects wider social forces. Effectively, bodies stand at the hub of theoretical and methodological tensions of social theory; and gender emerges as crucial too, because struggles over desire, sexual difference, reproduction and illness are all specific ways in which men control women:

> Sociological theory can be said to be organized around a number of perennial contrasts – agency and structure, individual and society, nature and culture, mind and body. Solutions to these contrasts – voluntarism and determinism – are simultaneously premature and lop-sided, because the contradictions are theoretically creative and productive. We can exercise agency, but we do so in the context of massive structural restraints. We are individuals, but our individuality is socially produced. Human beings as organic systems are part of nature, but their natural environment is also the product of historical practices.
>
> We are conscious beings, but that consciousness can only be realized through embodiment. The importance of the sociology of the body is that it lies at the axis of these theoretical tensions and it is thus a necessary component of any genuine sociology. (Turner, 1984:248–49)

Mary Douglas' contribution to the study of the Body concerns how cultural awareness of the self and its bodily boundaries provides a telling metaphor for public life as a whole (Douglas, 1970). Our bodies are microcosms of the macrocosm of society, and can be read as metaphors for our social and political concerns and fears: for example, questions of security, invasion, disease and contamination. Thus, there is a reflexive relationship between individual experiences of bodiliness, and wider social relations and power struggles.

Foucault and the Discipline of Bodies

The work of Michel Foucault has been tremendously influential for contemporary social theories of the Body, as well as theories of gender (Foucault, 1977, 1984; Arac, 1988). Foucault addresses the perennial questions of social philosophy: a concern for the nature of the modern world in the West and the problem of social order. The rise of the State has involved a series of coercive measures and institutions which control the population via a series of discourses, which may be medical, moral, theological or psychotherapeutic. This is not to say that there are not physical and economic injustices and constraints; but that knowledge, mediated by powerful scientific practices, becomes a crucial component of the state's maintenance of social control. But ideology is exerted at a somatic level as well as that of consciousness or propoganda: hegemonic institutions operate to coerce physically, via discourses of medicine, sexuality and morality. Definitions of sickness, perversion, insanity and sin are produced by influential institutions that reflect emergent forms of knowledge which serve to maintain strong (but culturally variable) lines of definition between the normal and mainstream, and the marginal and transgressive.

All history for Foucault is the struggle between these two tendencies. It is arguable that part of his refutation of 'humanist' and progressive narratives of history – like Marxism and liberalism – is that he cannot envisage a time when this struggle can be finally resolved. The passage of history is simply marked by new versions of the relationship: out of the struggle are born coercive and constraining practices and institutions – the clinic, the asylum and the confessional – which actually serve to 'create' the pathologies they seek to undermine. One example often cited is the emergence of the discipline of sexology and its 'discovery' and abnormalization of conditions like male homosexuality and female hysteria in England in the 1880s (Weeks, 1985; Caplan, 1987; Jackson, 1987; Mort, 1987).

The mechanisms by which knowledge is placed at the disposal of powerful social agents are most clearly played out in history upon various disciplines of the body: penitence, sexuality, incarceration. Science is thus a 'panoptic' discipline, acting to control and oversee individual bodies and entire populations; but the human self is only discernible through the operation of such discourses, and alternatives glimpsed dimly in their contradictions. Knowledge is never attained independently of its uses, which are to coerce or resist; such power/knowledge is exerted by constructing certain kinds of bodies and thus certain notions of the Self, which is presumed by the power and hegemony of the disciplining technologies to be the total revelation of a 'true self'. Yet there is, for Foucault, no true self, and no genuine or authentic body either: his story of Hercule/ine Barbin, the notorious transsexual, for example, is not a humanistic rendering of this unfortunate individual's wrongful assignation (which is generally how transsexuality is spoken of in our culture); all that is available to Barbin is a variety of ways of ordering his/her anatomical peculiarities.

Thus for Foucault, bodies are always already disciplined bodies; individuals are social subjects, knowable only through the representations of their own desires. This refusal to assert a constant human nature persisting throughout history characterizes Foucault's work: 'truth and the human subject that knows truth are not unchanging givens but are systematic differential productions within a network of power relations' (Arac, 1988:vii). Similarly, Foucault's favoured heuristic methods of 'genealogy' and 'archaeology', refusing singular causations, seeing knowledge as never able to transcend the conditions of its own production, preclude notions of a privileged knower or social actor who, once in possession of the truth, will thence be set free. However, although there can never be a final or definitive 'revelation' of absolute truth, many commentators argue that there is still space in Foucault's thinking to allow for dissent and transformation. Despite his avowed anti-humanism, the constant scepticism and deconstruction of fixed positions implied by his archaeological enquiries destabilizes dominant power relations and exposes the 'underground' discourses. Sawicki offers the following rendering of Foucault, one which implicitly connects him to feminist and poststructuralist understandings of subjectivity as a site of multiplicity, dissonance and dissidence:

> To suggest, as Foucault does, that the human is a social and historical construct is not to discredit every attempt to understand ourselves, but merely to discredit those that claim to be universal and to represent the Archimedean leverage point from which society might be moved . . . The Foucauldian views the relationship between the social and the individual not as one of univocal determination but as one of conflict and ambiguity. Individuals are the vehicles as well as the targets of power . . . Eschewing the notion of a core identity, the genealogist attempts to mobilize the many sources of resistance made possible by the many ways in which individuals are constituted. (Sawicki, 1988:174–75)

Once again, therefore, themes emerge of the self as contradictory but subversive; and embodiment as simultaneously a process of enclosure in dominant hegemonic discourses, and the refusal to bend to conscious, public exercises of power. The Body is shadowy in that there is no 'real' core self; but (perhaps because of that enigmatic and constructed nature), it is also portrayed as an agent of transgression and transformation of constraining technologies and institutions. The Body, at the intersection of the concerns of social theory, is simultaneously coherent, coercive and totalizing, and chaotic, subversive and fragmented.

Feminism and the Feminine Body

The tension between being a subordinated and manipulated body, and seeing embodiment as the basis for a subversive or transformative agency, is deeply relevant to feminist theory and practice. Those who identify themselves as 'radical' feminists have argued that patriarchal domination of women is practised through various and systematic forms of bodily coercion, among which are the appropriation and institutionalization of women's health, especially in the sphere of reproductive self-determination; men's violence towards women; sexual objectification and exploitation; and the denial of women's autonomous sexuality.

Radical feminism counters this with a deliberate celebration of women's unique and specific identity as founded in embodiment, and uses this as the basis of a woman-centred politics, spirituality and epistemology. It is clearly apparent in the writing of Adrienne Rich, Monique Wittig and Margaret Atwood, and in the artistic creations of Judy Chicago, as well as the psychoanalytically-derived analysis of Luce Irigaray (Delphy, 1987; Irigaray, 1985; Whitford, 1991; Jones, 1981; Hite, 1988).

However, the manner in which radical and cultural feminism has appealed to women's bodily experiences has been the source of fierce debate, and has been accused by critics of collapsing into a form of biological 'essentialism'. Such accounts, it is argued, reify women's bodies within an ahistorical and apolitical realm, rendering an unmediated connection between biological sex and gender identity. The effect of this is to reinforce the patriarchal association of 'woman' with 'nature', and to deprive feminist politics of valuable analytical clarity and political leverage which locates the formation of gender within human culture and agency (Jaggar, 1983:105–13).

However, the debates about the body in feminist theory and practice do at least challenge gender studies to take account of bodiliness as an integral element of selfhood, and require gender theorists to address questions about the relationship between embodiment, our inhabitation of a particular culture, and the experiences available to us in evoking specific ways of knowing and acting.

Writing the Body

'Writing the Body' is a feminist strategy which deploys a celebration of women's bodiliness in a direct challenge to patriarchal expropriation. Molly Hite points to the subversion of masculinist 'closure' of women's identity by feminists' evocation of a polyverse, diffusely sensual feminine morphology, thereby defying the deterministic and prescriptive accounts of patriarchy (Hite, 1988:121–22). Such a celebration and self-affirmation of feminine sexuality and embodiment is intended to reveal that woman cannot be controlled and enclosed in androcentric norms of difference and bodily representations.

Writing the body thus attempts to counter the effects of a 'somatophobic' Western philosophy, with its implicit dualism, its notions of a neutral (but covertly male) rational subject, and a consequent epistemology which seeks to invalidate or suppress somatic and psychosexual experience (Spelman, 1982:119). The Platonic tradition taught that only the soul and the mind could be counted upon as sources of true knowledge; and Plato pointed to women as imperfect beings insofar as their behaviour and preoccupations betrayed their bodiliness. Liberal feminism has tended to inherit this tradition, conceptually unable to reintegrate bodily experience into its notion of the subject, and excluding women's somatic oppression or welfare from its political manifesto. Radical feminism, however, argues that bodies are more than mere appendages to 'pure reason', and seeks strategies by which the implicit dualism of liberal theories of selfhood might be undermined, and with it the conventions that associate the feminine with the subordinate 'Other' of such a system.

As in the celebration of womanhood inherent in cultural feminism, this particular genre sets out to rescue women's sexuality and morphology from the dominant modes of patriarchal culture which objectify and expropriate women's sexuality, whether in censorious, romanticized or exploitative fashion. Given the common feminist argument that women's oppression in any society is frequently directed at freedom of sexual expression – be that lack of access to contraception and abortion, or practices like clitoridectomy, or sanctions against women who do not relate sexually to men, and so on – it is valuable to encounter a genre of feminism which both protests against the role of sexuality in women's subordination and focuses on valuing women's own pleasure and morphology as a source of protest and self-determination.

Nevertheless, the celebration of female morphology and the sense of living in a female body must not be assumed to be transparent and unambiguous. Part of the experience of being a woman in a man's world is that no experience is unaffected by society's prescriptions about what women should do, be and look like (Brownmiller, 1986; Lawrence, 1987; Wolf, 1991). Issues of bodily self-determination, pleasure for oneself, being satisfied with one's own bodily appearance, regardless of messages from medicine and the slimming and fashion industries, are important sites of feminist struggle; however, they simply underline the difficulty women face in gaining access to a body that is truly theirs, and expresses their personality and sense of being-in-the-world with some measure of authenticity.

The struggle to find a vocabulary by which women can articulate self-knowledge in a patriarchal culture that has so colonized women's experiences of themselves is clearly exemplified in the work of Luce Irigaray. She is one of a group of French-based feminists who draw upon the psychoanalytic school of Jacques Lacan to emphasize the significance of women's embodied sensuality in generating an alternative source of self-knowledge and authoritative speech.

For Lacan, the acquisition of gender and social identity is associated with the adoption of speech, which predicates a positioning relative to the 'Phallus', the symbol of a male-dominated society that disavows plurality, dissent or heterogeneity. Luce Irigaray argues that the construction of selfhood is centred around 'phallogocentricism', rendering women as 'void' or 'lack'. The adoption of a feminine identity in culture necessitates demotion to that which is mysterious, invisible and unvoiced. Women's inability to name themselves as autonomous subjects under patriarchy is the political and cultural stumbling-block to the autonomy of feminine subjects (see also Chapter Eight).

The female body, therefore, has no opportunity to create for itself a coherent identity. Instead, patriarchal thought essentializes it as 'Other' and immaterial, and represses the feminine into the male unconscious. However, Irigaray uses female morphology deliberately to create an alternative ontology. In opposition to the unitary logic of patriarchal phallogocentric speech, the female body possesses multiple sites of pleasure, fluidity of sensuality, and the two lips of the vulva as a substitute for the single focus of the phallus (Irigaray, 1980; Whitford, 1991:112–18). Thus, women gain access to *jouissance*: the polymorphous, uninhibited sensuality which characterizes the pre-Oedipal realm of pure desire. Such a celebration of female sexuality serves to prefigure the feminist Utopia in which the feminine is not repressed by the 'symbolic' or cultural realm, but released like the unconscious under analysis. A logic which conceives of one sex alone – male, with female as lack – is thus challenged by a feminist voice which appropriates the products of its own psychic imaginings (necessarily born of the body) and transforms them into concrete social relations of feminist solidarity and social change.

Irigaray's intention is to reinstate women as creatures of true essence, subverting Aristotelian systems which deny this. Irigaray's radical project to rewrite Western epistemology and ontology restores the significance of the body, passion, libido and the unconscious as legitimate foundations of knowledge and selfhood. Being able to think *about* oneself, rather than to be thought *of* by another, is the project of feminist thought for Irigaray. Whitford calls Irigaray a 'maximalist' of difference; not seeking to minimize sex difference beyond reproduction, as in 'liberal' feminism, but asserting it and thereby creating a powerful female symbolic to stand alongside the male (Whitford, 1989:120).

Such a quality is not biologically determined but rather positional in relation to patriarchal language. However, this is the main point of contention about Irigaray's thought: the precise connection between cultural silence and anatomical difference. For Lacanian psychoanalysis, possession and acquisition of language and privileged social speech-positions stand in for bodily difference. Similarly, Irigaray's feminine bodies are highly metaphorical, the site of a pre-Oedipal, pre-social unconscious. Thus, Irigaray develops femininity as an essentialist, metaphysical category because it is from precisely this mysterious status beyond patriarchal language and culture that women derive their subversive power. However, for this to work as a feminist strategy, such bodies must be socially inscribed. The risk is that the evocation of feminine *jouissance* takes place in a realm inaccessible to any productive or material human agency. By placing the female body outside patriarchal culture, the more effectively to challenge androcentric norms, Irigaray risks rendering women's bodies immaterial and rhetorical, rather than empirical and rooted in social relations.

Accusations of apoliticism and essentialism have been levelled at Irigaray. Many Anglo-Saxon feminists read her work as either espousing a form of psychic essentialism, with distinct and separate male and female libidos, grounded irrevocably in different kinds of bodies, or as reverting to a biologically deterministic account of femininity. However, Irigaray is better understood as a theorist of change who draws upon a metaphorical and philosophical reading of psychoanalytic theory. It is to the body as an alternative source of knowledge, and, ultimately, of feminist praxis, that Irigaray looks.

Martin Stanton supports Irigaray against her materialist critics by defending her emphasis on the body as the proper province of psychoanalysis:

> Luce Irigaray's work on alternative spacing for women has so far been principally concerned with morphology. Some of her critics . . . have suggested that this emphasis has again obscured the problem of political action by reducing everything to the level of process . . . Women do not want to be told how to analyse after the event but want a strategy to enable them to act effectively now. The space they want is freedom to walk the streets at night not some inner space to understand themselves. A moot point or nice aside but it totally fails to appreciate the location of Irigaray's ideas . . . What emotional effects are produced with the intellectual acceptance of set political positions. How women think in other words – are taught to think – they live with and in their bodies. The crucial question of what determines their identity and difference. (1983:80–81)

For Stanton, Irigaray and psychoanalysis, the crucial issue is one of morphology: the body is the site of the creation of identity, and is therefore very properly the focus of critical discourse. The task of feminist strategies is precisely to reinscribe the body at the heart of social theory, gender relations and epistemology. However, the risk of Irigaray's strategy is not so much due to her concentration on the body in itself, but more the way in which morphology is rendered as a pre-social, fixed essence which silences rather than invites further examination. Feminist strategies of writing the body may envision a feminist Utopia, but they are deployed in cultures where the perception of women as bodily, natural and alien to culture and philosophy is still all too familiar. While it may be right to relocate and explain gender relations and subjectivity in relation to the morphological, it is important to see that such territory is hotly contested.

Such feminist renderings of the body therefore deliberately draw upon the psychoanalytic fusion of psyche and soma: the body as no longer passive, but always holding the potential to 'speak' and disclose new self-knowledge previously repressed and now stored in the unconscious. It also serves to harness the element within psychoanalysis that sets civilization and desire at odds, and argues that bodies are simultaneously constrained and determined by society and social pressures, but also stand beyond and outside culture, threatening to undermine the surface order both of conscious rationality and of the social order. Arguably, it is this tradition, rather than a return to determinism and essentialism, that characterizes Irigaray's work.

Bodies as Sites of Resistance

Other studies have also attempted to document how a reclamation of women's bodily experience can be undertaken, with powerful implications for feminist politics. In particular, such studies explore the possibility of women's relationship to their bodies as potentially resistant to the closure of restrictive and punitive practices. (Foucault also conceived that 'disciplined bodies' might in certain circumstances be able to break out of such enclosures.) Not surprisingly, therefore, feminists have turned to evocations of bodies as sites of resistance – as active agents of transformative practice. In this strand, bodies are much less sites of restrictive technologies than metaphorical resources for subversion; the very mystery and otherness of the feminine body serving to destabilize patriarchal colonization of women's reproduction, sexuality and bodily integrity. Women are thus empowered to speak of their bodiliness for themselves, in opposition to patriarchal relations which have silenced them by only permitting men to do the defining.

Emily Martin attempts to bring the study of exotic and alien understandings of the body into the familiar and everyday. Her interviews with women in three age-groups and from different socio-economic classes in Baltimore in the mid-1980s aim to convey the taken-for-granted assumptions behind various pivotal experiences in women's lives. Menstruation, pregnancy/childbirth and menopause are not simple biological processes, but are stamped with the marks of medical discourse. The basic categories of 'society', 'personhood' and 'body' are social, and the metaphors employed to represent them reflect a patriarchal capitalist organization of activities such as work, medicine, families, homes and a gender dichotomy and gendered division of labour. The fragmentation and alienation of waged labour under capitalism are replicated in women's experiences of their own bodies as medicalized and mechanistic. Women's biology is represented in teleological terms; reproduction as the sole justifying function of their physiological and sexual well-being. Medicine is a practice which reflects hegemonic values, whereby menstruation, labour and menopause are impersonal inevitable events acting upon women who are powerless to affect them.

Nevertheless, those experiences do also present alternative avenues of experience, where loss of control and division of self from body are not inevitable, and it is possible for women to have a more active and self-possessed perception of themselves. One of Martin's claims is that the further away a group of women is from the dominant class, the greater the space for renegotiation and subversion of hegemonic meaning. Black working-class culture has generated entirely different ways of talking about and relating to those basic biological experiences, which depart from the medical discourse into more subjective realms. Martin draws upon the writers Dorothy Smith and Nancy Hartsock, who point to the possibilities of subordinate groups expressing values and perspectives of resistance to dominant ideologies via 'standpoint epistemologies' which transcend the dualisms of androcentric experience.

> What I would like to suggest . . . is that the seemingly abstract code of medical science in fact tells a very concrete story, rooted in our particular form of social hierarchy and control. Usually we do not hear the story, we hear only the 'facts', and this is part of what makes science so powerful. But women – whose bodily experience is denigrated and demolished by models implying failed production, waste, decay and breakdown – have it literally within them to confront the story science tells with another story, based in their own experience. (Martin, 1989:197)

Martin reiterates themes of the inherent rebellion lying dormant within bodies, which defies patriarchal discourses of dualism, and of the dormant possibilities to be found in the articulation of a selfhood which, whilst fragmented and contradictory, carries the germ of alternative understandings of what it means to be an embodied person. Women, living across the boundaries of public/private, mind/body, home/work, carry within their experience the conception of alternative means of organizing social reality. This is not an essentialist thesis, as Martin is at pains to emphasize: although biology is at the core of her analysis of their subordinate position, it is important to see bodily experience always as a function of wider social organization and as a bearer of meaning, both hegemonic and subversive. The relationship between morphology and meaning is, as Martin suggests, reflexive and malleable.

In concentrating on her subjects' accounts of their negotiation with medical treatments, Martin tends to leave unquestioned the actual specific processes by which scientific and medical orthodoxy is created and enforced. She recognizes that she has little access to a similar ethnography of doctors' understandings of the relationship between bodily experience, medical metaphors and social order. It is not clear, therefore, precisely what strategies might be available to women actually to realize alternative forms of knowledge in a political or policy context. Martin's women still appear to be on the receiving end of a fairly undifferentiated medical science, which, even if constructed, is nevertheless, phenomenologically speaking, 'hard fact', and supported by power relations which continue to subordinate women to the values and demands of capitalism. Martin's primary conclusion appears to be that, faced with the divorce of self from body under patriarchal dualism, all women can do is turn to poetry (1989:201–202). Furthermore, her earlier sceptical comments about the lack of critical accounts of women's health in the 'well woman' movement further suggest that she sees little creative space in such networks (1989:87–88). In fact, other accounts of such initiatives do appear to offer more hope by reporting women's attempts to bring their alternative experiences and constructions of their bodily experiences out of the subjective sphere into the public realm, and thereby actually persuading the medical establishment to consider new models of practice.[1] This serves as a corrective to the postmodern tendency, which regards alternative 'discourses' of bodily experience as no more than competing multiple narratives, and roots alternative generations of meaning in a strategy for political and policy changes.

The Male Body

The return to morphology in feminist theory represents a coming to terms with the effects of a gendered culture which has produced a characterization of human nature in which women are bodies, and are their bodies, in a way men are not. Men's bodies do not feature in social theory; psychoanalysis theorizes about the penis and the Phallus, but very little of the immediacy of men's own real lived bodies is visible. Critical studies of men and masculinity are beginning to engage with the issues of embodiment: but, as with feminism, there is a clear division between Marxist-orientated theorists and those more psychoanalytically and culturally influenced, who are in general choosing to concentrate on questions of style, desire and power (Brittan, 1989; Chapman and Rutherford, 1988; Nelson, 1992; Segal, 1990).

Studies of men-and-masculinity exhibit a marked consensus that masculinity may be understood as constructed around the denial of femininity and embodiment. Arthur Brittan remarks that Cartesian dualism represents the 'disembodiment' of reason, whereby the thinking, active (male) agent is assumed not to require a body in order to possess full selfhood. Masculine disembodiment is therefore only possible on the condition of feminine 'otherness', and women's only identity derives entirely from the inhabitation of their all-determining corporeality:

> A history of masculinity is the struggle to tame and subdue the emotional and sexual self and to recognise the ascendant and superior nature of reason and thought. The dominant meanings of masculinity in our culture are about producing our bodies as instruments to our wills. Flesh, sexuality, emotionality, these become seen as uncontrollable forces and a source of anxiety. Male sexuality becomes not so much a concern of our relationships with other people, but with ourselves; a struggle between our intellects and libidos. We live within a culture that alienates men from their bodies and sexuality. We learn to repress them because they are the antithesis of what it means to be masculine. It's a repression that we project onto others. Our struggle for self control is acted out as mastery over others. (Rutherford, 1988:26)

Whether the analysis is radical feminism's denunciation of all men as pathological by virtue of their inherently violent sexual natures, or

another understanding which emphasizes the importance of practice, cathexis and 'embodied intentionality' (Brittan, 1989:199), it is
actually male *bodies* that are agents of masculinity and patriarchy,
however such bodies are constructed, marshalled and exercised.
Thus, however elusive, the male body must not be allowed to be
obscured as an object of scrutiny for gender studies; and in fact, it
may be argued that a reassociation of men with the somatic begins to
break the hold of dualist rationality which denies men their bodies
whilst allowing women nothing else (Shilling, 1993).

Nevertheless, just as much theorizing about 'the Body' seems to
leave bodies as lived experiences strangely untouched, so studies of
masculinity seem to stop short of really engaging with the problem
of male bodies. Many commentators have noted how men's responses to feminism often manage to deflect attention away from
men and masculinity and back to women; as Irigaray has said, 'the
bodily in men is what metaphysics has never touched' (quoted in
Nelson, 1987:157). Masculinity is theorized as being about power,
race, sexuality and, latterly, consumption and style; but never,
ultimately, about what it means to live in a man's body, to practice
gender as an embodied – but culturally mediated – male. (Perhaps
this is the Phallus as the ultimate transcendental signifier!) What
might it mean for a man to 'write his body'?

Bodies and Practice

The body thus occupies a significant role in the generation of gender
identity and social relations. However, to 'reclaim' the gendered
body, analytically and strategically, is to be clearly differentiated
from biological determinism, partly because theories of gender have
become sceptical of 'biology' as a category of definition. Thus it is
possible to conceive of a return to the question of bodily difference as
something tangible but not deterministic: 'The body-as-used, the
body I am, is a social body that has taken meanings rather than
conferred them . . . The body, without ceasing to be the body, is
taken in hand and transformed in social practice' (Connell,
1987:87).

Rosi Braidotti confirms suggestions made earlier that much of the
debate about the body in feminism is about knowledge and ontology

(1989, 89–105). Feminist strategies of 'writing the body' would serve to claim unique and distinctive knowledge arising from the relationship between selfhood and/as embodiment, and epistemology. Such an appeal to embodied humanity is portrayed as providing the potential for a thorough deconstruction of Western androcentric philosophy and rationality. The affirmation of women as sexed and embodied is only essentialist within the constricting and closed controlling discourses of patriarchy; as both Braidotti and Whitford argue, feminists like Irigaray actually reconstitute the terms on which an appeal to the body is made. The body becomes a site of the unity and autonomy of identity, because the body stands at the intersection of self and society, psychic and material. Thus patriarchal definitions of ontology and epistemology are challenged by what Braidotti terms the 'feminist cogito', and with them evocations of women as inhabitants of fixed and closed realms of bodily existence, which have no positive content beyond being the negation of masculine, rational and normative subjectivity.

What is at issue, therefore, is not the facticity or materiality of sexual difference or anatomy, but the interpretations and symbolism that make reproductive difference so primary in determining social destiny. However, against deconstructionists who seem to wish the body to remain immaterial (literally) and destabilized to the verge of disappearance, the growing argument for the recovery of the Body also carries an implicit appeal to an ethic that chooses to ground itself in the very facticity of bodies to gender relations and politics. This is of itself an implicit denial of the dualism of determinism and categoricalism: bodies are neither irrelevant nor all-determining.

Chris Shilling refers to the body in social theory as an 'absent presence', referring once more to the paradox of the ubiquity of human embodiment amidst its corresponding undertheorization (Shilling, 1993:19–20). Similarly, I have already noted the tendency of many studies of the body, for all their concretion and materialism, to collapse into abstraction. A more useful perspective on 'The Body' may be on 'our bodies/my body' as sites of agency, construction and practice: 'We all have bodies and this constitutes part of what makes us human beings possessed of the ability to communicate with each other, and experience common needs, desires, satisfactions and frustrations' (Shilling, 1993:23).

Simone de Beauvoir's solution to the dichotomy of dis/embodiment is that of 'situation' (Butler, 1987:133). Bodies might be conceived as being both 'artefacts' or fabrications of culture; but also genuine 'vantage points' for renewed creative agency and transformative practice.[2] Bodies may well be texts, and sites of discourse; but they are also the vehicles and objects of coercion and injustice.

Similarly, Frank starts from the premise that the control of bodies is an especial site of gender oppression and argues for a gender politics which roots itself in this fact. Frank presents an ethical rationale for maintaining a commitment to a transformative politics, namely that human bodies suffer. He thereby attempts to counter the implicit anti-humanism of some perspectives which claim no constant or enduring 'human nature' outside of the discourses of power and oppression. Ethics should therefore take the 'fundamental embodiment of social action' as their point of departure. This requires us to take seriously the material realities of concrete practices which harm, neglect or coerce bodily people, and to construct a hermeneutic of gender which tackles the complex process by which bodies, via social practices, create social relations and institutions which themselves have already served to shape and construct social conventions of embodiment and selfhood.

> It is . . . disingenuous to write a history of sexual difference, or difference generally, without acknowledging the shameful correspondence between particular forms of suffering and particular forms of the body, however the body is understood. The fact that pain and injustice are gendered and correspond to corporeal signs of sex is precisely what gives importance to an account of the making of sex. (Laqueur, 1990:15–16)

Clearly, therefore, the story of how we inhabit our bodies in and against historical and cultural contexts, where meanings are contested by a variety of media – medicine, religion and politics, as well as whatever constitutes our sense of these categories we call selfhood, subjectivity and experience – is immensely complex. The fundamental claim of such enquiries yet remains: bodies are crucial actors in the cultural rendition of gender, even though critical access to them in order to analyse their participation in the process is fraught with difficulty.

Notes

1. One example would be the 'well women' movement, and models of obstetric practice which focus on the needs of the mother as well as those of the baby.

2. The work of Maurice Merleau-Ponty develops a similar understanding of the relationship of embodiment to existence and self-knowledge; see Merleau-Ponty (1945), and Kruks (1975).

7 · Ideas of Nature

Whatever 'nature' might be in itself, we can know it only as we construct it through vocabularies laden with social relations, political purposes, and moral commitments. (Flax, 1993:154)

In this chapter, I want to explore how repudiations of the so-called 'naturalistic fallacy' have fuelled debates in gender studies, concerning not only the social construction of gender as a cultural relation, but also the very certainty and reality of the realm of nature itself. From studies of historical appeals to nature as serving ideological ends, namely the rationalization of particular conceptions of the social order, to exposing appeals to the 'Eternal Feminine', to the taxonomization and pathologization of homosexualities in the name of 'natural' and 'normal' heterosexuality, scholars have identified critical ways in which the characterization of gender is called into question. Yet projects seeking new forms of gender relations are also challenged by such explorations, as in the debates over radical feminists' evocations of women's connectedness to nature as the source of transformative politics. Theories of nature would therefore appear crucial to theories of gender; but the relationship of women and the whole of humanity to nature, however problematic, requires critical attention which returns us to questions of knowledge, agency and identity.

In her introduction to an interdisciplinary set of essays on gender, Deborah Rhode identifies one of the central tasks of gender studies as examining, and exposing, the claims of naturalism (Rhode 1990:4). This she characterizes as the view that nature, rather than values, dictates human action. It can be understood as a kind of deterministic thinking, deriving its values about what is normative in human behaviour from that which it identifies as the 'facts' of nature. In the social sciences, such naturalistic thought is often characterized as a form of pre-critical, 'common-sense' reasoning, implicitly repudiating all other factors and denying sociological perspectives which, after Emile Durkheim, regard 'social facts as things'. Humanity's biological constitution serves as an all-encompassing and satisfactory explanation of all other phenomena, rendering all other levels of analysis redundant or illusory (Lewontin *et al.*, 1984).

Criticisms of the assumption that biological science tells us the 'truth' about ourselves, revealing the facts about our essential and fundamental nature, centre around the assumption of 'objectivity' by partial and biased perspectives. The status of science is dependent upon its value-freedom and facticity; but it is actually connected to power systems in wider society which use science to rationalize women's subordination and present particular renditions of gender as privileged. Scientific enquiry is therefore to be regarded as a form of social practice, reflecting the power relations and interests of a wider social order; clearly, it is necessary to examine critically the very category of 'Nature' to which such deterministic and reductionist analyses make their appeal.

There is a marked consensus within the human sciences over the universal tendency to characterize human activity according to a binary opposition between 'culture' and 'nature', although, as I discussed in Part Two, the terms of definition and boundaries between the two concepts are culturally variable. However, the ubiquity of such binary oppositions and their association with other dichotomies, including those of man/woman and masculine/feminine, makes such categories highly potent cultural symbols. Even if a perspective is adopted which refuses to essentialize such dichotomies, it is still important to examine the origins and dynamics of such bifurcations. What lies behind different ideas of nature, and why such 'ideas of nature' are crucial to gender studies and feminist theory, are essential questions in the development of a critical analysis.

'Nature' in Historical Context

R.G. Collingwood, in *The Idea of Nature* (1945), argues that there have been three dominant conceptions of nature in human history: Greek, renaissance and 'modern' views. The thesis underpinning his survey of how these ideas developed and superseded one another is two-fold: firstly, that such ideas evolve in dynamic interaction with scientific practice, and secondly that they are historically grounded.

Ideas of nature, according to Collingwood, never emerge in abstraction, but evolve out of reflection upon scientific activity. His work, and that of similar twentieth-century writers on the philosophy of nature (Leclerc, 1986), can be seen as an attempt to reunite the enterprise of philosopher and scientist. Before the renaissance, philosophers were scientists, and vice versa, because both regarded enquiry into the workings of the natural order as legitimate activity; but, after Descartes, when mind became seen as ontologically distinct from body, the two disciplines diverged, as philosophy became concerned with mental processes and epistemology. Collingwood aims to bring the two into interaction once more, by arguing that scientific experimentation and verification are inherently philosophical activities, because scientific practice and philosophical reflection proceed in concert with one another to generate theories of science and nature (Collingwood, 1945).

An attention to the philosophy of nature necessitates not just an interest in the history of ideas but in history itself, as events, actors and social contexts. Natural science consists of hypotheses and theories; but these are merely records of people's observations. Thus, they constitute historical events, and so notions of nature depend on particular temporal and social contexts for their existence. So, 'natural science as a form of thought exists and always has existed in a context of history, and depends on historical thought for its existence . . . We go from the idea of nature to the idea of history' (Collingwood, 1945:177).

A critical attention to ideas of nature thus necessitates a historical perspective. The meaning of the term 'nature' lies not in some dictionary definition, but in the various ways in which an appeal to nature is used to elucidate a wider world-view. The history of the term 'nature' is therefore one of its deployment within political discourse, and critical analysis involves an examination of the rhetorical qualities that nature comes to represent. Historical studies argue that, prior to the Scientific Revolution, nature as a category often carried diverse or even contradictory meanings (Brown and Jordanova, 1982; Bloch and Bloch, 1980; Offen, 1990). However, gradually nature became reified, with a unitary meaning, denoting the essential basic constitution of reality, embodying fundamental and immutable qualities. From the nineteenth century, arguments begin 'nature is . . .' or 'nature teaches . . .': nature becomes the absolute repository of universal laws, which are seen as fixed, ahistoric and unchanging givens. Nature might intervene in history, as in the theory of evolution, but essentially it was seen as a blind force that acted only according to its own laws and ends.

In interaction with changing philosophies were changing technological and economic trends, requiring greater examination and manipulation of natural resources. By abstracting 'nature' to an impersonal force, and separating it from human interaction, such intervention could be exonerated, because the natural realm was no longer a transcendent mystery, but an immanent storehouse, predictable on its own terms alone without recourse to a doctrine of divine power or control.

Thus social philosophers like Locke and Rousseau posited an idyllic state of nature alongside which culture seemed like a fall from grace; Hobbes by comparison regarded humanity's life-chances in a state of nature as 'solitary, poor, nasty, brutish and short', and regarded culture and the Social Contract as the force which protected humanity from itself. Theories of society thus required a clear separation from the realm of nature in order to sanction the immense economic and material transformations of the eighteenth century in Europe. However, it was necessary to maintain a rhetorical link between the accompanying social changes and the notion of an axiomatic and eternal nature, which underwrote and guaranteed the self-evident goodness of nascent social interests (Plumwood, 1993:41–68;104–19).

Historically, features conceptualized as belonging to a realm of pure nature, immune from human efforts, can be exposed as reflecting political and social preoccupations. Studies in Jordanova's *Languages of Nature* and Hubbard's discussion of Darwinism examine how discourses about nature in scientific accounts were invested with cultural conventions and presuppositions (Jordanova, 1986; Hubbard, 1981). However, even such evocations of nature are constructions: if the boundaries and characteristics of nature itself are historically contingent, then it is possible to concede that nature is not a fixed category. Arguably, theories of evolution themselves portray nature as evolving, adapting and developing in response to new conditions and imperatives. Val Plumwood's analysis perhaps comes closest to this when she argues that no concept of 'nature' is free of cultural construction. Historically, nature has been defined in opposition to 'reason'; and the 'idea of nature' in Western thought is necessarily a colonized and circumscribed nature. Thus, appeals to nature do not necessarily have to portray it as a blind, immutable force; it is a sign of the political intentions of such appeals that invariably they seem to do so.

Gender Relations and 'The Death of Nature'

Although nature and women are not ontologically connected, it is clear that historically the social practices of science, medicine and political philosophy have served to construct and communicate the central metaphors by which they have been linked. One particular historical approach that has caught the imagination, particularly of feminists, is the 'death of nature' narrative, as exemplified by Carolyn Merchant, and developed by Brian Easlea and others (Merchant, 1990; Jordanova, 1987; Easlea, 1980; Keller, 1985; Schiebinger, 1989).

Exposing the connections between the rise of scientific rationality and the objectification of nature and women in the name of the scientific enterprise has been influential in supporting the analysis of two strands of feminist theory and politics, namely radical feminism and ecofeminism. Both draw explicit connections between the domination of nature and the subordination of women, and seek to refigure the traditional connections between the two. For Merchant, the use of gendered imagery in the nature-culture debates of the Scientific Revolution reveals a process by which one philosophy of nature succeeded another. Merchant traces how the practices of capital accumulation and social domination effect a shift from a model of nature as a living organism on which humanity was deeply dependent to a model of a machine to be controlled. Thus social and material change contributed to the development of objectivist, instrumental values. Language serves to decode the patterns of wider social relations, in this case the metaphors depicting the process of industrialization and the development of modern science, and their subsequent impact on gender relations.

Merchant's analysis is both historically detailed and sophisticated. She argues that meanings of nature were often various and complex, so that evocations of a pastoral past of social harmony could co-exist with views of nature as unpredictable and savage. But these contested views of nature were actively deployed in the construction of social philosophies that then fuelled struggles for cultural hegemony.

The association of women and nature pre-dated the Scientific Revolution. Aristotelian notions of women as mere matter, contributing nothing to reproduction, reinforced perceptions of women as passive, irrational and uncreative. With the development of new technologies for controlling nature, and debates about the shape of new social and political orders, women could be excluded from science and education and from full citizenship via their traditional association with nature, the passive, inanimate and pre-social. Women could be venerated as the guardians of natural bucolic values; or feared as wanton, degenerate and subversive (Merchant, 1990).

Merchant avoids the risk of historicism by allowing space for discussion of the development of scientific practice itself, not simply as the site for imported ideologies, but as generating material and technological changes which contributed to the shaping of new social problems and philosophies (Merchant, 1990:42–43; 67;177ff;288). Nor is *The Death of Nature* merely a story of a pre-capitalist idyll of human co-operation and ecological harmony swept away by a bourgeois science intent on raping and plundering the earth. Merchant argues that science itself has always been heterogeneous, a pluralistic discipline, sensitive to changing social contexts and comprising a diversity of theoretical models and practical methods. The organic model has never been entirely eclipsed, either in post-renaissance science or today.

The language of nature also helped establish the claims of Enlightenment appeals to the primacy of reason. Lloyd traces the association between women and nature/irrationality, and argues that it is present in earliest Greek philosophy (Lloyd, 1984). However, historians of the eighteenth and early nineteenth centuries seem to agree that such binary representations gained political importance as they were deployed to establish and entrench the substance of the Scientific and Industrial Revolutions. Thus, as Brown and Jordanova argue, the eighteenth century was a period of sharpening gender divisions, where language linking women with nature was part of the strategy of constructing a scientific culture. The model of human nature assumed by the trends associated with the Scientific

Revolution and the Enlightenment equated human identity and self-determination with the possession of reason; in distinguishing the world of human agency, or culture, from that of nature, it was necessary to associate the natural with the non-rational. Women were assumed to be ontologically closer to nature than men, and therefore bound to the realm of bodiliness, sexuality, decay and finitude. The association of women with nature is therefore part of a dualistic system that excludes these elements from what Plumwood terms the 'master identity' of modern technical-rational society (Plumwood, 1993).

Women thus served as the metaphorical bearers of irrational, conservative nature; and because of their reproductive association with the natural, women were deemed unfit to participate in the public cultural activities of science and politics. This legitimated control and manipulation over nature, but also served to privilege scientific methods and epistemology by asserting reason over superstition (Brown and Jordanova, 1982:394).

Merchant's book further advances and places in context the argument that appeals to nature are inherently political and reflect the preoccupations of their time. The replacement of animistic, organic notions of nature with mechanistic, inert models signalled what she terms the 'death of nature' and the beginnings of its exploitation, a process that she blames for our current ecological crisis. Models of nature reflect dominant social values; thus modern mechanistic understandings are drawn from the values and practices of industrial capitalism. Then in turn, taken-for-granted cosmologies re-enter the political realm, and are used to sanction as 'natural', and therefore inevitable, particular structures of social relations and concepts of the self:

> The rise of mechanism laid the foundation for a new synthesis of the cosmos, society, and the human being, construed as ordered systems of mechanical parts subject to governance by law and to predictability through deductive reasoning. A new concept of the self as a rational master of the passions housed in a machine-like body began to replace the concept of the self as an integral part of a close-knit harmony of organic parts united to the cosmos and society . . . But mechanism as a metaphor ordered and restructured reality in a new way, eliminating some kinds of ideas and problems from its scope of explanation, and opening up new ones for investigation. Among its great strengths were that it served not only as an answer to the problem of social and

cosmic order, but it also functioned as a justification for power and dominion over nature. (Merchant, 1990:214–15)

The machine so exemplifies a neutral, passive, inanimate natural order upon which an omnipotent and detached humanity acts, that Western science appears to deny notions of knowledge as value-laden and context-bound. This eliminates any notion of effective relationships between knower and known; any notion of humanity as formed out of the application of its labour to the resources of the earth; and notions of social and political structures emerging from human practices. Merchant quotes Heidegger's critique of post-Cartesian philosophy, namely its obsession with power and control over the object of its own knowledge. What new forms of knowing and relating to our world might develop as an alternative? Merchant hints at new ecological orders emerging, which conceptualize nature as random, wild and unstable:

> Emerging over the past decade are a number of scientific proposals that challenge the Scientific Revolution's mechanistic view of nature · . . . The recent emergence of chaos theory in mathematics suggests that deterministic, linear, predictive equations, which form the basis of mechanism, may apply to unusual rather than usual situations . . . Chaos theory reveals patterns of complexity that lead to a great understanding of global behaviours, but militate against over-reliance on the simple predictions of linear differential equations . . . The mechanistic framework that legitimated the industrial revolution with its side effects of resource depletion and pollution may be losing its efficacy as a framework. (Merchant, 1990:xvii–xviii)

Ultimately, this interpretation risks becoming simply another chapter in the story of a reified nature, unless this version can carry with it a recognition of its own constructed and hypothetical character. Whatever the case, the mechanistic model is clearly under attack, with intriguing political and epistemological implications. If nature is perceived as dynamic, fluid and disordered, then appeals to the idea of nature would not necessarily mean essentialized, reified accounts, signifying foreclosive and deterministic traits. Similarly, the acquisition and generation of gender identity might be seen not as fixed but as 'context dependent' and non-essential. Gender dichotomy existed before the mechanistic world-view gained ascendancy, so it would be foolhardy to assume that the rise of 'new physics' will necessarily challenge existing gender divisions all by itself. However, it might give us new conceptual frameworks of selfhood, causation, objectivity, structural/individual relations and rationality which might assist changes in the social order which facilitate understandings of gender as a form of human practice, natural and cultural.

Such studies in the history of science serve to illustrate the notion that nature and everything that is understood to be 'of nature' is constituted in and by culture. Nature always has an author, even if renditions of the 'natural' like to claim that its genesis was divine or spontaneous. Scientific practices construct for us the universals and essences of nature, and therefore the fundamentals of human nature, but such science reflects values and practices of wider society: 'Facts are theory-laden; theories are value-laden; values are history-laden' (Haraway, 1991:77).

Historical studies of the specific contexts within which certain configurations of nature developed, and the relationship between images and concepts of nature and gender metaphors, reveal the complexity and often inherent contradiction of specific concepts of nature. Nature has a history, inscribed in social relations, especially social relations of medicine, family, sexuality, work and bodies, which deploy gender and nature metaphors to naturalize power relations. Metaphors of nature tell us about their authors: the state of nature is held to be whatever theorists desire about the ideal society.

The Social Construction of the Natural

The work of Kessler and McKenna (1978) applies the claims of ethnomethodology to the study of gender. They conclude that in terms of most people's taken-for-granted experiences, gender dichotomy is understood as the norm – even though significant evidence in the world around us fails to support this empirically (see Chapters One and Four). Gender is not an axiomatic natural fact, but the process by which society attributes either one or the other gender to an individual. In keeping with the theoretical emphases of ethnomethodology, Kessler and McKenna argue that the assumptions and criteria guiding us in the process of attributing gender are not objectively real, but socially constructed. The 'natural' world is assumed to be one in which gender is dichotomous and follows the dictates of dimorphous biological sex in a straightforward fashion.

Interpretation of physical evidence is shaped to conform with this taken-for-granted evidence, so the arbitrary nature of gender dichotomy is never exposed: 'Biological, psychological and social differences do not lead to our seeing two genders. Our seeing of two genders leads to the "discovery" of biological, psychological and social differences' (Kessler and McKenna, 1978:163).

Transsexualism serves further to illustrate the processes involved in the construction and maintenance of gender dichotomies, even at the point of their supposedly apparent breakdown. Transsexuals believe themselves to be the wrong sex in the wrong body; but, in aiming to 'pass' as their chosen gender, they confirm gender dichotomy by self-consciously conforming to established stereotypes of masculinity or femininity. Self-help material for male-to-female transsexuals gives advice on 'passing successfully' in a female role. In order for the transsexual to be successful in gaining surgical reassignment of sex, he/she must satisfy psychiatrists, surgeons and general practitioners of his/her plausibility as a 'conventional' woman, even if that requires considerable adjustments to habitual patterns of speech, body language and manner:

> If your appearance is perfect and your voice acceptable, your manner of behaviour can still betray you . . . Whatever one believes the respective social roles of men and women ought to be, simple observation can be very revealing as to what they actually are. Men are frequently condescending towards women and often interrupt them in conversation. Women rarely interrupt men, are used to having their opinions ignored, even on subjects they may know more about, and hesitate to correct men openly especially in public . . .
>
> It is well to realise that to deviate too strongly from the culturally accepted norm will defeat the object of blending inconspicuously . . . There is no simple formula to develop a pleasant and acceptable feminine manner but given time thought and observation it can be done. (SHAFT, 1981:5–6)

The reason for this may be self-protection, or even adherence to socially acceptable behaviour in order to be guaranteed treatment; but Kessler and McKenna also insist that transsexuals think of their behaviour and quest for 'corrective' surgery as strategies to restore order and dichotomy to the disorder of their ambivalent position in the gender system. Transsexuals' insistence on having a 'true' gender at odds with the one attributed at birth is therefore in keeping with a wider society which takes gender dichotomy for granted and assumes that an individual's sex is normatively innate, and that gender must be clearly and unambiguously derived from the natural facts of biology.

A more recent article by Suzanne Kessler further serves to indicate how, in phenomenological terms, we act not according to observed empirical facts, but through the filter of our taken-for-granted presuppositions about the world. From a case study of medical staff working with intersexed infants, she concludes that practice operates to ensure phenomenological conformity to a 'realist' notion of two clearly differentiated genders. Physicians pride themselves on the speed and incontrovertibility of their clinical judgement as to whether a child is truly male or female, and on the effectiveness of subsequent treatment. Nor is this a strategy designed simply to mollify anxious parents of intersexed children; physicians in counselling parents generally reassure them that social factors and upbringing are the most influential in determining gender identity. Yet despite this, and despite the complexity and often indeterminacy of the analytical procedures involved in assigning biological sex – analysis of hormonal and gonadotrophic levels, chromosome measurement, cytological and genitographic screening – physicians base their decisions chiefly on the viability of genital reconstruction and appearance. Kessler argues that physicians maintain they are bowing to parental pressure, but in fact deproblematize sex/gender by behaving as if they are 'discovering' a child's sex rather than constructing it:

> Although the deformity of intersexed genitals would be immutable were it not for medical interference, physicians do not consider it natural. Instead they think of, and speak of, the surgical/hormonal alteration of such deformities as natural because such intervention returns the body to what it 'ought to have been' if events had taken their typical course. The non-normative is converted into the normative, and the normative state is considered natural. The genital ambiguity is remedied to conform to a 'natural', that is, culturally indisputable, gender dichotomy . . . Language and imagery help create and maintain a specific view of what is natural about the two genders and, I would argue, about the very idea of gender – that it consists of two exclusive types: female and male. The belief that gender consists of two exclusive types is maintained and perpetuated by the medical community in the face of incontrovertible physical evidence that this is not mandated by biology. (Kessler, 1990:24–25)

Intersexuality is, like transsexuality, therefore, an exception that proves the rule: intersexed children have a gender (re)constructed in such a way as to eclipse the fact that gender is always constructed, and that the biology said to underlie gender identity and dichotomy is also often ambiguous and complex.

The 'Eternal Feminine'

The political significance of repudiating arguments from nature has already been noted. Critical studies of gender have exposed how characteristics attributed to women and men are portrayed as innate and universal, and dualisms as mirroring natural imperatives rather than products of human discourse. One of the most systematic efforts in this area, and exemplifying feminist challenges to ahistorical essentialist evocations of the 'feminine', was Viola Klein's *The Feminine Character*, first published in 1946.

Karl Mannheim was Klein's colleague and mentor, and his intellectual influence is apparent, as her interpretative and critical framework springs from the sociology of knowledge. In investigating the debates about the 'Woman Problem' at the end of World War Two, Klein argued that attention must be directed to the interests of the ruling classes in taxonomizing and theorizing femininity. Klein was concerned that evocations of women's natural abilities and propensities were being used to bolster certain economic and social policies, in particular to reverse the mass entrance of women into the labour market during the war years. If femininity could be rooted in discrete, tangible and essential qualities which pointed to women's innate capacity for nurture and maternity, social policy could then be grounded in unequivocal empirical evidence.

Klein examined what femininity meant for a variety of social thinkers, and argued that it was always subject to historical and intellectual trends. Femininity is never static and essentialist, although many thinkers make use of Kantian philosophy (Sayers in Klein, 1989:xix). Even notions of bisexuality and androgyny work from the assumption that fixed essences can be chosen or combined. Klein rejects this. She also identifies the impact of Darwinian evolutionary biology on Havelock Ellis, Otto Weininger, Sigmund Freud and W.I. Thomas, and its conception of an all-pervasive force of nature propelling human development. 'Whatever is in harmony with Nature is beyond good and evil' (Klein, 1989:43). However, evidence is selected as significant only if it conforms to *a priori* standards of evolutionary function: 'any trait which is in harmony with the general trend of evolution will be natural and organic; all other characteristics will be artificial and transient' (Klein, 1989:43).

There is also an implicit Romanticism in the perception of a natural harmony between the sexes, thus enabling views of gender as complementary but separate. Just as nature ensured harmony in all its elements, so sexual reproduction, in order to be functional and successful, was required to be the unity of opposites. However, that which is predisposed as natural is itself a selective reading of the 'truth' of nature. As Anne Dickason's survey confirms, the characterization of the relative qualities of male and female derive from assumptions about male dominance and female submissiveness as existing in nature and primitive human societies and that such traits are eternal and essential in human behaviour (Dickason, 1977).

In conclusion, Klein notes that there is no list of feminine traits held in common by the theorists surveyed. All, however, are influenced by dualistic concepts, whereby woman is the reverse or the opposite or the 'double' of man. Klein again comments that dualistic categories of thought may impose some kind of heuristic order, but do little justice to actual human experience (Klein, 1989:169–70). There may be physiological and constitutional differences, but they must be identified with care and with attention to the influence of culture and environment. Klein however is no social constructionist; as Sayers remarks in her appraisal, she was ahead of her time in pleading for a model of human nature and of gender identity that eschewed reductionism of any kind (Sayers in Klein, 1989:xxii;89).

It may also be noted that even a focus on the possibility of an 'Eternal Feminine' presupposes that such a category might be distilled from a very diverse set of scientific enquiries, and that it might exist independent of history or social relations. A very different strategy might be to identify relations between women and men as the important issue in determining the fate of women in society, rather than seeking to root it in an abstract concept. However, this simply serves to foreground the contrast between the relational and contextual nature of gender, and theories which imply that such issues can be approached via fixed definitions of masculinity and femininity.

Other critical studies of gender relations have focused on the relationship between that which is prescribed as 'natural' and the policing of desire around activities associated with sexuality, consumerism, and the management of bodies and lifestyles (Armstrong and Tennenhouse, 1987; Coward, 1984). Here, again, a Foucauldian analysis shapes the debate: that which we perceive as the most intimate and authentic about ourselves is, paradoxically, the most public, scrutinized and engineered. Subjectivity is constructed via a series of discourses about that which is most desirable and desired, but each discourse also serves to 'naturalize', and therefore rationalize, itself as innate and immutable.

Feminism and the Problem of Nature

The historical association of women with nature is regarded within feminist theory as central to patriarchal social relations. Strategies for reclaiming or reframing cultural evocations of nature are therefore crucial to feminist programmes for the transformation of gender relations. However, feminist theorizations of nature are no less problematic than those which they seek to replace, and serve to indicate the ambiguities and complexities of political and strategic harnessing of the concept.

One issue for feminist theorists has been the extent to which the traditional identification of women and nature is something they wish to perpetuate, albeit on different terms. The approach of liberal feminism has been to divorce women from any association with nature; to emphasize the shared capacity of women and men for reason; and to demand equality of access to the public, cultural sphere (Tong, 1989:31–38).

A different stance is adopted by feminists like Shulamith Firestone. Whilst arguing that women's oppression rests in biological difference and the subordination of women's sexuality and reproductive capacity in patriarchy, she also envisaged liberation coming from the appropriation of childbirth by biotechnological means, thereby relieving women of the burdens of the 'natural' functions of reproduction which serve to exclude them from full participation in the cultural realm (Firestone, 1971).

However, later strands of radical feminism have criticized Firestone for failing to see the colonization of women's bodies by new technologies and hegemonic medical practices, and have chosen instead to venerate the connection between women and nature. Science remains a patriarchal institution; and women cannot expect liberation from this source. The abuse of nature is endemic – so women, rather than opting into the gyno/ecophobic system, must forge an alliance with nature (Daly, 1978; Griffin, 1980).

Thus, cultural feminist theorists such as Susan Griffin and Mary Daly exhort women to identify with nature and the cosmos against men and create a new, sane order free of the pathologies of patriarchy. Here, the analysis uses the traditional association of women with nature alongside a more recent emergent 'ecological' concern to argue that women's connectedness with nature offers new ways of knowing and living that will rescue them from militarism, environmental crisis and sexism. Both theoretical strands, therefore, illuminate the problem for feminist thought and practice: is the woman=nature equation inherently oppressive, or can it provide the source for an autonomous woman-centred politics?

It is arguable that neither approach is entirely satisfactory. Both can be accused of simply perpetuating the dualistic metaphors of women=nature and men=culture: liberals by advocating the wholesale adoption of androcentric culture and values; radicals by simply inverting the old Aristotelian and Thomist metaphysics. Certainly, Daly, and to a lesser extent Griffin, effectively reify a female identity, and appear to reduce the identities of women and nature into timeless essentialized phenomena. As many critics have remarked, this fails to take account of the differences and divisions between women, of class, race, religion and sexuality (Jaggar, 1983:249–302; Tong, 1989:95–138). It is therefore essentially a romantic and organic view of nature, albeit harnessed to a very different political agenda than that of the Romanticists; but, apart from this rather questionable metaphysical basis, it also fails to address the practical problem of what women's relationship with real-life technology should be. An assertion of the uniqueness and distinctiveness of women's experience still requires careful interrogation for the sources and grounds of such an epistemological claim.

One account of the relationship between the oppression of women, the development of modern science and the primacy of scientific rationality which exhibits some of these flaws is one by Evelyn Fox Keller, influenced by object-relations psychoanalysis (Keller, 1982). Keller's central criticism is of the concept of 'objectivity', which she sees as characterizing scientific epistemology as a result of the masculine gender identity emerging from the separation of subject and object. Nature is objectified as female, and knowledge as male. Women are excluded from science as unfit to be knowers; and nature is exploited as the male personality expresses its will to dominate.

Yet Keller's account tells the story in terms of fixed innate identities that leave little room for subversion or contradiction. Are all male scientists and philosophers inevitably prisoners of a particular standard of Oedipal objectivity? Similarly, Keller suggests that, via the device of 'co-mingling', women's values of empathy and relatedness might merge with those of reason and cognition. However, this is another example of a union, not a deconstruction or transformation, of dichotomous (and stable) gender identities, and reiterates themes of Romanticism rather than contributing to a renewal of the scientific enterprise. The relationship with nature is interesting here: it is either to be domination or 'ecstatic communion' – echoing the alternatives of the castrated boy and the pre-Oedipal girl – but there is no attempt to transcend the inevitability of these choices, or to consider that, if Merchant and Plumwood are to be believed, human interaction with nature and the underlying metaphysics have always been more complex than a simple choice.

The problem with the adoption of the 'death of nature' story by radical feminists is that it still leaves the boundaries of nature and culture unexamined. However, what has emerged consistently from the discussions above is that it is the drawing of the boundaries between the categories of nature and culture, and the implications of how each is defined in relation to the other, that serve to support particular social and ideological interests. Women may gain power and ecological connectedness from subverting the time-honoured associations of women=nature; but this does not 'unmake' the patriarchal practices and meanings which executed thousands of women for witchcraft by the same logic, although it may 'unmask' the history of that discourse. The danger is that it removes women from the same cultural frame as men, rendering culture a monolith and refusing any critical windows into the shared gender regimes of women and men. Nature and culture are still in antipathy; by separating women and men ontologically and sociopolitically, little critical leverage is gained in terms of the actual dynamics of that differentiation (Jaggar, 1983:18–22; 27–47;110–13).

Nature and Woman therefore remain rhetorical, rather than empirical or analytical, categories within this theorizing; the critique has absorbed Merchant's polemic, but not her attention to the shifts and subtleties of history and socioeconomic context. Linking domination of nature with suppression of women still does nothing to explain the specific historical relations which made the exclusion of women expedient to new developments in scientific practices, or to analyse the general cultural context which enabled metaphors drawing parallels between women and nature to claim people's attention powerfully and persuasively. It presupposes the existence of gender power in the process of trying to explain its origins.

This analysis also assumes that if women and nature are both subjugated under patriarchy, then women can be subsumed under the category of nature. Although this reminds us that humans are part of a living and changing creation (indeed this is one of its key political and ethical implications), there is a danger of regarding women as no different from any other part of oppressed 'nature', be that rainforests, rivers, mineral deposits or giant pandas. Like any other form of life – animal, vegetable or mineral – women certainly inhabit a nature that has been expropriated and defined by culture. However, unlike other (non-human) beings of nature, women also occupy culture in a more direct way by virtue of their common humanity with men. Forms of feminism which evoke women= nature and men=culture risk portraying men as the sole creators of culture, thus mimicking a central tenet of patriarchy. They deny women's productive and reproductive work, and ignore the social relations and interactions – personal, corporate and structural – between women and men that constitute culture. 'Patriarchy' may be androcentric, but it is not homosocial.

The perpetuation of the old nature/culture dichotomies in much feminist theory is discussed by the 'ecofeminist' Ynestra King (1989). She argues that we must regard the history of women as both natural and social. The revolt against women as 'natural' was important in that it exposed the myth of complementarity, by which women were simultaneously venerated and constrained as inhabitants of a 'natural' sphere and effectively kept separate from the public world of culture (King, 1983, 1989). However, at a time of grave environmental crisis, it is vital for feminists to restore human relationality with nature to the heart of social theory and practice. What is required, she argues, politically and metaphysically, is an end to the dualism of nature and culture. Ecofeminism starts from the premise that women stand at the boundary of nature and culture, but that this is a historical construction rather than the result of natural law. A refusal to countenance the relegation of women into nature gives rise to a new theory of the person that is embodied and dialectical rather than dualistic:

> An ecological feminism calls for a dynamic, developmental theory of the person – male and female – who emerges out of nonhuman nature, where difference is neither reified nor ignored and the dialectical relationship between human and non-human nature is understood. (King, 1989:131)

In practice, this does not involve wholesale repudiation of science and technology, but rather their adaptation for uses which do not build on domination and exploitation, either of human or non-human life. Here, King echoes strands of feminist epistemology in her claim that 'the will to know and the will to power need not be the same thing' (1989:133). She is arguing that a renewal of social relations will enable a shift in metaphysics; but that qualities like empathy, spirituality, affectivity and nurture must be restored to the public sphere and affirmed as legitimate aspects of human rationality. Such qualities remind us of our origins in non-human nature, rather than being relegated to the 'dirty little secret' with which women are archetypically entrusted, namely the 'socialization of the organic'.

Similarly, whilst serving to expose the ideological uses of the term 'natural' and to root gender divisions in the social realm, feminist use of the sex/gender distinction also has its problems. As I have already demonstrated, it excludes study of the body as a medium of selfhood and experience, and ignores the extent to which biology, the body and nature are simultaneously 'givens', yet profoundly subject to cultural definitions and representations.

Such problems raise questions for feminist theory in attempting to reinvent new ways of talking about the self and its relations to human and non-human biology, which are not essentialized and reified, but do not escape the embodied and ecologically-connected practices of culture. Levitas and Jaggar both consider the claims of feminist theory in terms of what they imply about human nature

(Levitas, 1983; Jaggar, 1983). These are ontological and metaphysical questions about what makes us what we are; the kinds of causal explanations we want about the human and the non-human; and what heuristic processes are available to analyse but not to reify or objectify that which is to be observed, namely nature.

In turn, this raises questions about what women's relationship with nature should be. Arguably, just as nature has been historicized, so too has women's association with things natural. Jane Gallop says that historical studies of motherhood and mothering should enable feminists to assert women's reproductive role as positive without any fear that such a claim will simply push them back into the realm of nature (Gallop, 1989). Women's 'biology' can then be seen to be as contextual and as cultural as men's. Women are no closer to nature than men; it is only historical discourse that renders their reproductive differences significant. This is helpful, although we do well to learn a lesson from historians of science: knowledge is deployed in the service of political ends. In this context, plenty of those who use pro-family and anti-feminist appeals to nature are prepared to realize their claims to the naturalism of women's reproductive role through anti-abortion legislation; cuts in family planning provision; erosion of women's right to choose between different methods of childbirth; and the freezing of child benefit; all of which amount to coercive and constraining influences on women's experiences of mothering.

If there is no one reified notion of nature, but a series of historical relationships between human agency, and scientific and epistemological practices, then there is no one single way of relating or associating with nature. It does not necessarily mean either domination or innocence – both of which, as evoked in feminist theory, still essentialize and romanticize nature. Instead, there is the possibility of conceiving a variety of relationships with nature which essentialize neither nature nor women. Plumwood advances the idea of nature as 'co-creative other', encapsulating a notion of 'intentionality' (value-directedness, context and teleology). Nature is characterized as distinct, yet in relation to human agency and culture; as connected to, but not colonized by, human labour (Plumwood, 1993:124;154–57). Nature may therefore be identified as different from, but not Other to, humanity.

Donna Haraway's motif of the 'Cyborg' as an emblem of our postmodern relationship to science is another possibility (Haraway,

1991:149–81). Cyborgs, who are hybrids of machine and organism, represent the blurring of boundaries between humanity and technology, human and non-human and physical and non-physical, which is a feature of late twentieth-century science. They inhabit the boundaries of organic origins and human technological construction, neither creatures of nature nor pure cultural artefact. It is not possible for Cyborgs to abstract themselves from the contradictions or ambiguities of their own hybrid being, or hope to transcend the practices and discourses that created them in the first place. For Haraway, the Cyborg is a fitting metaphor for postmodern feminists, and offers a model of being and knowledge in an ecological age. Dualistic patterns of objectification and identification are redundant:

> Certain dualisms have been persistent in Western traditions; they have all been systemic to the logics and practices of domination of women, people of colour, nature, workers, animals – in short, domination of all constituted as others, whose task is to mirror the self. Chief among these troubling dualisms are self/other, mind/body, culture/nature, male/female, civilized/primitive, reality/appearance, whole/part, agent/resource, maker/made, active/passive, right/ wrong, truth/illusion, total/partial, God/man . . . High-tech culture challenges these dualisms in intriguing ways. It is not clear who makes and who is made in the relation between human and machine. It is not clear what is mind and what body in machines that resolve into coding practices. (Haraway, 1991:177)

Absolute boundaries and bipolarities are born of control mechanisms, so totalizing visions – including the radical feminist search for the organic unity of women with nature – are not appropriate. The task is to live within the present contradictions and work therein for transformation. One feature that does emerge is a different awareness of, and relation to, the stuff of which we are made: we can no longer assert which is organic and which is machine. Such a dichotomy is no longer tenable; but in its dismantling we glimpse a new relationship to that we once called nature. Like ecofeminism, Haraway's vision sees humanity as learning once more to interact with nature as a living partner in the created order. It seeks neither domination nor pre-Oedipal bliss with Mother Nature, and does not imagine that we can live in innocent ignorance of all the destruction that humanity has inflicted on nature. Haraway states, 'I would rather be a cyborg than a goddess' (1991:181) – meaning, I think, that she sees no possibility of transcending or denying nature; instead, humanity overcomes the dichotomies of nature/culture, subject/object, separation/union, reason/emotion via a constant process of play, or negotiation with a living being of nature, which is itself in flux, changing and developing. Haraway envisages such a philosophy of nature:

> Ecofeminists have perhaps been most insistent on some version of the world as active subject, not as resource to be mapped and appropriated . . . Acknowledging the agency of the world in knowledge makes room for some unsettling possibilities, including a sense of the world's independent sense of humour. Such a sense of humour is not comfortable for humanists and others committed to the world as resource. Richly evocative figures exist for feminist visualizations of the world as witty agent . . . The Coyote or Trickster, embodied in American Southwest Indian accounts, suggests our situation when we give up mastery but keep searching for fidelity, knowing all the while we will be hoodwinked. I think these are useful myths for scientists who might be our allies. Feminist objectivity makes room for surprises and ironies at the heart of all knowledge production; we are not in charge of the world. (1991:199)

In a similar fashion, other writers evoke psychoanalysis to emphasize the inherent disorder and instability of human selfhood and knowledge, and the impossibility (and pathology) of models of knowledge built on self-possession and objectification. Toril Moi concludes an evaluation of Evelyn Fox Keller's vision of a feminist science based on a synthesis of masculine objectivity and feminine connectedness by arguing that the logic of binary structures itself needs deconstructing, and that Keller's criticism of science is trapped by the very binary structures she wishes to displace, namely organization of categories into fixed dichotomies. A more thoroughgoing deconstruction of the metaphysics of identity represents a refusal to deal in binary oppositions and allows our definitions of identity and selfhood free play. This, she argues, is truer to the psychoanalytic imagination, one which regards the unconscious and the somatic as constantly subverting and destabilizing self-containment and self-control. Our very cultural predispositions to oppose emotion and reason, body and mind are subverted by the energies of our unconscious drives:

> Self-defeating, always frustrated by the limitations of the body, the Freudian drive for knowledge is structurally incapable of achieving

total insight or perfect mastery: the philosopher's dream of self-contained plenitude is here unmasked as the imaginary fantasy it is. Freudian theory posits the drive for knowledge (epistomophilia) as crucially bound to the body and sexuality. If reason is always already shot through with the energy of the drives, the body and desire, to be intellectual can no longer be theorized simply as the 'opposite' of being emotional or passionate. (Moi, 1989:203)

Thus the solution might be to enable us to reframe our notions of what it means to be human. At the moment, we have available a dualistic model: the dominant ideology that privileges masculinity, distances itself from nature, relates to others via hierarchy and domination and knows through rational objectivity. By contrast, radical feminists appeal to a femininity that embodies connectedness to nature, nurturance, affectivity and intuition. Both wish to assert a normative model of humanity that is biologically derived, and which places gender traits in some sort of evaluative hierarchy. However, it may also be possible to conceive of a model of human nature and virtue which does not reproduce value-differences between character attributes, and which enables people to affirm a connectedness to nature; but not in a way that implies that women are, ontologically speaking, any closer than men to nature (Plumwood, 1988). Thus, again, a solution is proposed which places the formation of gender identity firmly in the sphere of culture and agency, yet allows for both women and men to affirm that their experience is always already constituted from elements often termed 'natural': birth, sexuality, affectivity, bodies and psyches. It involves transcending present dichotomies in what is understood as normatively and correctly human towards a model of personhood that draws on new evaluative criteria.

8 · *The Challenge of Difference*

The answer is not in stabilizing gender; not in rendering past lives more coherent and less conflictful than they were; not in reasserting the equivalence of race, class, gender and their primacy over sexuality and ethnicity. Rather than retreating, we must keep moving; we must recognize the instability of all categories, the contested terrain of all historical sites, the dangers in all political projects, and then shape a human history that captures both the messy multiplicity of lived experience and the power relations within which those lived experiences are played out. (Hewitt, 1992:317)

Historically, feminist theory and practice has displayed a tension between what are often referred to as the strategies of 'equality' and 'difference'. This has informed many of the analyses already examined. For example, criticism of research into 'sex differences', especially within biology and pyschology, has aimed to expose the bias towards reporting (often statistically inconsequential) variations at the expense of shared characteristics. 'Difference' is thereby used as a key pillar of gender inequality, by portraying gender traits as biologically given, not culturally learned, and by presenting differences in such a way as to privilege masculinity.

Politically, an orientation towards equality aims to facilitate the greater entry and recognition of women within social institutions, through equal opportunities legislation, enhanced education or political empowerment. However, as critics have noted, such a project assumes that the objective of feminist action is to assimilate women to a man's world, thus neglecting to challenge the fundamental terms of patriarchal social relations and the grounds on which prevailing constructions of the identities of 'women' and 'men' are based.

Such programmes highlight the paradox which lies at the heart of feminist political claims: in asserting equality with men, feminists refer to shared experience of oppression, which is identified as unique and distinctive to women alone. Feminist projects to gain access to society failed to dislodge male-defined norms of success and the nature of institutions; in response, feminists began to consider what specific qualities women might bring to public life in order to challenge norms of humanity which equated it solely with maleness. This has generated another strand of feminist thought which seeks to develop an understanding of women's difference from men, as a means of articulating feminist opposition to present values and structures in areas as diverse as medical practice, philosophy, sexuality and scientific practice. Feminism cannot be truly effective and critical, as Mary Midgley argues, without an acknowledgement of women's 'difference' from men:

> Reformers attacking the subordinate status of women have naturally appealed to the idea of equality, because it was already recognised as a powerful tool of reform. But in other situations – for instance asserting a mother's special right not to be deprived of her children, or in offering characteristically female insights to correct a narrowly male view of life – they have equally naturally appealed to the idea of a distinct female nature. (Midgley, 1988:31)

Midgley's argument is that feminists must not be afraid of the concept of difference. The source of their reluctance is what she terms 'standardization', or 'the failure to value a difference', in the name of what Midgley considers an over-hasty impulsion towards blanket equality with men. She attributes much of this to a suspicion of biological and psychological determinism and a desire to repudiate all traces of anything tainted by the dangerous notion of 'natural sex differences'. Thus Midgley asks feminists to reconsider the possibility of differences between women and men, mainly because the strategic project of feminism requires some appeal to notions of women's specific needs and perspectives.

There is much in this that is true; but, in calling for greater attention to difference in feminist politics, Midgley fails to ask what such a concept might mean. She believes that to assert the facts or reality of difference is simply a healthy, common-sense admission of the axiomatic truth of our experience:

There is nothing fishy about simply admitting the reality of the difference, or that of the physical causes which – alongside cultural ones – help to produce it. To insist on denying the reality of such causes is to draw a bizarrely hard line between the physical and the mental aspects of a human being – a line which does seem sometimes to be drawn in the social sciences, and may prove handy in academic feuds between them and biology, but which seems very badly suited to the realistic description of our lives. (1988:40)

However, Midgley avoids the most critical question, which is the meaning and significance of difference and the role it plays, especially in the defence of gender inequality. She also leaves unexamined the question of the actual generative source of any difference. An admission of the 'reality' of difference may be simply a matter of identifying and cataloguing self-evident facts which feminists have been too ideologically blinkered to admit; alternatively, the crucial issue may be, as some of my previous analysis suggests, that the very nature and presentation of that reality is shrouded in epistemological and ontological difficulties.

Midgley's argument, therefore, whilst valuable in reintroducing the concept of difference as an integral part of feminist politics and analysis, fails to recognize that the inhibitions surrounding the term arise not from a wish to disregard or abandon it, but from a desire to assess its proper potency, and to appreciate its many dimensions, before deploying it within feminist discourse. Contrast Midgley's statement on difference in feminist theory and practice with that of Josette Féral. For her, 'difference' as currently constituted and theorized is ideological and functional – patriarchy conceives women as 'Other' to silence them in the name of a particular system of gender identity:

Thus difference has always been construed and perceived through a set of binary oppositions that leaves no room for an authentic difference set outside of the established system . . . Society itself is made possible by this repression of woman; it is founded upon the negation of her difference, upon her exclusion from knowledge and from herself. (Féral, 1980:89)

What such an 'authentic' difference might be is something which of itself raises further questions, which will be addressed when I scrutinize the work of the poststructuralist French feminists more closely later; but Féral reflects a preoccupation within feminist writing which seeks to expose the falsity of prevailing constructions of masculinity and femininity, and thereby the supposed distinctions or differentiations between them. Far from satisfying us that it is a self-evident term which provides the key to all explanations of gender, such an approach identifies 'difference', and in particular how it is generated and maintained, as a critical focus of enquiry.

This chapter will therefore examine how various appeals to difference are being made in theories of gender, and the interpretative strategies they represent. In particular, the very status of the term 'difference' – and in particular the contrast between what might be termed 'categorical' and 'relational' notions – will be placed at the centre of critical understandings of the process by which gender relations are forged.

I will be discussing three usages of difference: first, voices within feminist theory which repudiate notions of a singular difference between women and men in favour of multiple differences amongst women, and the consequent fragmentation of feminist objectives. Second, I shall examine feminist appropriations of psychoanalysis which found a notion of difference on a distinct and unique feminine identity based upon the repressed unconscious of a patriarchal social and symbolic order. The relationship of this analysis to materially embodied gender relations is problematic; it is still a categorical and inflexible rendition of difference. Thirdly, I shall use analysis from poststructuralism which sees difference itself as unstable and enacted, the process by which social interests are entrenched. What Nancy Hewitt calls the 'tracing' of differences emerges as the central critical strategy in gender theory.

Differences and Diversity

The question of differences between women is not a recent discovery within feminist theory; historically, as Alexander and Bacchi argue, campaigns for women's equality have consistently been confronted with rival interpretations of ultimate objectives and intermediate strategies, as well as a recognition of the diversity within their constituencies (Alexander, 1984; Bacchi, 1990). However, contemporary feminism has been most exercised by a consideration of the significance of differences of race, class, sexuality, nationality and religion. The pluralism of women's situations is expressed through a diversity of analysis and agendas for change – even in terms of what it means to theorize, as 'womanist' (Black feminist) writers turn to forms of narrative and poetry to delineate their experiences of racism, colonialism and sexism (Barrett, 1987; Grosz, 1990).

The argument that no one single definition of 'woman' can inform feminist theory and practice, that gender identity and loyalty is historically and culturally contingent, requires renewed attention to the options of equality and difference. Black, third world and woman-identified women articulate the inadequacy of projects of equality which reproduce white, androcentric standards of virtue, success and experience; but an insistence on diversity further problematizes the terms on which women might claim a distinct and unique identity as an alternative. An identity is not simply determined in reference to some notion of 'women's experience'; instead, difference itself is multiple, conditioned by the factors of class, region, sexuality and culture. However, many feminists are concerned that such an analysis deprives women of a clear and compelling source from which to articulate oppositional politics; that the contingency of gender difference robs it of its ethical imperative.

This dilemma may derive in part from an attempt to hold together the diversity and plurality of experience with a drive to maintain a unity and coherence to gender as a theoretical and analytical category; but another problem is that feminists are required to choose between difference-as-uniqueness and difference-as-diversity. Insofar as the problem is defined as difference as an absolute category, this suggests that such an assertion of difference is too one-dimensional. 'Difference' is thus unable to reflect the complexity of lived experience at the same time as sketching a theoretical reconfiguration. I shall return to this issue at the end of this section; but I now turn to another rendition of difference which, while offering a distinct and unique source of gender identity, also carries similar problems in terms of the actual deployment of such a vision of difference.

Speaking of Difference

Jacques Lacan is a key figure in feminists' appropriation of postmodern philosophies. He has inspired a school of French feminism which owes to him a renewal of the classical psychoanalysis of Freud, a concern with language and writing as constitutive of gender identity, and an analysis of patriarchal power as generating itself primarily in the symbolic representations of language and speech (Sayers, 1986; Mitchell and Rose, 1982).

Lacan eschews any trace of biologistic explanations for human consciousness, emphasizing instead the crucial point of psycho-sexual development as occurring at the recognition of sexual difference. He proudly claimed to be instituting a 'return to Freud', although his work also bears the clear marks of French structuralist semiology and linguistics, after Claude Lévi-Strauss and Ferdinand de Saussure. Lacan therefore takes Freudian understandings of human identity – especially sexual identity – as formed upon the entry to, and adoption of, culture, into the realm of symbolism and linguistic expression. For Lacan, the person is primarily a speaking subject, and therefore identity – gender identity in particular – is formed in and through language.

The ungendered infant exists initially in the world of the 'Imaginary', a pre-cultural pre-Oedipal world. Its first step towards self-consciousness occurs when it glimpses its own reflection in the mirror. Secure in the arms of its mother, the child receives an image of itself as whole and complete, inseparable and undifferentiated from the world around it. However, says Lacan, this is an illusion, because we are actually not perceiving the real self, but only a reflection of ourselves as constituted via the desire of others.

Lacan departs from Freud in replacing the penis as the key signifier of sexual difference with the 'phallus': this denotes the symbolic and social power of men, expressed (after Lévi-Strauss) in the exchange and subordination of women. At the mirror stage, when the child can only authenticate itself as the object of another's desire, the phallus becomes the symbol of that desire. When the 'Law of the Father' – namely the cultural repression of uninhibited desire – intervenes to disrupt the mother/child relationship, the child is forced into a choice between desire for the mother and desire for the Phallus. Because the phallus is society's 'privileged signifier', and it, not the mother/child dyad, represents complete and unitary identity, the child represses the early identification with the mother and transfers it to the phallus. However, neither girl nor boy can actually be the phallus, having to be content with language as a mere substitute for the privileged signifier.

At the resolution of the castration complex, the child becomes a speaking, cultured and sexed subject. It is at this point that the child realizes simultaneously its alienation from itself, the repression and banishment of instinctive, primal desire and the relativity of all speech to the absolute privilege of the Phallus. The boy child resolves this by abandoning his desire for the mother and identifying with the father in his relation to the Phallus, in the hope of sharing, albeit in a fragmented and secondary way, in the privileges of patriarchy. The girl recognizes herself as the site of absence, lack and negativity; of 'otherness'. The Father (or Phallus) comes to represent the only source of completeness, unity and satisfaction; all else is an incomplete realization of identity.

Lacan reinterprets Freud's usage of the term 'penis' to denote not anatomical difference, therefore, but differential locations and relations to the symbolic and semiotic power of the Phallus. The phallus is the 'privileged signifier', the term which differentiates all other terms, due to its visibility, its unity, and its (symbolic) link with male sexual power. It is the presence or the absence of the phallus which indicates a speaking subject's position under the Law, and therefore constitutes gendered subjectivity.

By the same process, the child's unconscious develops: the unconscious for Lacan is repressed desire but also the remnants of *jouissance*; and this too, works like a language, illusory, partial, ceaselessly moving from one signifier to the next in an effort to achieve true and final meaning, which is of course impossible given the fragmented and alienated nature of speech.

Sexual difference, denial of the primal identification with the mother, acquisition of language and entry into culture all coincide, as they are all dependent upon the transfer from the Imaginary to the patriarchal, or 'Symbolic' order. The Phallus comes to represent this separation from maternal pleasure, and the consequent repression of such desire. With this repression comes the unconscious, evident in the child's newly acquired use of language, in which, in keeping with Saussurean linguistics, the speaking act simultaneously asserts one position whilst necessarily denying all others.

Irigaray, Cixous, Wittig, Kristeva

The emergence of a new school of francophone feminist theory can be traced back to the foundation of the 'Psychanalyse et Politique' group in Paris after the demonstrations of May 1968.[1] Broadly, it emerged from a feminist philosophical tradition which emphasizes the influence of the body upon consciousness, the structures of culture and language which shape our speech and our relationships, and the importance of the unconscious in creating the individual. The notion of *jouissance* is central to their analyses, signifying the pre-Oedipal, pre-Symbolic innocence which, silenced under patriarchy, stands for the re-emergence of an unrepressed and authentic gender identity.

Whilst maintaining the traditional cultural stance of much feminism in adopting a 'woman-centred' or 'woman-identified' position, the French writers eschew any notion of difference as meaning inferiority. Simone de Beauvoir's notion of man as Self and woman as 'Other' has been influential here. However, any sense of negation and ontological incompleteness has been reversed, so that women's otherness becomes a compelling vantage point for a greater self-possession and identity. Indeed, the francophone feminists argue that difference can also be a subversive term: difference as radical Otherness, beyond patriarchal definition, by virtue of its reduction to silence and marginality by patriarchal discourse. Thus difference in the hands of women is celebrated as something which evokes a multiplicitous heterogeneous identity, rather than an absolute point or line which demarcates male from female, masculine from feminine.

Cixous and Irigaray emphasize the differential experience of their bodies by women as the source of *jouissance*, which serves to subvert phallogocentric culture; Wittig argues for a woman-identified or lesbian politics as the locus of feminist revolution; and Kristeva sees the identity of women as associated with all marginalized subjects under patriarchy.

Exploring the boundaries between philosophy and psychoanalysis, Irigaray focuses on the ubiquity of the tradition, from Plato to Freud, of woman as absence and lack. In Freudian theory, reflecting gender construction under patriarchy, woman is 'Other', only existing as a negation or reflection of man's own self-image. Irigaray uses the image of the 'speculum' (a concave mirror used in vaginal examinations) to express the androcentric nature of patriarchal representation; the masculine gaze on women sees only a reflection of itself. Women's difference has therefore been rendered invisible in order to privilege male-centred being; woman thus exists outside representation. To find the authentic woman requires stepping into non-identity, and perceiving woman as non-being, absence, loss of self in an almost 'mystical' experience of surrender of self-identity.

This notion of women's speech and writing constituting a 'space' outwith patriarchal categorization and objectification is a strong unifying element in French feminist neo-psychoanalysis. It reappropriates and subverts the phallocentric evocation of Woman as invisible void, lack or essence and reiterates such space as the source of women's self-determination. However, the exact nature of such a space – whether it is political, metaphorical, psychic or linguistic – remains contested and indeterminate. Yet here, in the space to which patriarchal discourse cannot penetrate because there is no longer anything to reflect, women can discover a purposeful and autonomous self-determination.

Irigaray uses women's bodily experience as a metaphor for their differential self-knowledge, which serves as the resource for oppositional epistemology. Thus she contrasts the unitary monolithic phallogocentricism of men with the dual, self-reflexive anatomy of women, using the imagery of water and blood to signify their life-giving properties in opposition to the pathology that is masculinity. Difference becomes more than anatomical: women themselves embody alterity, duality: 'the sex which is not one' is thus understood as women who are defined as absence (not a substantive group or sex, but the 'Other'), which thereby defies the logical, linear, single identity definitions thrust upon them by patriarchy, and of itself offers a self-composed, pluralistic notion of self. Thus women's morphology, through its very lack of penis, constitutes alternative feminine identity; bodily experience – the two lips of the vulva and multiple sites of libidinous pleasure – is all that women have to construct their self-consciousness.

Woman's morphology offers an alternative mode of expression and selfhood, where ambiguity, heterogeneity and inner space demarcate her as the site of 'difference', which offers a return to the Imaginary. For many critics of francophone feminism, however, such an evocation of bodily experience suggests a collapse into biological essentialism. However, it is important to see the exposition of women's *jouissance* as a highly contrived rhetorical strategy, echoing other radical programmes that regard free expression of sexuality as politically subversive. Thus, the French feminists are making an ironic comment on the patriarchal characterization of women as inherently sexual, and using that to articulate an alternative perspective. Irigaray's evocation of polymorphous sensuality is

> in no way a 'true' or accurate description of women. Its function is not referential but combative: it is an image to contest and counter dominant, phallomorphic representations . . . It does not designate a female essence or anatomy but subverts the dominant male conceptions of women's essence. (Grosz, 1989:116)

Like Irigaray, Cixous argues for a specific psychosexual identity for women, and for the transparency of bodily experience (Cixous, 1981; Moi, 1988). Her primary contribution is a critical analysis of binary systems of thought, where masculine and feminine are juxtaposed in opposition; this very binary forms the derivation of meaning of one via the suppression, even destruction of the other. In a patriarchal value system, the active, powerful masculine destroys the passive subordinate feminine. Thus femininity is characterized as death, invisibility and negativity; and Cixous seeks to undo this chain of connection and assert femininity as positive and life-giving.

Cixous claims to reject fixed essential notions of femininity as products of the very logic she seeks to undermine, and relies instead on the Freudian hypothesis of the individual as inherently 'bisexual'. What she terms 'the other bisexuality' refuses marks of difference as binarity, choosing instead to evoke and embody multiplicity and openness of identity. However, this celebration of polyversity is undermined somewhat by the strictures of Cixous' standards, by which writing can in fact qualify as bisexual: in practice, bisexuality is a position only open to women, because only they can detach themselves from the compulsions of binarity and categorization. Men are unable to do so because of fears of castration, of transgressing what Cixous terms the 'Realm of the Proper', akin to Freud's 'Reality Principle' or Lacan's 'Symbolic' realm. Binary oppositions contrive to construct women as 'Other' in the language of the Symbolic where the unitary Phallus holds sway; but by self-consciously perfecting a fluid, erotic style of writing, women can draw upon a different sensibility (Cixous, 1981). It also serves to throw into question the notion of difference as oppositional, polarized and hierarchical.

Wittig's analysis and strategy focuses specifically on the identity of the lesbian as the one to expose the false logic of patriarchy (Fuss, 1990; Butler, 1990:79ff). Again, Wittig employs the notion of women as defective men under patriarchy: women only achieve identity as men's 'other', which renders them negative and deficient. The only acceptable status they have in heterosexist society is through their relations with men, as wife, daughter, sister, etc. But the lesbian, in her refusal to align herself with male-centred relations, exposes the constructedness and falsity of the heterosexual economy: she claims the status of woman for herself in defiance of the 'Straight Mind' which equates gender with conformity to a particular sexual orientation. Thus, argues Wittig, 'we are compelled in our bodies and our minds to correspond, feature by feature, with the idea of nature that has been established for us . . . "men" and "women" are political categories, and not natural facts' (Wittig, 1981, quoted in Butler, 1990:115).

Kristeva's studies are chiefly on the nature of language, rather than psychoanalysis specifically. Her interest is in speech and language as discourse, existing only at particular times and places, as spoken by particular people, inscribing particular interests and subject-positions. Meaning thus has no final closure: it can be reopened. The primacy of meaning thus rests on the speaking subject, who can be supposed to have a social and political context.

As with Lacan, language is formed within the realm of the Symbolic, and involves the repression of the Imaginary into the unconscious. Kristeva's equivalent terms are, respectively, the 'symbolic' and the 'semiotic' (Moi, 1988; Butler, 1990:79–93). It is this distinction which, for her, constitutes gender difference in speech and the nature of gender difference. Semiotics thus corresponds to a pre-Oedipal state, a sphere of undifferentiated, unspoken (and unspeakable) unity, which is repressed in the transfer into the symbolic. Yet the semiotic realm remains, as a chimeral and spectral presence, hinting at the idyllic Imaginary order in the midst of the repression that is the patriarchal Symbolic. In another spatial metaphor, the semiotic is likened to Plato's *chora*: a 'receptacle, unnameable, improbable, hybrid, anterior to naming, to the one, to the father, and consequently maternally connoted' (Kristeva, 1982, quoted in Grosz, 1989:42).

Kristeva eschews discussion of 'feminine' or 'feminist' identity or politics, because she rejects any claim to coherent stable subjectivity. She is not interested in attempting to assert a brand new feminine identity against the old phallogocentric order. What she does propose, however, is a sense of marginality subverting the centre, of silenced powerlessness hinting at the overthrow of the powerful. In contrast to Irigaray's or Cixous' notion of femininity as absence and lack grounded in a pre-Oedipal or morphological experience, Kristeva maintains that the semiotic is enacted from a social and cultural position; through, and not outside, the Symbolic. If 'Woman' or 'women' have any meaning, therefore, it is as oppositional and strategic terms: women are privileged in standing outside the phallic economy because of their lack of power and social mediations of motherhood which give them a role in the care of pre-Oedipal children; but she is at pains to emphasize an active, assumed and strategic feminine identity, rather than a transcendental and pre-existent self-consciousness.

Indeed, of all the francophone feminists, Kristeva is most ambivalent to the equation of female gender identity or morphology with women as a politicized group. For Kristeva, the feminine – that which subverts the Law of the Father and upon which the 'difference' of oppositional gender identity is founded – is not a fixed subject position, but alterity, transgression and indeterminacy (Kristeva, 1981). She emphasizes, in true Lacanian fashion, the linguistic structuring of social relations and subjectivity: how language is both a metaphor for the positioning of an individual in society (as a 'speaking subject') and is crucial to the acquisition of gender identity. Yet it is the instability of language – represented by the notion of 'difference' as produced by the foreclosure of meaning yet constantly threatened by destabilization – that leads Kristeva to look for strategies and historical examples of the subversion of language – and thus, of fixed identity and social hierarchy. She identifies some of those spaces in 'madness, holiness and poetry' (Grosz, 1989:52): the margins of language, often seen as 'hysterical' discourses, where unified and rational meaning begins to break down, and space is created for alternative forms of subjectivity and meaning. The device of 'writing the body', prominent amongst other francophone feminists, is displaced by Kristeva's greater emphasis on language. This renders her less vulnerable to charges of essentialism, but also arguably less located in women's experiences of embodiment, however mediated.

Critique

Critics of Lacanian psychoanalysis argue that its emphasis on language and sign/symbol risks abstraction, and carries little reference to concrete practice. Critics have argued that there is a tendency to privilege a consideration of the structures of the unconscious at the expense of a social critique (Rose, 1983; Moi, 1988:167–72). The central 'speaking subject' of Lacanian psychoanalysis, for example, is too abstract and ahistorical, coming from no particular class or race (Butler, 1990:45ff). It may also be argued that Lacan, whilst recognizing that the phallus represents material power and male privilege, allows his theories on the primacy of language to obscure the politics which underpin speech and provide a social context for the speaking subject: in other words, to risk collapsing the signifier into the signified, and forgetting that the phallus is merely a metaphor for a wider set of gender relations. It is debatable therefore whether Lacanian analysis is truly an account of the entry into the material external world or merely a description of an interior psychic process.

Some critics argue that the distinction between Phallus and penis – that between culture and language as the determinant of gender and that of biology and anatomy – is not a successful working difference, and to Lacan they are effectively identical. Does the symbolic power of the Phallus precede material male power or vice versa? How does one generate the other? Lacan seems to argue that a phallocentric social order generates male privilege; but also that the phallus is only a privileged signifier because it 'speaks' of patriarchy. Thus doubts are already being cast on Lacan's claim to rescue Freud from biologism; and, in fact, the accusation of 'essentialism' is the one most frequently aimed at this school of thought.

> It is true that the phallus is not the penis in any simple way; as a signifier it operates as a sign in a signifying chain, a symbolic metaphor and not a natural fact of difference. But it is also true that this metaphor derives its power from the very object it symbolizes; the phallus is pre-eminently a metaphor but it is also metonymically close to the penis and derives much of its signifying importance from this by no means arbitrary relation. It is precisely because a woman does not have a penis that her relation to the phallus, the signifying order, the order of language and the law, is so complicated and fraught with difficulties. The privileging of the phallus as 'transcendental signifier' (the signifier without a signified) has led to charges that

Lacan is endorsing the phallocentricism he purports to critique.
(Fuss, 1990:8)

This kind of writing is very successful in asserting a particular
expression of difference, whether it derives from the morphology of
'writing from the body' in Irigaray and Cixous, or Kristeva's
retrieval of traces of the 'semiotic' on the margins of language, or
Wittig's universalized lesbian – a 'transcendental signifier' from
whom all other women draw their meaning. However, the grounds
of such difference, even in the pursuit of feminist identity, can still
be criticized for positing a pre-gendered self which exists outside the
structures of language in a 'pre-discursive' realm. The implication of
this, it is argued, is a return to the ontological schism between male/
Symbolic/mind/world and female/semiotic/ body/nature. The question is whether these differences are conceived as formed independently of human agency and culture or posited as political, psychic
and linguistic constructions. Writers such as Kristeva may be seen as
attempting to resist appeals to fixed identity, by refusing metaphysical or morphological categories; however, she has also been
criticized for disregarding the political agency of specific social
groups in favour of a more diffuse form of protest (Grosz,
1989:94ff). Clearly, 'difference' functions best when it delineates
some kind of experience or vantage point – perhaps some kind of
psychic, political, linguistic or morphological 'space' – from which
new forms of speaking and acting can arise, rather than simply
returning us to essentialism.

Deconstruction and Difference

The post-Lacanian school represents a strategy which subverts
patriarchal assertions of difference by reappropriating them in the
service of a woman-identified *poesis*. Thus, it is clear that the issue is
not how difference is conceived, but who defines difference and on
whose behalf. French feminism refuses to adopt an androcentric
prescriptive difference; but the danger of collapse into forms of
essentialism nevertheless alerts critical attention to the extent to
which difference is still deemed a fixed and in some way pre-
discursive category. Other forms of poststructuralist thought concentrate on difference as positional and relational, enabling a more
thorough destabilization of the conditions under which gender
identity and difference are generated.

Jacques Derrida is commonly hailed as the 'founder' of a particular school known as Poststructuralism and the general methodology of 'deconstruction', although a number of commentators have noted the continuity between Derrida and earlier critics of structuralism, especially those from a phenomenological and existentialist background. His general theory, and in particular his concept of *différance*, will occupy this section, as they are of considerable importance in later psychoanalytic/poststructuralist writing on gender (Weedon, 1987; Dews, 1987; Derrida, 1987).

Derrida's philosophical method begins with a critical appreciation of the structuralism of Ferdinand de Saussure, and in particular with the foundational premise that meaning and interpretation are produced through systems of binary opposition. Structuralism privileges systems over constituent parts, and thus language is regarded as a self-contained structure, composed of interlinking and interdependent signs. Each sign is made up of a 'signifier' (the sound or written image, the manifestation of the sign) and the 'signified' (the meaning of the sign). The relation between the two is arbitrary, and sustained by convention rather than immutable laws. Whereas Saussure believed that once signifiers were assigned to signifieds, then meanings were assured of fixity, Derrida claims that the relationship between signifiers and signifieds can change, and that for meaning to be maintained by rational self-consciousness implies a view of human agency and identity that has been untenable since Freud (Weedon, 1987:25–27).

The implications of this 'deconstruction' of meaning can be seen in Derrida's critique of a fundamental concept of structuralism: that of binary opposition. In Saussurean semiology, the sense of any term is generated via its differentiation from its opposite: such dualism is apparent in gender terminology and has inhabited Western philosophy since its inception. However, for Derrida, such binary pairs are not stable, because traces of *deferral* will always co-exist within the production of *difference*: in establishing what a word positively means, it is necessary to remember that it carries with it nuances and reminders of what it is not.[2] Thus any word bears both positive meaning and its own negation, and meaning is therefore unstable and shifting, forever referring to other, absent signifiers. In an almost paradoxical way, the harder the attempt to assert absolute and transcendent meaning, the more such expressions undermine themselves.

Derrida coined the term *différance* to express this process of simultaneous assertion and negation of meaning: it sums up not only the sense of differentiation and oppositionalism implicit in meaning, but also the endless transfer and deferral by which the overall structure of language coheres. Thus, there is also an implicit denial of finality or privileged authority, both in terms of a 'transcendental signified' by which all meaning comes to rest, and in terms of any understanding of the author of a text having more control or intent over its meaning than anyone else. Thus, although Derrida may resemble many of the more radical figures in hermeneutics in his commitment to models of language as generated in human discourse, he differs from them in refuting any inevitable discovery or interpretation of 'true' meaning, or any notion of privileged ownership or authorship of meaning.

Thus, as Chris Weedon notes, we are already provided with a theory of language which denies any natural affinity between the signifier 'woman' and any of the qualities which are commonly associated with her; a significant tool for feminist 'deconstruction' of gender (1987, 40–41). Derrida's profound scepticism toward views of meaning as fixed and absolute enables all discourse to be exposed as provisional, and appeals to 'truth' and 'consensus' as illusory. Binary oppositions, especially those which characterize masculine and feminine as fixed, self-authenticating 'metaphysical presences', are undermined as unstable, slippery concepts which deny any notion of language as revealing a reliable external 'reality'. Any assertion of 'difference' as an ontologically stable or reliable index of identity, therefore, has to come to terms with a theory which allows language alone as the medium of expression, and thus denies the prospect of attaining such metaphysical certainty.

> From a feminist poststructuralist perspective the battle for the meaning of gendered subjectivity and the many attempts made by conflicting discourses to fix meaning once and for all is doomed to failure by the very nature of language itself . . . The precariousness of any attempt to fix meaning which involves a fixing of subjectivity must rely on the denial of the principles of difference and deferral. The assertion of 'truth' involved is constantly vulnerable to resistance and the redefinition of meaning. From this point of view particular versions of femininity and masculinity are never inevitable. (Weedon, 1987:105–106)

Deconstructionist philosophies and strategies claim that 'equality' and 'difference' are not absolutes, but are themselves constructs. They emerge from human discourse, and exist within a context of power relations and material practice. To attempt to impose absolute and unchanging meaning upon gender relations is to assert an abstraction which returns us to metaphysics. Derrida's notion of *différance* as something referential, relational and unstable may therefore be seen as a corrective to more categorical understandings, in which difference is conceived as an absolute. However, if difference is relational and positional, it may be regarded as in some way generated by human action, material or symbolic. Derrida's work is about identifying the linguistic patterns by which indeterminate and pluriform expression is given unitary meaning and reference as a result of the speech-act. Every act is an imposition of meaning, itself constructed according to cultural convention; but meaning constitutes an abuse, because it necessarily represses and silences some aspects of speech in order to assert and privilege others.

This pattern of dominant/other as the fundamental dynamic of meaning is also reflected in Foucault's work, by which the parameters of legitimate knowledge are traced in accordance with the controlling interests and objectives of a dominant class or group. Indeed, such knowledge is itself deployed in order to provide the rationalization for constraint, by creating supposedly objective and universal demarcations by which difference is brought into being. Both Derrida and Foucault, then, see the generation of identity (and therefore difference) as forged by historical and material human agency, and the boundaries between self/other, dominant/subordinate, meaning/non-meaning as traced along 'fault-lines' of difference, which are drawn in order to defend the privileged position of the powerful against the incursions of the alien other. Part of any critical analysis will therefore be an examination of how bodies, science, reproductive technology, sexual imagery and the language of nature and culture act as the vehicles and agents of difference, and in particular how such practices serve to articulate and enforce the values upon which the fault-lines of difference are drawn.

This way of thinking propels us towards an understanding of difference as a means towards further analysis, rather than a fixed marker separating inherently different beings; difference thus promotes enquiry, but is not an answer in itself. Theories may be patriarchal constructions, but feminist epistemology must move beyond unexamined discourses of difference to new perspectives. Toril Moi comments on projects which attempt to identify 'gender differences', in this case in language use:

> It would seem that the pursuit of sex difference in language is not only a theoretical impossibility, but a political error. The concept of difference is theoretically tricky in that it denotes an absence or a gap more than any signifying presence. Difference, Jacques Derrida has argued, is not a *concept*. Differences always take us *elsewhere*, we might say, involve us in an ever proliferating network of displacement and deferral of meaning. To see difference primarily as the gap between the two parts of a binary opposition (as for instance between masculinity and femininity) is therefore to impose an arbitrary closure on the differential field of meaning. (Moi, 1988:153–54)

In the past, difference has fuelled and crystallized important feminist projects, and what is sometimes known as 'identity politics' should not be derided for its previous achievements, even if we do wish to subject its philosophical and ontological assumptions to closer examination. Indeed, one of the main criticisms of the poststructuralist impetus within feminism is that it deprives the women's movement of a clear identity upon which to build a political programmme; it is thus seen as a withdrawal from engagement, a theory devoid of practice, and a collapse into the very metaphysics which it claims to deconstruct.

Many feminists, writing a decade after 'The future of difference' (Eisenstein and Jardine: 1980), reflect on the new choices facing a post-deconstructionist (postfeminist) movement. It is surely significant that the growth of the movement engaged in critical studies of masculinity, hardly apparent before the mid-1970s, has developed using many of the theoretical and critical tools of deconstructionism and poststructuralist psychoanalysis (Jardine and Smith, 1987; Chapman and Rutherford, 1988). Lynne Segal, surveying the growing field of studies of masculinity and sexual politics, recognizes therein a similar questioning of categorical certainties and allegiances as has taken place within feminism. Yet, as she points out, the richness and multiplicity of diversifying identities may be something to be welcomed, but it tends to muddy the political and strategic waters, leading to the dangers of relativism and fatalism, or of lapsing back into rhetorical territory which is best relinquished:

> But while the notion of masculinity becomes ever more complex, the 'problem of men' becomes ever more pressing. We may come to

understand sexual difference in terms of a shifting reality – a multiplicity of meanings rather than simple opposition – but the cultural,
social and political domination of men over women persists . . . A
similar paradox in relation to men lies in the importance of challenging the existence of any fixed essence of 'man', while at the same time
insisting upon the continuing practical problem of men. The danger
here is that we may end up dismissing the diversity and changing
meanings of 'masculinity', some of which we might need to help
strengthen as a challenge to the more traditional ones. (Segal,
1990:206)

Beyond Essentialism: A Return to Praxis?

One of the arguments of this chapter is that 'difference' as a concept
needs to be closely examined, but that it is not a term which
feminists need to shun. It has also become clear that many of the
French advocates of women's 'difference' make recourse to varieties
of essentialism in order to defend their visions of alternative realms
of reality. Thus, something of a paradox seems to emerge: philosophical schools which undermine fixed human rationality, or any
distinction between subject and object, and reject notions of a
coherent and knowable 'self' in order to dismantle many of the
assumptions of the modern age, end up positing a pre-social,
essentialist force or source of knowledge as a basis from which to
construct alternative epistemologies.[3]

However, it is possible that some of the critical tools and perspectives of poststructuralism might be retained while seeking to avoid
such unreconstructed romantic regressions to essentialism. A profound scepticism about rational, fixed selfhood may still be compatible, logically and politically, with a view of human agency which
does not have to call upon abstract rationality, essences or experiences. This position would accept that selfhood is constructed
according to coercive forces, and that language is arbitrary and
provisional, but would seek some positions of authority and coherence for a subjectivity which is both constituted, and open to further
challenge, by concrete practice. Thus it would help to counter the
charges of nihilism considered above, whilst putting to the test
understandings of gender identity and formation as generated by
human agency. Such a debate seeks to recover political strategy in
the light of deconstructionist critiques of subjectivity, rationality
and meaning.

Two recent works develop this line of thinking, and attempt to move theory and practice beyond the entrenched polarizations between essentialism and constructionism (Fuss, 1990; Butler, 1990). Diana Fuss argues that the two concepts are more closely linked and interdependent than is normally assumed; and Judith Butler seeks strategies of gender reconstruction which, whilst cognizant of deconstructionist claims, move beyond the impasse of political immobility. Both argue for a reworking of essentialism, to supersede the fixities of former identity politics, where 'woman' is assumed to be an unproblematic and universal category. Instead, Fuss calls for a recognition of the essentialisms underpinning constructionism – particularly the determinant role of 'culture' – and the constructed nature of essentialism, so that it is possible to see the two concepts as mutually interdependent rather than dichotomous. To assume that the natural is always fixed and pre-given and the social always constructed, she argues, is to fall prey to a variety of determinism which fails to see the artificiality of the two terms. Once essentialism, as an appeal to a fixed, ahistorical, universalized ontology, is recognized as a constructed discourse, not itself beyond history, it can be deployed in the service of gaining identity and self-determination within specific political struggles. She talks of this, after Stephen Heath, as the 'risk of essence' (Fuss, 1990:18).

Essentialism thus becomes just another construct, as unstable and constrained by discourse as any other category. Not all talk of 'difference' has to be essentializing. The political and theoretical challenge for feminists is to retrieve and reappropriate difference without, as Simone de Beauvoir terms, becoming 'enclosed' in, or by, difference (Simons and Benjamin, 1979:330–45). As Fuss argues in defence of Irigaray, her assertion of an essentialist vision of women is a liberatory strategy in the face of Aristotelian philosophy, which has never even allowed women an essence to start with.

Similarly, Butler explores the possibilities of identity politics which subvert and parody existing power structures and hegemonic gender regimes. This implicitly denies the plausibility of gender Utopias which exist somewhere outside the present system, but also serves to avoid charges of metaphysical lapses into pre-discursive essences that cannot be retrieved in any practical programme of transformation. Such a strategy carries with it revolutionary implications for understandings of the generative factors of gender, which transcend notions of determinism versus free will, essentialism versus social construction:

> Construction is not opposed to agency; it is the necessary scene of agency, the very terms in which agency is articulated and becomes culturally intelligible. The critical task for feminism is not to establish a point of view outside of constructed identities; that conceit is the construction of an epistemological model that would disavow its own cultural location and, hence, promote itself as a global subject, a position that deploys precisely the imperialist strategies that feminism ought to criticise. The critical task is, rather, to locate strategies of subversive repetition enabled by those constructions, to affirm the local possibilities of intervention through participating in precisely those practices of repetition that constitute identity and, therefore, present the immanent possibility of contesting them. (Butler, 1990:147)

Butler singles out many gay and lesbian strategies as prefiguring the practices of parody and subversion that she recommends. In terms of claiming specific sexual identity for political purposes, Jeffrey Weeks has long affirmed the centrality of political programmes as fundamentally constitutive of, and not just consequential to, homosexual and lesbian identity (Weeks, 1987). Sexual identity is therefore simultaneously crucial to the self-development of marginalized groups, and necessarily open to scrutiny as culturally and historically constructed and variable. This is not to say that identity leads inexorably from activity (which might be a criticism to level at Butler). The experience of health education workers in the AIDS era, who target one particular 'at risk' group not as homosexual or bisexual men, but as 'men who have sex with men', is indicative of the presence of other forces which inhibit a straightforward correlation between individual action and political identity. Clearly, actions have to be interpreted through a framework of political identification, and not as the immediate consequences of unreconstructed desire.

Poststructuralist discourse theory, therefore, enables us to see not just patriarchal repressive ideology as representative of power relations, but feminist emancipatory analysis as reflecting strategic and practical commitments. Even the conventional distinction between 'sex' and 'gender' advanced by Robert Stoller and Ann Oakley might be seen as a historical strategic assertion of the non-natural character of gender, a claim which enabled the early women's movement to advance its vision of women 'made not born', but which now needs to be surpassed by a more complex configuration of the relationship between 'nature' and 'culture', and in particular by the development of an analysis which recognizes 'nature' as simultaneously constructed by, and foundational to, a gendered universe:

> Gender ought not to be conceived merely as the cultural inscription of meaning on a pregiven sex (a juridical conception); gender must also designate the very apparatus of production whereby the sexes themselves are established. As a result, gender is not to culture as sex is to nature; gender is also the discursive/cultural means by which 'sexed nature' or a 'natural sex' is produced and established as 'prediscursive', prior to culture, a poltically neutral surface on *which* culture acts . . . This production of sex as the prediscursive ought to be understood as the effect of the apparatus of cultural construction designated by gender. (Butler, 1990:7)

Theorists of gender must therefore concern themselves with the question of difference as a core element of their enquiries. Yet a preoccupation with difference actually halts the process, and deflects us from an enquiry into how difference is actually generated and sustained by human practice and ideology. This section has outlined the beginnings of a debate which calls for a constructed essentialism, one which has recourse to a notion of fixed coherent identity, but only as a strategic and enacted category. One of the issues around the re-emergence of essentialist identity politics is the recognition that it is a representative metaphor, entailing human agency and practice, rather than a realist retreat into nature against which human beings are powerless. The perspectives of poststructuralism offer an analysis which exposes the ways in which fixed and rhetorical notions of difference serve to uphold dominating and coercive gender relations; critical attention begins with an interrogation of how human agency and practice go to 'make the difference'.

Notes

1. The group was later renamed 'Politique et Psychanalyse'.

2. Derrida's critique of the authority of interpretation is also influenced by his reading of the phenomenology of Hegel and Husserl; see Dews, 1987:4–11.

3. Arguably, in this respect poststructuralist thought betrays its debt to Nietzsche: contrast his rejection of an external and coherent physical 'reality' and the prospect of any reliable truth, with the supposition of the 'will to power', a metaphysical force subtending and validating human existence (Hollingdale, 1977).

9 · *Knowledge: Feminist Epistemologies and Philosophies of Science*

> Whether we like it or not, we are within philosophy, surrounded by masculine-feminine division that philosophy has helped to articulate and refine. The problem is to know whether we want to remain there and be dominated by them, or whether we can take up a critical position in relation to them, a position which will necessarily evolve through deciphering the basic philosophical assumptions latent in discourse about women. *The worst metaphysical positions are those which one adopts unconsciously whilst believing or claiming that one is speaking from a position outside philosophy.* (le Doeuff, 1977:2)

This chapter will discuss in more detail how feminist philosophers of knowledge, as well as feminist practitioners in the natural and physical sciences, have since the early 1970s approached questions of the nature of scientific enquiry, experimentation, validation and methodology. It is clear that in contesting the scientific basis of gender difference, theorists have been required to consider how knowledge itself may be 'gendered'.

Chapter Four discussed how biological science in all its manifestations, but particularly as bodies of knowledge representing the 'truth' about the relative qualities and abilities of women and men, and in its 'applied' guises via medical and technological practices, is regarded by feminists as a key agent of gender divisions and a powerful mechanism of patriarchal oppression.[1] Science – particularly the various branches of biology and especially evolutionary biology after Darwin – was deployed to portray women as 'naturally' fitted for certain roles in order to serve certain social and political ends at a time of growing pressure for women's emancipation (Harding, 1991).

Janet Sayers suggests that the natural and physical sciences have replaced religion and morality as the arbiters of gender difference, and the respective 'natural' roles of women and men. At crucial historical moments, science has advanced 'theories' which restrict and confine women's influence, and portray them as passive objects of nature, rather than active agents of culture, politics and the public world. Such appeals to the authority of science to rule on matters of social policy rest upon science's claims to 'objectivity' (Overfield, 1981). To this day, scientific research and evidence appears weighted against feminist aspirations, espousing instead theories of gender difference which serve, to feminist eyes, to exaggerate and reify gender dichotomy (Sayers, 1982; Harding, 1986:15–110).

One way in which women experience patriarchal knowledge at its most powerful and excluding is via its manifestations in science and technology. Judy Wajcman examines how even new and supposedly gender-neutral disciplines such as information technology are rapidly becoming male preserves: 'Most women never approach the foreign territory of these masculine areas' (Wajcman, 1991:151).

The new reproductive technologies are another area of scientific innovation that is extremely contradictory for many women. Such advances in medical and scientific knowledge promise women greater control over their own fertility, to the extent of making it possible for many childless women to have a baby. However, reproductive technology is still controlled by medical professionals and the state, meaning that treatment is driven less by women's needs than by medical and scientific values and social policy considerations (Stanworth, 1987; Hanmer, 1993).

Science, as knowledge and practice, therefore, has often appeared to be the implacable foe of the women's movement and a highly influential and significant factor in the construction and maintenance of patriarchal ideologies and policies. Proper scientific knowledge is portrayed as pure, objective and value-free, reflecting a notion of rationality as encapsulating pristine logic, untainted by the interests or perspectives of the knower. Such a view of rationality is typically associated with the world and activities of men: objectivity, domination, creativity and intellect are qualities associated with the building of culture. Inevitably, they become opposed to the characteristics equated with women: subjectivity, irrationality, affectivity: the qualities of home and family. Science is therefore culturally associated with masculinity, and with the public realm of the masculine.

> Masculinist rationality is a form of knowledge which assumes a knower who believes he can separate himself from his body, emotions, values, past and so on, so that he and his thought are autonomous, context-free and objective. (G. Rose, 1993:7)

The sphere of instrumental technical reason has traditionally been defined as a male activity – as an intellectual space into which women may not stray – and is predicated on an exclusion of all that is irrational, emotional, subjective – and 'feminine'. Here again we encounter the dynamics of exclusion and foreclosure; in order to circumscribe the (exclusively) androcentric sphere of reason, all ambiguity and alternatives are rendered 'Other' and alien.

Not surprisingly, therefore, many feminists have turned their attention to possible programmes for reform in order to dislodge the primacy of patriarchal science. One way of making science more 'woman-friendly' might be to promote a greater equality of access for female scientists. It is argued that women practitioners would rectify the androcentric bias and produce an altogether more 'balanced' science. Yet, increasingly, feminists have cast doubt on such a strategy. Individual access to a discipline or profession in itself will not change the fundamental character of scientific discourse, which is constructed to serve patriarchal society. Women in science are constantly disabled by the fact that, ultimately, they are still women in a men's world.

Feminist Empiricism and Value-Neutrality

Another perspective has therefore been advanced, in an attempt to gain some purchase on the connections between women's relative absence in scientific practice and the nature of science's own structures of knowledge. 'Feminist empiricism' advances the criticism that current science is failing to observe its own norms and criteria for value-free, objective knowledge by allowing androcentric values to creep into its procedures. Thus feminist empiricism challenges androcentric research as 'bad' science. A clear example of this process, already encountered, would be the feminist critiques of sociobiology, in their condemnation of that discipline's excessive anthropomorphism, ethnocentricism and poor logic. Other examples of feminist-empiricist correctives to androcentric science are discussed elsewhere (Harding, 1986:24–25;33–56). The norms of objective and stringent observation of experimental procedures, it is argued, have not been upheld; feminist research serves as a 'corrective' to value-neutral science, by pointing out the intrusion of sexist values which betray the integrity of science.

Yet, as Harding in particular has pointed out, feminist empiricism carries the seeds of its own contradictions: in the name of a value-neutrality which eschews the intervention of the researcher's own biases as a disruption of scientific objectivity, feminists expose the androcentric distortions of much research. Yet the impetus for these 'exposés' comes from a politically committed perspective: that which protests against the exclusion and denigration of women within the (less than objective) scientific world-view!

Feminist empiricism therefore itself founders on the myth of value-neutrality, although it reveals the means by which androcentric science uses an appeal to objectivity to cloak its own biases. Yet to admit that the very nature of science reflects its social and cultural context enables explicit connections to be drawn between androcentric values in science and wider gender divisions. The historical development of scientific enquiry has always reflected socially conditioned definitions of what is problematic. Even 'pure' sciences, like physics and mathematics, are affected by social factors, such as the language and symbolism required to express simple equations, so as to render any notion of a value-neutral science implausible, even by the standards of its own practice.

Towards a Woman-Friendly Science

Thus feminists have come to a position of arguing that neither equal opportunities policies nor empiricist strategies of encouraging 'bad' science to become 'better' reach to the roots of science's most fundamental knowledge-claims. The focus for feminist critiques has come to rest upon questions of method, methodology and epistemology, and the recognition that all three constitute a gendered scientific discipline.[2] Thus, androcentric science is not simply about lapses into subjective procedures of experimentation and validation; the whole of the scientific enterprise exhibits a series of choices as to what sort of knowledge is privileged, what elements of human experience are regarded as problematic and worthy of exploration, and to what uses such scientific 'discoveries' are put.

Two issues seem most important in terms of a feminist critique: firstly, that science does reflect its social and political surroundings, and that its social context includes a dichotomous and hierarchical gender regime. Thus, feminist critics of science maintain that the sexist nature of science cannot be considered apart from a wider society in which gender hierarchy conditions all experience. Effectively, knowledge is connected to more pervasive power relations between women and men, and we have to see scientific epistemology as somehow both reflecting and perpetuating male superiority. Kathy Overfield argues that there cannot be a 'woman scientist' because science is constructed around the exclusion of the feminine. Science is built around domination and around separation from the material and the sensual, because the rise of objective science coincided with historical shifts in gender relations, which rested upon a severe dichotomy and hierarchy of gender roles. Thus, scientific imagery and claims to knowledge are integral and functional aspects of patriarchy:

> In fact, the construction of our political philosophy and views of human nature seem to depend on a series of sexual dichotomies, involved in the construction of gender differences. We thus construct rationality in opposition to emotionality, objectivity in opposition to nature, the public realm in opposition to the private realm. Whether we read Kant, Rousseau, Hegel, or Darwin, we find that female and male are contrasted in terms of opposing characters: women love beauty, men truth; women are passive, men active; women are emotional, men rational; women are selfless, men selfish – and so on and on through the history of western philosophy. (Fee, 1983:11)

The connections between masculinity, scientific objectivity and patriarchal power relations have been traced by many feminist writers on the philosophy of science, and have served as a crucial analytical perspective. Elizabeth Fee criticizes the conventional notion of science as pure, objective and value-free, as reflecting a liberal notion of rationality as encapsulating pristine logic, untainted by the interests or perspectives of the knower. For her, this already reveals an epistemology that is rooted in a gendered world, because such a view of rationality depends upon a dichotomous and oppositional organization of reality, one which associates men with the privileged and abstract, and women with the subordinate, constrained and material realms. Science thus betrays its incipiently political and gendered character, because such categories of know-ledge and practice depend on the creation and maintenance of gender dichotomy and hierarchy for their definition. They identify themselves with those gender qualities traditionally attributed to men: objectivity, domination, creativity, intellect and the building of culture. Inevitably, they become opposed to the characteristics equated with women: subjectivity, irrationality, affectivity. Science is therefore culturally associated with masculinity, and any woman entering the field is thought to be surrendering her 'true' nature. Such a process of definition is therefore part of a wider system, which uses gender dichotomy to exclude women from public activity, cultural definition and social power:

> Man is seen as the maker of history, but woman provides his connection with nature; she is the mediating force between man and nature, a reminder of his childhood, a reminder of the body, and a reminder of his sexuality, passion, and human connectedness. She is the repository of emotional life and of all the nonrational elements of human experience. She is at times saintly and at times evil, but always she seems necessary as the counterpoint to man's self-definition as being of pure rationality. (Fee, 1983:12)

Therefore, implicit within all scientific enquiry, within the very way in which the discipline is formed, is a dichotomy of human experience into separate and opposite categories. Some feminists therefore adopt the oppositional nature of male science and female invisibility, and develop an analysis that sees a feminist alternative as originating in the repressed and marginalized values currently represented by women. Such a perspective equates objectivity and domination with male control and consciousness, and argues for a renewed woman-centred epistemology, which affirms the 'feminine' qualities of empathy, closeness to nature, co-operation and nurturance.

Other varieties of interpretation attempt to connect constructions of science as built around one half of a dichotomous system of gender attributes by associating particular forms of subjectivity (consciousness) with psychoanalytically constructed patterns of gender 'difference'. Evelyn Fox Keller chooses to invoke object-relations psychoanalysis, which engages with innate sex drives and actual relations with others, to produce an analysis which explains how early experiences help to shape subsequent states of subjectivity.

Following writers such as Nancy Chodorow and Dorothy Dinner-stein, Keller presents a genealogy of masculinity grounded in the disruption of intimacy with the mother, and the establishment of personalities rooted in control and domination (Keller, 1982). Patterns of early mother-child relations are held to be central to the development of the mature adult, and the psychosexual influences of the initial sensual maternal bonds, and the implications of the psychic processes required to achieve separation from the mother in order to become a mature adult, are held to be crucial. All persons are caught in the tension between connectedness, intimacy and sensual/sexual loss of self in enjoyment of another, and separation, self-definition and achievement of autonomy through rational self-control and self-possession. Masculinity as culturally constructed rests upon a denial of the feminine, and a distancing from the mother as representative of the 'Other'. Femininity can afford to be more closely identified with the mother, as mothering is the female child's eventual destiny. Thus, boys growing into men must assert self-definition, distance between self and other, rational objectivity and domination. Hence the connection between masculinity and object-ive science, although it still begs the question as to which precedes which, causally speaking.

Although Keller argues for the possibility of a feminist science, grounded in non-repressive practice (invoking Marcuse's notion of an 'erotic' science which seeks to restore the split between connection and separation), and although she is clearly presenting a model of gender which is constructed, 'compelling' men to occupy the sphere of rationality and women that of subjectivity and nature, it is difficult to see how such transformative science can take place when both male and female practitioners are so trapped in their respective states of consciousness. Again, beyond relating back to structures of child-rearing, this approach does little to bring analysis to bear upon questions of how configurations of scientific knowledge relate to economic and power relations, for example in the sexual division of labour, questions of greater male expertise in technology, and the social control of women via agencies of the law, education and medicine. It rather subordinates epistemology to child-rearing practices, and begs the question of whether particular understandings of science are simply functions of our psychosexual dispositions, or whether both the gendered division of labour in the family and the scientific structures of knowledge are not themselves products of more general gender relations.

Rita Arditti argues that women's values of co-operation, nurture and affectivity serve as a corrective and redemptive influence upon androcentric science (Arditti, 1982). Feminism offers alternative procedures of organizing and knowing: greater integration of mind and body, socially useful knowledge and a refusal to operate within a dualism of mind and body. Women give science its 'soul', because they offer it a radically different set of experiences upon which to build its claims to truth.

Arditti also traces women's exclusion from the scientific elites, and concludes that androcentric science is a major pillar of patriarchy. By articulating alternative values, rooted in feminist understandings, women can renew scientific practices, inducing social responsibility, instigating new methods, and widening definitions of what can effectively be known, all by an appeal to women's experience.

However, there are several problems with this view. Firstly, if equal opportunities are difficult enough, how feasible will it be for women to engineer wholesale shifts of values? A social constructionist understanding of science must also take account of the extent to which research priorities, funding and application are determined by wider social forces, such as government policy and the research and development programmes of transnational corporations.

A second problem with Arditti's view of women inserting 'human' and holistic values into science has been raised by Longino (1987). Arditti maintains the gender polarizations of 'hard' objective men, and 'soft' caring, co-operative women. For many women scientists, this sounds just like another version of women being told that they are incapable of proper science. Joan Rothschild, whilst critical of the gender dichotomy upon which an association of 'feminine' values and a feminist contribution to the history of technology are based, does argue that at least this approach highlights the way in which technology has been defined around one half of a dualism, and renders the discipline itself more holistic by drawing attention to previously repressed values of irrational and affective knowledge, subjectivity and ecological responsibility.

This positive contribution notwithstanding, however, Rothschild's perspective fails to engage with the gendered nature of society, because its appeals to knowledge still reflect a sexist division which places women in the affective, caring and interactive sphere. This is a form of analysis which enables a greater descriptive clarity (in that psychic subjectivity is a part of a gendered world which privileges certain kinds of reasoning), but fails to transcend the dichotomies from which such gendered characteristics originate. Women give science greater responsibility for nature, greater social concern, greater connection between the knower and the known. The problem emerges that the connections between the subordination of women, certain kinds of gendered experience and such differential knowledge remain unspecific. There needs to be a greater rigour than that offered by Rothschild concerning the origins of such experience: is it innate, and therefore an absolute and axiomatic source of an alternative epistemology? Or is it forged through social experience and therefore eternally self-reflexive, always open to charges of relativism? In seeking what various other commentators have termed a feminist 'successor science', the grounds upon which such an enterprise will rest its epistemology, and the terms on which it makes an appeal to the distinctiveness of women's (or feminist) experience and apprehension of the world, become most crucial:

> Some radical feminist theorists . . . reject reason because they identi-fy it with the instrumental, quantitative, technocratic and supposedly value-free conception of reason that began to become dominant with the scientific revolution of the 17th century. If this is reason, radical feminists want no part of it, and many rush in reaction to identify women with feeling, emotion, nature and wildness . . . It is ironic to note that, by accepting these historically bound definitions of reason and of emotion, which are both conceptually and politically inad-equate, radical feminism in fact takes over one of the most funda-mental of the patriarchal dualisms that it wishes to reject. A more fruitful approach for radical feminism would be to reject the domi-nant conceptions of reason, of emotion and of the relation between them and instead to develop new conceptions that would be more coherent, comprehensive and appropriate to feminist values. (Jaggar, 1983:115–16)

Feminist epistemology is becoming increasingly wary of setting up any appeal to a category of differential experience or knowledge that is beyond critical scrutiny. Longino and others stress the diversity of women's experience, and begin to suggest that, so long as feminist epistemology emphasizes the content of science, as opposed to its processes and practices, epistemology is going to be restricted to debates about women's and men's 'differences' in a way that abstracts and psychologizes the actual social and material contexts of scientific knowledge.

Thus many theorists have challenged the essentialist flavour of such analysis, and argued that women's experience of themselves as closer to nature is part of the rhetoric out of which modern science itself was constructed. Such arguments maintain that women need equal access to power, material and ideological, in order to change both the patterns of definition and the material relations which underpin them. Therefore many writers look to the principles of the organization of women's labour as the source of their 'difference' and as the reason for their alienation from the scientific enterprise. This is the kind of argument advanced by the 'standpoint' feminist epistemologies.

Standpoint Epistemologies

This perspective has been explored by those who are searching for alternative systems of knowledge not characterized by seemingly 'essential' dualisms, with some relation to women's distinctive experience, but also with some potential for the transformation of knowledge. The claim, in Sandra Harding's words, that science has always borne 'the fingerprints of its human producers' (Harding, 1986:137) may lead to relativism, or may offer the possibility of recovering sources of knowledge which reveal their sources not in the dualistic subjectivities of gendered beings, but in actual social and practical contexts. Thus, standpoint epistemology has evolved as a particular feminist strategy; speaking from the specific and immediate perspective of women, with a clear political and strategic agenda. Feminist standpoints start from Hegel's Master/Slave dialectic, whereby the privilege and special claims to knowledge of the dominant group is achieved at the expense of any autonomous identity of the oppressed. The more powerful group can designate to themselves the activities which constitute 'reality', and project onto the subjugated classes those undesirable functions which are then categorized as worthless.[3]

Feminist standpoint epistemologies have been advanced by writers such as Nancy Hartsock, Dorothy Smith and Hilary Rose, who maintain that patterns of women's work place them in a distinctive relationship to the world, where interconnectedness and caring characterize women's labour (H. Rose, 1983; Harding, 1987). It is argued, therefore, that theories of knowledge have to be seen as connected with theories of labour; consciousness is not an abstract concept, but rooted in material practice. This is derived from Marx's theory of historical materialism: that knowledge arises from the basic processes of humanity's transformation of raw 'nature':

> The sensuous world . . . is not a thing given direct from all eternity, ever the same, but the product of industry and of the state of society; and indeed in the sense that it is an historical product, the result of the activity of a whole succession of generations . . . (K. Marx, *The German Ideology* (1848), quoted in Rose and Rose, 1976a)

Androcentric science, therefore, derives from specific circumstances of the gender division of labour under capitalist patriarchy. The undervaluation and invisibility of women's work – and its expropriation through ideologies of 'caring' – results in the denial of the experience and knowledge which is generated by women's labour. Science, by contrast, is true knowledge, and rests upon the very antithesis of women's experiences of caring labour: intimacy, involvement, relationships. The deskilling of women's labour, so that it ceases to qualify as real labour, means that women are alienated from the sources of their own experience and satisfaction.

Nevertheless, women's subordinate experience also carries a germ of critical protest. Rose argues that women's labour, as well as being alienated, also offers a source of real satisfaction. By generating and leading a new understanding of the material world, it offers a transformative epistemology (H. Rose, 1983:87–90). This contains the seeds of a new vision, although Rose acknowledges that it is still dependent upon a dualistic and gendered world-view, because it arises from women's experience within patriarchal conditions of labour. Smith also explores the implications of women's contradictory experience under patriarchy: they are as much creators and bearers of culture as men, yet are denied the credit for that work. However, the discontinuity between women's own material experience of the deployment of their own labour, and that invisibility in culture, creates what Smith terms a 'fault-line', which gives rise to a renewed and critical consciousness. Subordinated experience of itself serves to challenge the givenness of androcentric accounts of reality (Smith, 1979, quoted in Harding, 1986:157).

Thus, feminist standpoint epistemologies offer a programme that is explicitly transformative, because it serves to criticize the subordinated position of oppressed groups. Such a perspective brings into the open a factor which, as has already been mentioned, renders feminist empiricism inadequate: that all knowledge reflects some specific and value-laden perspective. However, feminist standpoint writers tend to assume too ready and automatic links between subjugated positions, the development of distinctive knowledge and transformatory strategy. Harding exemplifies confidence in the belief that one's world-view will unambiguously direct one to change the world:

> The questions an oppressed group wants answered are rarely requests for so-called pure truth. Instead, they are queries about how to change its conditions; how its world is shaped by forces beyond it; how to win over, defeat, or neutralize those forces arrayed against its emancipation, growth, or development; and so forth. Consequently, feminist research projects originate primarily not in any old 'women's experiences', but in women's experiences in political struggles. (Harding, 1987:8)

It may therefore be important to distinguish between *feminist* science and *feminine* science when attempting to construct feminist epistemologies which do not cede the realm of rationality back to men, and which fully acknowledge women's participation in the creation of culture and social relations. A certain caution is required before claiming that women's consciousness will necessarily and axiomatically be transformative; at the very least, a distinction between transformative and conservative feminist standpoints should be drawn. The need for this distinction rests in my opinion on the lack of definition between a feminist and a feminine standpoint, and whether 'women's experience' needs to be distinguished from feminist epistemology. For example, whilst regarding the material conditions which generate women's alienation as socially constructed functions of patriarchy, Rose still seems to offer hostages to the fortunes of essentialism in failing to indicate sufficiently clearly whether the opposition between women's knowledge and men's is something essentialized and absolute, with women – again – as the innate bearers of pure virtue and responsibility. Rose seems no closer to a strategy of transcending such a gender dichotomy, because the difference in epistemologies still seems to rest in values and psychic dispositions, rather than in making the connection back to where she started, in social and material relationships.

> Masculinist knowledge takes the form of a peculiar emphasis on the domains of cognitive and objective rationality, on reductive explanation, and on dichotomous partitioning of the social and natural worlds. It is this masculinist knowledge which has produced today's deadly culture of science and technology and which seeks to relegate women and women's knowledge to the realm of nature. By contrast, a feminist epistemology derives from women's lived experience, centred on the domains of inter-connectedness and affectual rationality. It emphasizes holism and harmonious relationships with nature, which is why feminism has links with that other major social movement of our time, ecology. (H. Rose, 1986:162–63)

Although such special knowledge arising from women's subordinate position is of itself part of a gendered world, materialist feminist standpoint theorists like Rose insist that such experience is the product of patriarchy in that it derives from the division of labour (which constructs feminine subjectivity), rather than residing in innately feminine traits. This reintroduces problems concerning the nature of women's experience; how reliable and authentic it can ever be under conditions of patriarchy; and how to ensure that feminist epistemology can transcend the conditions which, paradoxically, have gone to create it.

Thus, the advantages of feminist standpoint epistemologies are various, but some aspects of them lack clarity and lapse into a rather essentialized and absolute appeal to women's experience. It is undoubtedly important to connect structures of knowledge with social divisions of gender and individual subjectivity, because knowledge is something generated by people. Yet often such analyses assume that science is purely about clashes of oppositional values held by particular groups of people, and neglect to explore whether such connections have not themselves been socially constructed (and, indeed, sanctioned by certain kinds of scientific research). There is still therefore a tendency to regard experience as axiomatic: like the 'feminizers' of science, they regard reform as a validation and continuation, rather than a subversion or deconstruction, of existing gender divisions. Women do certain kinds of work because they are oppressed: this obviously creates their alienation, but what does it mean to claim that knowledge is privileged if it is knowledge arising from the tasks and experiences that patriarchy discards? Where does the new gender order come from?

Therefore, there seems to be little attention to the strength of the ideology which, whilst identifying the pervasiveness of existing gender dichotomy and hierarchy, appears to resist the search for a more fundamental dynamic or rationale. The result seems to be that women are inherently unable to share in any science which actually seeks to commandeer the privileges normally accorded men. This poses the question as to whether any form of rationality is possible under feminism, albeit integrated with those qualities of intuition and connectedness traditionally excluded from scientific epistemology.

Elizabeth Fee argues that some kind of engagement with science by women must not be abandoned, and that there are some valid criteria for scientific enquiry which can be affirmed within a feminist enterprise. These include the principles of understanding the world in rational terms; of putting knowledge to critical scrutiny; of acknowledging the provisionality of any findings; of collective and collaborative enquiry; and accountability to a wider, 'lay' community (Fee, 1983:22–24). However, I think Fee would argue that these are values and qualities which pertain in a de-gendered epistemology, and that the task is to create the social conditions which make it possible for such a science to be sustained. This neither unravels the connections between scientific practice and gender symbolism, social relations and subjectivity, nor gives us a purchase on the processes of causation.

Such debates seem therefore to be stuck at descriptive levels; they posit connections between certain configurations of gender and the internal structures of scientific practice and epistemology, and they offer some kind of explanation as to why science serves society's interests in underpinning and rationalizing gender inequality. However, they tell us little about the actual relationship between gender ideology and social structure in any other than functionalist terms. Nor do we gain much insight into the possible constructionist nature of 'culture' and 'nature', and how they first became, as it were, 'gendered'. Part of the difficulty may be that such perspectives concentrate on the content of science, and the ways in which certain kinds of rationality or affectivity serve as metaphors for wider gender divisions. Yet gendered subjectivity, as in the analyses informed by object-relations psychology, becomes dominant and pre-eminent at the expense of any autonomous processes of scientific production. It is therefore necessary to move beyond a preoccupation with content and values, to emphasize scientific practice and process.

However, although it is argued that concepts of 'nature' and 'culture' are arbitrary and do not portray any 'real' dichotomies, it is clear that such polarities have infected virtually every human society. What is more, there seems to be a similar propensity to categorize such dichotomies as hierarchical *and* gendered. If we are able to trace arguments which resist the explanation for this as lying in ontological differences between women and men, and chains of causation which are more or less biologically determinist, we still need to begin to construct plausible theories which trace alternative patterns of causation. This involves the development of epistemologies which recognize that our accounts of 'nature' are constructed, rather than reflections of an objective reality, but nevertheless enable a theory of knowledge-claims that can be counted as in some sense reliable. Feminists have therefore drawn upon postmodern accounts of knowledge to deconstruct androcentric defences of objectivity, by challenging notions of fixed, rational and unitary accounts of language, knowledge and science.

Feminist Postmodernism: The Challenge to Epistemology

The dilemma for feminist epistemology in seeking an alternative to androcentric science and knowledge-claims lies in its exposure of all knowledge as socially-constructed and subjective. Thus, there is no knowledge that is value-free or context-independent, and no objective grounds on which to privilege feminist epistemology. Although feminist standpoint strategies carry a promising degree of understanding of the complexity of the creation and generation of women's experience, a successor science based on such a category would arguably not be sufficiently transformative. Such subjugated knowledge as women may possess in certain social contexts may certainly destabilize established and powerful claims to truth; but the postmodern impetus suggests that those very standpoints of women must be subjected to constant scrutiny, as being no more rational or true than any other form of knowledge. All science, sexist or feminist, is simply a 'text'. Yet clearly a postmodern scepticism can lead to relativism; if all we have in science are competing narratives, within which a subordinate standpoint knowledge has no automatic primacy, how do we decide between rival discourses? Does a postmodern perspective on epistemology effectively rob us of any transformative impetus? In seeking to resolve this impasse, I shall now turn to perspectives which are mindful of all the debates reviewed above, and which attempt to transcend some of the inherent difficulties.

Mary Hawkesworth (1989) reviews feminist theories of knowledge within the natural sciences, with special reference to feminists' projects to analyse connections between gender and ways of knowing. Having reviewed the categories of feminist empiricism, standpoint theories and postmodernism, Hawkesworth moves to consider how an epistemology sensitive to gender and to questions of the socially mediated nature of scientific knowledge might be developed. In this, she is clearly concerned to assimilate the challenges in particular of postmodern perspectives in epistemology, which speak of the impossibility of a stable, universal and wholly rational quest to secure true knowledge.

A critical (and transformative) perspective is required, which identifies the equations of scientific objectivity with gender divisions and knowledge with power; yet such an epistemology must not surrender a political and moral commitment to a transformative project as well. Thus the transitional nature of all prospective feminist epistemologies without collapsing into mere relativism is a prerequisite. Hawkesworth argues that feminist epistemology has concentrated upon questions about 'knowers', reflecting feminists' struggles to establish women's experience of the world as of equal import and significance as prevailing androcentric perspectives. The rationality of women, long denied by dualistic gender metaphors which inform the organization of knowledge, has therefore of necessity been a central emphasis of such critiques. However, Hawkesworth makes some perceptive criticisms of the implications of such a pattern of reasoning, in particular how the processes by which rationality and objectivity are culturally attributed to men result in an analysis which serves to psychologize the social construction of knowledge.

> In focusing attention on the source of knowledge, that is, on men, rather than on the validity of specific claims advanced by men, the terms of debate are shifted toward psychological and functionalist analyses and away from issues of justification. This in turn allows a

number of contested epistemological assumptions about the nature of knowledge, the process of knowing, standards of evidence, and criteria of assessment to be incorporated unreflectively into feminist arguments. (Hawkesworth, 1989:539)

Effectively, Hawkesworth is challenging a crucial element of many feminist critiques of androcentric knowledge, and in particular those informed by object-relations psychoanalysis. She is also disputing the claim that reason is gendered, and that scientific claims to rationality and objectivity are intertwined with the construction of gender identity. Hawkesworth's critique of an unexamined path of analysis which locates the ideological and pathological nature of scientific knowledge in the psychic formation of one gender is significant. She reminds us that epistemology cannot be reduced to psychology, and patterns of scientific practice – which have been recognized as critical, in terms of creating an area of the social relations of science – cannot be reduced to the issue of male psychosexual development.

The result of such analyses, argues Hawkesworth, is that debates about knowledge become conflated into one particular conception of instrumental rationality, supposedly serving and justifying psychic drives to dominate and objectify. Far from disentangling reason from symbolic, social and subjective configurations of gender, such an analysis simply succeeds in further entrenching epistemology in gender dichotomy, especially as feminist strategies for change frequently rest upon an association of alternative knowledges with supposedly 'feminine' qualities of relatedness, respect for nature, intuition and co-operation. These analyses rest upon over-optimistic claims both to the transparency of self-knowledge (especially by women within a patriarchal society) and the liberating potential of knowledge rooted in women's unique qualities or experiences that, similarly, are themselves products of the gendered society which such knowledge is attempting to transform. Effectively, therefore, Hawkesworth is arguing that such feminist strategies are still rooted in essentialist and ontological analyses; whereas what is needed is some sort of politics.

Starting from a subjectivist approach to epistemology that focuses on issues pertaining to the faculties and sentiments of knowers as the source of knowledge, feminist inquiry arrives at an impasse. Presuppositions concerning a 'natural' subject/self capable of grasping

intuitively the totality of being, and a homogenous women's experience that generates a privileged view of reality, fail to do justice to the
fallibility of women's experiences, and to the powerful ways in which
race, class, ethnicity, culture, and language structure individuals'
understandings of the world. Claims concerning diverse and incom-
patible intuitions about the essential nature of social reality premised
on immediate apprehensions of that reality overlook the theoretical
underpinnings of all perception and experience and consequently
devolve into either authoritarian assertion or uncritical relativism.
(1989:546)

We have reached a familiar impasse, similar to that encountered in
my previous critique of the French feminists of 'Difference': in the
search for a distinctive and critical-transformative source of experience and knowledge, feminists run the risk of appealing to sources of
authority which are themselves atrophied in essentialist or gendered
categories. Yet Hawkesworth sees an epistemology which can both
honour the differential circumstances of women and men in a
gendered and hierarchical world, and account for the various and
socially mediated means by which knowledge itself is generated. In
this respect, it attempts to account for the self-reflexive nature of
identity and knowledge. Her solution resembles some other suggestions at which I have already hinted, namely analyses which centre
upon the question of human *practice*. Hawkesworth's discussion of
practice is therefore worthy of some detailed attention as a way of
further developing this perspective.

Knowledge as Human Practice

By adopting a conception of cognition as a human practice, a critical
feminist epistemology can identify, explain, and refute persistent
androcentric bias within the dominant discourses without privileging a putative 'woman's' perspective and without appealing to
problematic conceptions of 'the given' (Hawkesworth, 1989:538).

Hawkesworth's criticisms of standpoint and psychoanalytic feminist epistemologies rest on their insistence that knowledge is ontological and essential – existential knowledge – rather than enacted
and mediated: political and strategic acts of knowing. In her insistence upon knowledge and cognition as human practice, Hawkesworth draws upon an intriguing set of sources: anti-foundationalist
philosophers, such as Richard Rorty and Richard Bernstein; deconstructionists like Jacques Derrida and Michel Foucault; and the

moral philosophy of Alasdair Macintyre. Together these perspectives dismantle notions of knowledge as providing absolute and final access to established truth via deductive reasoning. Deduction itself rests upon faulty assumptions about the fixity of linguistic propositions necessary to support basic and primary premises; it ignores the role of prior theoretical commitments in conditioning empirical enquiry, and the social context of the observer – all aspects of what Wilfrid Sellars calls 'the myth of the given'. By contrast, after Macintyre, Hawkesworth proposes a renewed attention to knowledge as a form of human practice. Knowledge thus becomes something clearly bound by language, rules of procedure, validation and theorization, all of which have their origins, not outside or beyond that which is known in some Platonic realm of ideal reason, but within the realm of human agency:

> In this view, 'knowledge' presupposes involvement in a social process replete with rules of compliance, norms of assessment, and standards of excellence that are humanly created. Although humans aspire to unmediated knowledge of the world, the nature of perception precludes such direct access. The only possible access is through theory-laden conventions that organize and structure observations by according meanings to observed events, bestowing relevance and significance on phenomena, indicating strategies for problem solving, and identifying methods by which to test the validity of solutions. Knowledge, then, is a convention rooted in the practical judgements of a community of fallible inquirers who struggle to resolve theory-dependent problems under specific historical conditions. (Hawkesworth, 1989:548–49)

Thus all knowledge is bound by the conditions of human cognition: and this underwrites many of the feminist critiques of scientific objectivity, which tries to separate the products, agents and social contexts of knowing. As Donna Haraway observes, a commitment to empiricism which tries to persuade itself that its discoveries are 'brute facts' represents an impossible form of human knowledge because it denies its own embodied and 'situated' character (Haraway, 1991:188). She argues that all of us perceive from somewhere or other, even though patriarchy may attempt to delude us that it (represented by 'masculinist' scientists, technologists and militarists) likes to favour knowledge that abstracts its perspective, whilst projecting onto subordinate (and feminized) groups the stigma of embodiment. Whereas Hawkesworth uses the theme of practice,

Haraway evokes the metaphor of vision – as embodied and situated. The idea of infinite vision, of seeing all in a universal and final perspective, is plainly ridiculous, and to make such a claim is, effectively, to 'play God'. Thus an epistemology modelled on such assumptions should be rejected. Instead, Haraway argues that an insistence on the 'particularity and embodiment of all vision' comprises 'a usable, but not an innocent doctrine of objectivity' (Haraway, 1991:189).

This phrase 'usable but not innocent' contains great potential. It means that we recognize the specificity of our knowing, the tentative and provisional nature of our claims to 'truth', yet we still maintain a commitment to 'usable knowledge' as a working and strategic hypothesis. Furthermore, I would suggest that the thorny feminist problem of the role of the body in constituting and offering access to experience and knowledge is also resolved: we can see bodies as 'vantage points' from which we advance hypotheses about the world, rather than ontological essences which make absolute claims about the fixity of reality. At the same time, the materiality of *situated* knowledge allows for a moral imperative, because the knowledge which ensues does clearly have direct reference and relevance to concrete human situations. And, as Haraway remarks, this model of knowledge is stimulating and exciting, not irrational or irresponsible. Objectivity is dangerous, because it represents a distorted and partial vision. Its ideological function rests in its attempt to cloak its own situatedness behind the rhetoric of transcendent and disembodied vision.

Varieties of standpoint epistemologies endorsing this perspective – which involve a self-critical vision which refuses to absolutize or decontextualize the source of one's subordination as, for example, resting in 'nature' – can therefore be favoured. According to Haraway, they are *a fortiori* unable to deny the 'critical and interpretative core of all knowledge'; in other words, the situated, contextual and strategic nature of knowing.

How is this kind of analysis particularly pertinent to gender studies? Hawkesworth argues that to see knowledge as a human practice enables feminist epistemologists to expose appeals to abstract objective and universal claims to truth as cloaking sectional perspectives and interests. Yet equally, knowledge as practice validates the deployment of critical analyses of scientific claims to truth in the service of political ends; and it is interesting to note how writers like Hawkesworth and Haraway – and indeed Harding, Jaggar and others who propound standpoint theories or the 'practice' theories I have just been discussing – all insert claims to some kind of moral and political commitment to gender equality and the full participation of women in order to dispel accusations of relativism. However, we should expose the insertion of values into feminist epistemology with a critical eye. What does it mean to put at the heart of one's claims to knowledge a commitment to, in Hawkesworth's words, 'women's full participation in social, political, and economic life'? Is this fulfilled regardless of their role, as mothers, or as prostitutes, or as laboratory assistants conducting tests on non-human animals? Surely such an ethical/political system needs further qualification; and risks charges of universalizing women's experience and glossing over inequalities of race and class. Both standpoint and practice epistemologies look for validation in political and enacted notions of truth: theories or notions of what counts as acceptable knowledge have to lead somewhere, to contribute to a wider social vision, just as they have to be understood as originating in a social context of values, power relations and gender regimes.

It is this insistence that, for all its transitional and provisional nature (Harding), its specificity (Haraway) and its location in human agency (Hawkesworth), knowledge still has the power to judge and transform, that characterizes developments within feminist epistemology. Such epistemologies employ a kind of *a priori* commitment to the full participation and humanity of women in order to sustain a claim to the inherent superiority and adequacy of feminist science. Although, superficially at least, this may appear a long-winded way of saying that feminist science is feminist because it serves feminism, this perspective also raises important questions about the nature of knowledge and its relationship to gender. These concern the power relations which condition the differential access of women and men to scientific and cultural knowledge; the gender subjectivity which structures the opportunities for both women and men to articulate their own experience which has already been shaped by a gendered culture. Consequently, structures of knowing, in particular our categories of different modes of knowing, thinking and feeling, are conditioned by gender dichotomies and symbolic configurations. This analysis of the inter-relationship between power, knowledge and gender roots all those elements in human practice, and returns us to points already identified in previous sections: of difference as created and enacted, not given; of gender difference as relational, not ontological and absolute; and the reflexive – as both cause and effect – permeation of gender relations in every aspect of human activity.

Notes

1. See Hubbard, 1981, Rothschild, 1983, and Sayers, 1982 for further elaboration of the ways in which science and technology exclude women's contributions from their practices and accounts of adequate knowledge.

2. Harding advances three different aspects of the philosophy of science to which feminists must direct scrutiny. *Method* refers to techniques for gathering evidence – and is particularly relevant to feminists who wish to pay attention to women's own accounts of their lives as a means of privileging experience. *Methodology* is the theory and analysis of how research should proceed, especially in the use of a particular theoretical perspective – for example, phenomenological and ethnographic approaches as particularly suitable to feminist methods of research. *Epistemology* refers to the theories of knowledge, and what it is possible to know, to verify and how; in particular, perhaps whether women are held to be as reliable a group of 'knowers' as men, in the light of androcentric understandings of the gendered nature of rationality (Harding, 1987:1–15).

3. For a fuller discussion of the master/slave dynamic in Hegel, see Harding, *Feminism and Methodology*, Conclusion. Another less explicit influence in the stance of the standpoint epistemologists is Critical Theory, in its refutation of value-free knowledge and endorsement of practical and strategic claims to truth that explicitly favour the subordinated and oppressed. There also seem to be resonances with the analysis advanced by Jean Baker Miller, from a more psychoanalytic perspective. The tasks associated with embodiment, waste and death – all aspects of human life which patriarchy wishes to repress because it reminds it of its early connections with the mother – are repressed and marginalized. Women are associated with such tasks and their labour is therefore undervalued because it has no status in patriarchal concepts of reality (Miller, 1976).

10 · *Making the Difference: Towards a Theology of Gender*

> Men and women always remain somewhat alien to one another. Simply in virtue of having different bodies and social upbringings, the sexes are bound to find one another strange, perhaps even weird on occasion. To negotiate this strangeness and discover a humanity as rich, and in its own ways as rational, as one's own is one of the greatest challenges and delights that human beings can experience. (Carmody, 1994:58)

I have been reviewing some of the debates current within the social and human sciences which adopt a critical stance towards conventional wisdom surrounding gender identity, relations and stereotypes. Much of this originated in social science research into the status of women, which discovered that the assumptions, methods and models of verification were not neutral and objective, but 'gendered'. They were derived from male-centred experience, which did not simply exclude women from research, but presented them as secondary, lesser and 'Other'. This finding has informed critical studies of gender, which have exposed the ideological role of scientific studies in rationalizing and fuelling a social order founded on gender inequality.

A comprehensive engagement with theories of gender reveals some important insights, and challenges some traditional views. Firstly, a significant aspect of the study of gender relations across the disciplines is the almost universal extent to which gender is expressed in dualistic or binary terms, despite – as I have detailed – considerable scepticism towards the psychological and biological evidence for absolute polarities. Anthropologists have detailed the ubiquity of gender dichotomy, and how it imbues other categories: nature/culture, raw/cooked, domestic/public, gathering/hunting, profane/sacred. Men are seen as controlling public and social arenas, possessing clear status, occupying dominant roles, whereas women are confined to the margins, defined only in terms of their relationships to men.

In a commonplace sense, the tendency to refer to 'the opposite sex' reflects a taken-for-granted tendency that gender characteristics are not only tangible and quantifiable, but oppositional and dichotomous. However, studies of the psychological and biological sciences' measurements of 'sex differences' suggest that a false bipolarity has often been imposed on a selected sample, dampening the similarities between male and female and suppressing other non-polar diversities of character, ability and disposition. Male and female are thus portrayed as inherent opposites, as discrete categories of being – almost as separate species – rather than as persons with statistically overlapping qualities who share a common humanity. Yet, as much epistemological critique makes clear, the dichotomy of gender is naturalized by its extrapolation from a biological bipolarization of sex, which is itself highly questionable.

The exposure of patriarchy's association of women with subordinate, secondary and prescribed qualities has also enabled the repudiation of gender as a quality or relation of complementarity and symmetry. The material subordination of women, their social and symbolic marginalization and invisibility, and their objectification in culture are the tangible expressions of their devaluation within patriarchal societies, which place maleness as the norm. Thus, studies of gender reveal the ubiquity and centrality of power relations at the heart of all transactions between women and men.

As well as challenging the scope of gender difference, critical theories of gender have also questioned prevailing accounts of their ontogeny. Much of the impetus of early feminist engagements with the biological, psychological and social sciences derived from their repudiation of accounts of the personality traits of women (and men) and the origins of social divisions between the sexes as determined by the innate forces of 'nature'. The relative roles and characteristics of women and men were deemed to be directly deducible from empirically-grounded genetic, anatomical, hormonal or evolutionary dispositions. Similarly, deterministic theories of gender development, as in crude versions of Freudian psychoanalysis, portrayed the acquisition of gender identity as conformity to inevitable, predetermined and tangible patterns of behaviour in response to the logic of anatomical difference.

As alternative patterns of causation, gender theorists adopted perspectives like 'social role theory' and the sex/gender distinction. Such analyses emphasized the social construction of gender and offered accounts of the ways in which the stereotypes and expectations of masculinity and femininity are transmitted, learned and upheld by social institutions such as education, the media, religion and the family. Together they provide elements of the 'script' of gender.

Arguably, however, this option of social constructionism is still reliant on a form of (social) determinism. The characteristics to which males and females are required to conform are still assumed to be in some way sociologically or ontologically 'given'. Whether the categories of masculinity and femininity are biologically or socially derived, the individual is still a *tabula rasa* on which the forces of nature or social conditioning are inscribed. The content of sex roles, and the substance of gender characteristics, are not themselves seen as constructed or negotiable. They are as categorical as they would be if nature had decreed them. Gender roles are conceived as acquired within a social realm; but they have still been created outside human relations and then mapped onto passive beings.

Histories of nature and medicine, philosophies of science and sociologies of knowledge have all exposed the infirmity of the distinction between sex and gender: the properties of nature have been revealed as themselves the artefacts of culture. The association between metaphors of nature, scientific accounts of gender difference and particular forms of social relations demonstrates how definitions of 'nature' are human constructions, rather than self-evident categories.

A valuable new departure in recent critical work on gender has been a concerted effort to correct the relative invisibility of men in matters of gender relations. The predominant emphasis was formerly on the study of women, portraying women as the gendered, sexed, embodied, constructed category, leaving men still as the normative, unproblematic species. However, emergent studies of men and masculinity are subjecting the categories of 'men' and 'masculinity' to scrutiny, and identifying how they too are socially constructed and historically contingent. Such studies begin to examine critically how men have represented, and related to, one another, as well as how they have represented and related to women; and to see *all* situations as bearers and generators of gendered relationships, meanings and symbolism. They also begin to detail the differences within 'masculine' identity, and how power and difference pervade relationships between men as much as those of men to women.

Thus, notions of gender difference as deriving from fixed and innate characteristics, and women and men as occupying ontologically separate spheres by virtue of something called 'biological sex difference', have been contested by an alternative which sees gender as a relational rather than an abstract or reified term, and gender divisions as one fundamental dimension of the wider order of social relations. Culture is the creator, rather than the precursor, of gender; the ontological dichotomies of which gender has appeared to be an integral factor are themselves the products of a gendered system of thought: 'As observers of gender we are also its creators' (R. Hare-Mustin and J. Marececk quoted in Doyle and Paludi, 1991:341).

Thus, it is clear that gender is a fundamental form of social organization. Gender is but one manifestation of human social relations; it is not an ontological state, nor an intrinsic property of the individual. Theories about gender identity, gender regimes and the symbolic representations of gender are therefore theories about the formation of human culture; being a gendered person is about inhabiting a particular culture. Such social relations – and thus gender as a form of social relations – are generated and maintained by human *practice*, symbolic and material.

The notion of gender as a form of social relations entails a perspective which implicitly rejects a Platonic realm of human qualities which 'cause' or 'determine' gender difference. It challenges unicausal understandings of gender, and requires instead a critical attention to all dimensions of human interaction and activity that are constitutive of culture. Thus, theorists have turned to alternative explanations of gender relations, which affirm the importance of human *practice*[1] in the process of making gender difference. Gender is therefore not an innate or ontological category, but the product of human action and social relations, forged by the transformation of the world around us into material and ideological systems. Flax refers to this process as one of 'gendering':

> Power is required to produce the categories of gendering such as male, female, and difference. These categories are not present in

'nature' waiting for us to stumble upon them. They are not consequences of neutral empirical observation. We are not simply forced to acknowledge their existence through our investigations of other 'natural objects' such as human bodies . . .

Both men and women are implicated in the production and circulation of these categories and in the social relation in which they are embedded. (Flax, 1993: 24–25)

The emphasis of such practice is one of transformation, and here it connects with theories that refute the ontological distinction between nature/culture, biology/environment and male/female. However, as Connell argues, these categories are not denied so much as transcended: practice creates something new – social relations – out of the interaction of human agency and object (Connell, 1987:76ff). This allows for a reintegration of the divided realms of human agency, language and rationality and those of biology, embodiment and nature, with practice as the transformative agent. It then becomes impossible to distil any notion of the disembodied pre-cultural pristine self or innocent 'virgin' nature from the entirety of social/gender relations.

An understanding of social relations as the generator of gender differences, and of practice as the creator of a particular social order, is not to be mistaken for voluntarism. However, it is a rejection of determinism. Rather, the experience of living in any human society is one of being an active, creative agent, whilst simultaneously recognizing the constraints and sanctions – be they moral, material or ideological – which proscribe a wider set of choices or lifestyles. Any gender system is generated by the practices and conventions of science, technology, work, reproduction and cathexis, familial relations and religion; but these are all self-reflexive activities, involving acts of will and free agency as well as being constrained by the moral and material sanctions of institutions and structures.

Feminist psychoanalysis recognizes some of the implications of this in attempting to develop theories of gender formation which account for resistance, contradiction and change, and which provide a framework for an interplay between the individual's capacity to create a psychosocial world and the social and structural pressures into which he/she is born and socialized. In this respect it is possible to discern the extent to which gender is necessarily self reflexive: allowing for human agency and critical scrutiny whilst not underestimating its power to determine our lives. So a theory of practice needs to reflect such complexity and self-reflexivity at the heart of human experience.

Thus, human bodies, the practices and conventions of science, religion, language, work, reproduction, families and other social institutions are effectively the agents of gender, in that they are the vehicles by which personal identity is forged within a socially-constructed everyday world. This process is entirely cultural, a constant process of generation and regeneration of social relations:

> The origin of gender is not traceable to a definable origin because it itself is an originating activity incessantly taking place. No longer understood as a product of cultural and psychic relations long past, gender is a contemporary way of organizing past and future cultural norms, a way of situating oneself in and through these norms, an active style of living one's body in the world. (Butler, 1987:131)

The strategy of 'writing the body' in francophone feminism reminds us that gender cannot be an intellectual construct alone: it involves us as psychosomatic beings, inhabiting bodies as well as minds. The presence of such autonomous expressions of women's sensuality and bodily self-possession in a society which privileges Cartesian dualism and disembodied rationality is refreshing and challenging. This alternative perspective roots our gendered identities in the embodied and material practices of work, intimacy, reproduction, ageing and everyday social relations.

However, such a strategy of itself cannot rest unexamined; as critics have argued, no woman's experience of herself and her body is as transparent and unambiguous as many feminists would claim. Such a metaphysical evocation of subjectivity effectively collapses women's identity and the processes of gender differentiation back into biological difference. If women's difference from men rests not in social relations and human practice but in some pre-discursive, pre-Oedipal sphere, the source and nature of gender is effectively placed beyond critical scrutiny. Gender is once more theorized as a precondition to social relations, rather than their product.

Thus, even to talk about 'causes' of gender is misleading, because it assumes some kind of chronological or unilinear process whereby an ungendered (either totally sexed or completely androgynous) being is gradually converted into either a masculine or feminine person. However, the complex and reflexive nature of gender confounds this: gender is not a set of fixed attributes or certain traits in the possession of individuals, but a dimension of the culture in which we all live. It is more appropriate, therefore, to talk about the generation of gender traits; and of gender relations not as ossified or abstract sets of differences, but as a performative reality. This makes the business of being a gendered person the consequence (although also the precondition) of inhabiting a particular culture.

Structural anthropology, after Claude Lévi-Strauss, conceives of culture as formed out of the practices which delineate and circumscribe fundamental, but not ontological, binary oppositions. The boundaries by which such bifurcation is executed tell us about the values upon which the power relations and organizational structures of any culture are founded. Human practice establishes and reinforces the conceptual dichotomies of marginalization and inclusion upon which the material, political and symbolic relations of any culture are constructed:

> Ideas about separating, purifying, demarcating and punishing transgressions have as their main function to impose system on an inherently untidy experience. It is only by exaggerating the difference between within and without, above and below, male and female, with and against, that a semblance of order is created. (Douglas, 1970:15)

Similarly, poststructuralist theorists such as Derrida and Foucault give accounts of the ways in which human discourse, whether linguistic or institutional, creates the boundaries between truth and falsehood, meaning and non-meaning, subordinate and dominant, normative and pathological. These are inextricably linked to the deployment of power and the establishment and defence of power relations. Derrida understands 'deconstruction' as the critical strategy that lays bare the generation of truth and meaning engendered by the assertion of *différance*. Paradoxically, that very scrutiny undermines conceptions of those boundaries as fixed. Similarly, Foucault's historical excursions of archaeology and genealogy aim to identify the 'dividing practices' (Dews, 1987:197) upon which power and knowledge intersect.

Institutions, customs and individuals are thus informed and directed by values and principles which construct, defend and assert the fault-lines between normative and deviant, truthful and aberrant, dominant and 'Other'. They are the agents by which cultures construct their structures of meaning and power. Practice thus generates systems of gender identity, power relations and representations, or what Connell has termed 'gender regimes'.

In patriarchal gender relations, the boundary of 'difference' marks the trajectory of human practices which render a deviation from a masculine norm as absolute difference, enabling the subordination and objectification of the group thus rendered 'other'. The practices of inscribing gender difference as dichotomous and immutable are functional insofar as they reify the power relations and interests of male domination. Critical analysis would follow the 'fault-lines' of difference to see how categories were actually delineated, enforced and naturalized, and how the imposition of such fault-lines – within the discourses of science, religion, medicine, sexual practices and the metaphors of gender – facilitate the creation of dichotomy and fixity out of heterogeneity and polyversity.

Thus, 'difference' is a heuristic and not a reified category, created and deployed in order to maintain and entrench prevailing power relations. However, as the debates surrounding the feminist 'politics of difference' indicate, it may also be that difference can be retrieved in the pursuit of oppositional projects. The naming and assertion of a distinctive self-determined subjectivity in a reversal of the coercive programme forms a precondition of the articulation of the grounds for a 'politics of identity'.

Part of the allure of an understanding of gender as naturalistic and immutable is its pervasive and ubiquitous presence as a deep and intimate feature of both personal subjectivity and corporate structures. Individual experience is fundamentally associated with the axioms of being either one gender or the other; and the testimonies of transsexuals indicate how fundamentally society and individual self-image is built upon gender polarity. The phrase 'always already', often used by poststructuralist critics, expresses the notion of the reflexivity of our experiences as women and men. It further reinforces the argument that gender is not a set of traits created outside human affairs and then transposed onto passive human objects. It is essential therefore to abandon models of analysis which – either by attempting to withdraw from culture to a supposedly objective and detached standpoint which is itself neither gendered, nor part of culture, or by trying to abstract principles or single causative factors – implicitly privilege notions of gender as non-relational, acontextual and reified.

Although gender is profoundly social and complex, it is also personal and all-pervasive. There are no genderless persons in contemporary Western culture. Gender belies the notion of personhood as individualistic, independent and voluntaristic. Gender is instead fundamental to the experience of becoming a cultured being, and we cannot refuse its impact upon the structuring of our subjectivity, relationships, life-chances and practices. However, as many contemporary theorists of gender are suggesting, there may be room for negotiation, subversion and critique, because many theories of gender also point to ways in which the gendering process is incomplete, contradictory or contingent (Butler, 1990; Fuss, 1990; Flax, 1990, 1993; Morgan, 1992).

Therefore, critical studies of gender must appreciate it as a paradigm of the very foundations and dynamics of human personality and culture. Stories of the acquisition of language, the influence of early parenting, of embodied and sexual experience, procreation and social relations, the practice of science, the pursuit of knowledge and the application of technology upon the non-human world, are simultaneously accounts of the creation of culture and of the processes by which, according to the theories of gender surveyed, we acquire and generate gender relations and identities.

Towards a 'Theology of Gender'

An enquiry into the nature of gender roles, development of gender identity and the scope of gender relations therefore goes far beyond simple questions about the differences between women and men. Rather, critical attention to gender is concerned with difference as a category of social relations, as formed within the sphere of human practice, and not an ontological characteristic. Gender is a complex, dynamic and self-reflexive phenomenon; and a 'theology of gender' will not be a straightforward application of selected categorical statements about empirical differences.

Instead, theology itself must engage with the pluralism and complexity of interdisciplinary theories of gender at a profound level. Critical theories of gender confront fundamental philosophical questions about the nature of human existence, agency and social organization: whether it is possible to talk about a single or universal 'human nature' (ontology); what are the foundations and sources of personal consciousness and selfhood (subjectivity); whether know-ledge of the world is innate or phenomenologically – or even politically – constructed (epistemology); how purposeful and every-day transformation of the world around us effects the material and symbolic relations that underpin social systems (agency); and what might be the possibilities and grounds for an emancipatory know-ledge and action based on some notion of ultimate good (teleology).

Firstly, such a perspective portrays a 'human nature' that is not essential, but existential. Many of the theoretical perspectives which have influenced theories of gender in this respect portray a scepti-cism concerning the status of an extra-cultural or universal 'human nature' enduring throughout history and across diverse social con-ditions. Whatever human nature may be, it is inaccessible to our understanding beyond the medium of our own culture and agency. The challenge of this concerns the ethical and political implica-tions of the dissolution of self-evident standards of human need and value; and whether it is possible to understand human identity as contingent and contextual but also enduring and constant.

Such a rejection of an essential human nature outside the relations and interactions of human culture bears significant implications for theological anthropology, and for the Christian doctrine of the *Imago Dei*. It challenges notions of an eternal, pre-existent human nature, and suggests that theological teachings concerning a God-given order of creation or Natural Law which pre-ordains separate functions for women and men may be untenable. The challenge is to contemplate human nature as contingent and contextual, but also to consider the ethical and political implications of such a 'non-realist' understanding. Does such a dissolution of the subject, and a dis-avowal of any notion of personhood that is independent of human discourse, inevitably lead to an anti-humanism? Or can ethical and political value-commitments be founded on some enduring notion of the person that does not collapse into metaphysics or essentialism?

However, whilst gender is a complex and constructed phenom-enon, it is not merely an incidental aspect of our experience of being human. The decisive impact of gender as a form of social relations is suggestive of a model of human nature as profoundly relational, requiring the agency of culture to bring our personhood fully into being. This resounds with other perspectives that emphasize such an identity as thoroughly compatible with a Trinitarian model of God.

In a recent version of this, the multivalent and interactive nature of the divine is reflected in human relationships of mutual and non-coercive affirmation (McFadyen, 1990). Authentic human being is thus only fully realized – recognized and made concrete – within human communities that respect the dynamism and provisionality of personhood. Such a perspective may be further investigated in the light of gender relations.

Similarly, notions of the nature of human action in the world are challenged by voices from gender theory which regard agency as a gendered concept. Models of action that presuppose rationality, atomized selfhood, autonomy and freedom of self-determination have been exposed as particular and historically-conditioned accounts, dating from the Enlightenment and the Scientific Revolution. The most outstanding example of these altered notions of agency has arisen from feminist theories which identify human action and knowledge as profoundly embodied. Bodies are conceived as the primary source and medium of our relationship to the world around us; the 'situation' or 'vantage point' from which we effect change, interact with others, relate to non-human creation and manipulate technology. However, critical studies of gender maintain that while bodies are agents, they are also historical and cultural objects.

Theories of gender also undermine models of selfhood which rest upon a unitary, rational subjectivity. Postmodern perspectives which dethrone axioms concerning the transparency of language, the unity of consciousness and reason, and the self-possession of the individual portray instead notions of a personal identity that is contradictory and fragmented. The individual's struggle to establish personal integrity and self-determination is destabilized by competing discourses of fulfilment, satisfaction, identity and self-worth. Any account of ourselves is always already compromised by its situatedness in a world of coercive power relations. If subjectivity and selfhood are contingent upon the individual's inhabitation of culture, then individual consciousness cannot be divorced from social structures, because there is no pristine self independent of social relations and language.

In their use of gendered metaphors for God, therefore, theologians are reminded that gender is an artefact of human culture, and not a metaphysical category. However, faith-communities can only use human terms and images by which to apprehend the divine. The substitution of 'feminine' terms to replace patriarchal images of Father, King and Lord in inclusive liturgies and prayers are no more 'value-free' than patriarchal language, although arguably they represent important aspirations on the part of worshipping communities to count women's experiences as equally holy, and worthy of imaging the holy, as those of men.

However, they do nothing to dispel the fundamental limitations of using human experience to apprehend the divine, but rather remind us of the provisional and metaphorical nature of all 'God-talk'. Some of the most creative work in Christian liturgy and hymnody goes far beyond the corrective of 'God as Mother' to interpret truly inclusive language as embodying a much greater plurality of imagery, as in Brian Wren's recent writing ('Bring Many Names', Wren, 1989:137ff; see also Morley, 1988).

Gender theories also require critical scrutiny of the nature of knowledge and truth-claims in the light of such an understanding of human reality. They affirm the self-reflexivity and situatedness of human agency and critical knowledge, and repudiate notions of knowledge that are absolute, universal and abstracted from the material and relational circumstances of their production and generation. In this respect, knowledge itself – especially scientific knowledge – is properly regarded as a form of practice: transformatory, heuristic and contingent.

Feminist critiques of androcentricism in disciplines such as the philosophy and practice of science confront questions of epistemology, and especially the question of whether knowledge is inherently gendered. Those who argue for a differential feminist science as the outcome of a distinct and unique women's nature – whether socially, morphologically or psychically constructed – are claiming that gender and social location have a profound influence on the human capacity for reliable knowledge. Feminist proposals for forms of strategic knowledge, based on an understanding of emancipatory truth in the service of human equality and liberation, are thus adopting varieties of philosophical pragmatism, by arguing that the social application of knowledge, as well as the positions and sensibilities of its knowers, are inseparable from its claims to truth.

Critical studies of gender also refute the implicit Idealism and dualism of the rational intellectual self unencumbered by embodied subjectivity. Authentic analysis of gender must be informed by accounts of human bodiliness. However, it has been the rule that embodiment is regarded as an exclusively female quality, and that the female gender is marked with the signs of carnality, non-rationality and biological determinism. The challenge is to find ways of speaking which cast bodies as the primary source and medium of our relationship to the world – as a kind of 'vantage point' for experience, whilst lending diversity and provisionality to such accounts. It may well be that there is a definitive difference between inhabiting a male body and a female one; but we must recognize the extent to which our understanding of our bodies, and of ourselves *as* bodies, is always culturally constructed and mediated.

Thus, whilst bodies are creative agents through which we effect change, experience sensory perception, manipulate technology and interact with others, they are also constrained by relations of objectification and patterns of finitude. Theological traditions that have disregarded bodily experience in the articulation of spiritual and ethical verities may well need to be reformulated as a result. This is especially true in areas of sexual and reproductive ethics, but may also be relevant in areas of pastoral care associated with women and medicine, ageing, sexuality, celibacy, body image and violence against women.

The challenges within critical theories of gender to an essential human nature, the transparency of Self and language, and to Platonic categories of masculinity and femininity are mirrored within a wider body of social theory, where feminist and poststructuralist 'deconstructions' of metaphysics have produced similarly contingent and reflexive models of value, meaning, identity and truth. Critical studies of gender are therefore no less vulnerable to the challenge of generating new sources of principle and value in the wake of the dissolution of metaphysics, natural law or objective truth as 'foundational' epistemological criteria. Yet the debate is gradually moving towards the simultaneous rejection of essentialism and categoricalism with the hope of deriving clear and binding ethical and political principles from sources other than such varieties of foundational thinking.

Gender, Theology and Christian Practice

I have already related how models of gender identity and relations are perceived as grounded in processes of human practice. It is significant that many commentators are turning to accounts of 'truth' and 'value' as grounded in the purposeful and value-directed practices and activities of human communities. The impasse of postmodernism is resolved not by turning away from its critique of metaphysics and dominant rationality, but by insisting that purposeful, coherent and binding values can be articulated from within the core of human activity and value-directed practice (Benhabib, 1992; Browning, 1991:2–10).

Such a perspective translated into theology would speak of the contingency and situatedness of human existence and knowledge, and the provisionality of our apprehension of the divine. 'Truth' would be understood as realized within and through human practices and material transformation. Theologians may recognize the similarities between the kinds of 'situated' and purposeful models of responsible and value-directed knowing outlined in Chapter Nine, and forms of praxis developed within theologies of liberation. Thus, the centrality of practice – as self-reflexively reflecting and constructing gender identity, relations and representations – is confirmed as the focus of critical attention for a theology of gender. It would however add a feminist critique of such claims to truth and value by attending to latent aspects of domination and exclusion in the formulation of such values.

If the 'causes' of gender are constituted in, and enacted through, material, embodied and symbolic praxis, then the role of religious practices and ideologies in the creation and maintenance of gendered systems becomes a crucial area of study. How do religious practices, institutions and symbolic practices serve to reflect, reinforce and create particular dynamics of gender identity, gender roles and representations?

Contemporary pastoral theologians are turning to forms of congregational studies, often informed by ethnographic and anthropological perspectives, to identify the essence of the fundamental values, visions and attitudes of a faith-community (Browning, 1991; Hopewell, 1987). It is claimed that the stories members tell, the aspirations they absorb from their cultural environment and their interpretations of significant elements of the faith tradition, all constitute a corporate ethic out of which they forge their collective life. However, the gendered nature of these elements – whether such values are essentially founded on gender dualism or gender exclusion – has been conspicuously absent from such analyses. Thus, there is a project which amounts to what I might term a 'critical phenomenology of pastoral practice', which examines the assumptions concerning human identity and destiny, ultimate values, power relations, forms of authoritative knowing and acting embodied implicitly in all the activities by which faith-communities order their affairs. These effectively constitute the 'gender regimes' of religious faith and practice.

However, a number of recent works do provide pointers towards forms of critical theological studies of gender, and suggest ways in which a theology of gender might be constructed from the vantage points of human practice. James Nelson's (1992) study of the male body in theological perspective reflects some of these perspectives.[2] He seeks a rediscovery of embodied identity, and how this might inform ministry. The Doctrine of the Incarnation suggests for him that sexuality and physicality must affect spirituality and identity (1992:21–28). This is not a colonization or acquisition of feminine identity by proxy, but an exploration of non-competitive masculinity grounded in phallic sensibility: vulnerability and gentleness as embodied in the flaccid penis, not the power and aggression of the erect phallus. Thus, men will relearn more generous patterns of intimacy, friendship and spirituality, founded upon a truly embodied subjectivity. The implication for Christian practice would be the transformation of this renewed commitment to embodied selfhood into patterns of spiritual direction:

> Men, I truly believe, are hungering for a more incarnational spirituality. Christians have long been called the people of the incarnation. But so often we have been embarrassed by God's embodiment and our own . . . But if we do not know the gospel in our bodies, we do not know the gospel. (1992:8)

Caroline Walker Bynum's work on the historical construction of the female body within religious discourse also stands as a significant contribution to this field. She emphasizes the contingency of our embodied experience, and the tension between constructivism and agency, and affirms the centrality of morphological metaphors to theological formulation (Bynum, 1989, 1992).

The gendered nature of human experience also challenges many of the presuppositions of Christian pastoral care. That patterns of ministry have been shaped by androcentric expectations is one of the central claims of feminist critiques of pastoral care (Graham and Halsey, 1993). The Western churches' agenda of pastoral concern has not heard sufficiently clearly the voices of women: as mothers, in the workplace, as lesbians, as single women, as Black women. New perspectives expose the gender biases in the giving and receiving of pastoral care, but also attempt to reconstruct a new agenda of women's pastoral needs and the possibilities of new methods of pastoral agency (Graham and Halsey, 1993:210–34). Such voices argue that accredited functions of ministry need to be reshaped to take account of women's experiences: of operating at the boundaries of church and society, exploring new and changing dimensions of women's lives and finding new expressions and vehicles of Christian values. However, these are regarded as forged within the complex interplay of biological and cultural forces: not simply the passage of women's life-cycle, but the social and economic conditions that shape their lives. Even the most intimate familial and sexual relationships take place within social constructions of women's experiences as mothers, daughters and lovers; but equally, social policy is informed by sexist, and racist, images of women as 'natural' carers (Graham and Halsey, 1993:9–65;69–117).

Life Cycles (Graham and Halsey, 1993) reconstitutes the pastoral agenda and questions whose interests it reflects and serves. It challenges the patterns of power and difference in patriarchal estimates of what counts as proper pastoral care. Women's care has traditionally been seen as 'natural' and spontaneous, and therefore discounted. So long as women were excluded from leadership and formal ministry, their activities were never really designated as 'pastoral' and received little official sanction. But now, as women gain more confidence and prominence in Christian communities, women's liturgies and preaching, patterns of feminist spiritual direction, and new ways of 'being church' are emerging as legitimate expressions of Christian vocation and being recognized as powerful vehicles of pastoral care (Graham and Halsey, 1993:144–165).

Victoria Erikson's contribution to critical theological studies of gender is through a feminist analysis of the role of religion in creating and sacralizing gender relations: 'how religion participates in the creation of gendered identity, and then how it produces the violent forces that threaten to destroy . . . women's spiritual, moral and physical lives' (Erikson, 1993:xi).

In a scrutiny of classic texts in the sociology of religion (reminiscent of Morgan's study of sociological constructions of masculinity), she identifies the failure of writers such as Durkheim and Weber to address the patterns of gender stereotyping that oppress and exclude women. She exposes their implicit and unexamined biases such as dualism (equating women and men respectively with 'profane' and 'sacred' realms), a logic of history underpinned by asceticism and rationalization (again, serving to exclude women from participating in social agency) and gender blindness (androcentric perspectives and activities as normative).

Thus, the classical sociology of religion – and the role played by religious belief and practice in facilitating social order and social change – is always already a theory of gender. Erikson's interrogation of the social theory of religion reveals the hidden values concerning the identity of women, their subordination in gender relations, and their representation as synonymous with the non-rational and non-sacred.

It is perhaps significant to note that Erikson's own vision for further studies in this area recommends small-scale detailed studies of women's religious groups, such as 'Women-Church' communities, in order to discern how they are resisting and re-creating gender roles. Erikson focuses on new women-centred rituals which seek to break out of the inherited repression of women's experiences, a tradition which denies them the right to be considered 'holy', and which represent liberative practices that resacralize women's lives (1993:195–98).

Durber and Walton portray women's preaching as a form of value-directed practice that self-consciously speaks from a gendered perspective. They argue that women's sermons represent a challenge to patriarchal epistemology by exposing the androcentric nature of preaching. Women's sermons constitute effectively a form of 'situated knowledge' (see Chapter Nine) because they recognize their own locatedness – physical and strategic – and forge new styles of proclamation that call upon feminist values of knowing and acting:

> As women speak from their position from outside the mainstream of their culture, they will shake the apparently solid foundations of what we had previously held to be authoritative . . . Women will speak not from the high and lofty pulpit, above contradiction and dispute, but from their own place in the church and world with openness and provisionality, with wit and wisdom. (1994:xvi–xvii)

However, such styles of speaking from a gendered vantage point recognize the necessary tension between retrieving women's distinctive experiences of birth, nurture, and sexuality, and recognizing that women occupy the intersection between powerlessness and playful renegotiation. Echoing psychoanalytic and deconstructionist theories of language, Durber and Walton locate practices of 'speaking from the margins' as exposing patriarchal foreclosure of meaning and difference. They affirm patriarchy's ability to 'enclose' women in discourses of bodily difference and biological determinism, yet see resistance and empowerment in women's attempts 'to speak holy words from their bodies' (1994:3).

A 'theology of gender' must therefore address itself critically to the contribution of Christian practices, values and theological metaphors to the creation and maintenance of specific gender ideologies and relations. In formulating alternatives, it must look to the practices of the Christian community as the source of both received wisdom and future reappropriations. Practical strategies in the form of pastoral care, worship, adult formation and direction, social action and preaching, might serve to foster the values, relationships and truth-claims of a more 'gender-inclusive' community.

Notes

1. Connell argues that the notion of 'practice' has attained prominence in social theory, and is especially valuable in theories of gender, because it insists upon a model of social relations as both historical and material structures and as the products of human agency and construction. Such a perspective seeks to resolve the perennial tension in social philosophy and sociology, between what are often termed theories of 'social action' and 'social structure', or what Connell identifies as the twin problems of 'voluntarism' and 'categoricalism' in gender theory. The most sustained example of such practice-based theories is perhaps found in the work of Anthony Giddens, and his concept of 'structuration'. Giddens develops a theory of social action in which practice is never divorced from its enactment within the constraints, conventions and power relations of social structures; but practice itself also serves to construct and maintain a concrete social order. For the debate between social action and social structure (or 'social system') perspectives in sociology, see Daws, 1978, and Sharrock, 1986. For discussions of theories of practice and structuration, see Giddens, 1976 and Connell, 1987:61–64, 92–99.

2. Nelson's work is one of a number of recent welcome contributions by men to theological debates, often in response to feminist theology. See Pryce, 1993; Holloway, 1991; McCloughry, 1992.

Bibliography

Ahmed, L. (1992) *Women and Gender in Islam: Historical Roots of a Modern Debate*. Yale University Press.

Alexander, S. (1984) Women, class and sexual differences in the 1830s and 1840s: some reflections on the writing of a feminist history. *History Workshop*, **17**: 126–49.

Allchin, A.M. *et al*. (1992) *A Fearful Symmetry? The Complementarity of Men and Women in Ministry*. London: SPCK.

Allen, P. (1985) *The Concept of Woman: The Aristotelian Revolution 750 BC – AD 1250*. Montreal: Eden.

Anderson, R.J., Hughes, J.A. and Sharrock, W.W. (1986) *Philosophy and the Human Sciences*. London: Routledge.

Arac, J. (ed.) (1988) *After Foucault: Humanistic Knowledge, Postmodern Challenges*. New Brunswick, New Jersey: Rutgers University Press.

Archer, J. and Lloyd, B.B. (1985) *Sex and Gender*. Cambridge: Cambridge University Press.

Ardener, E. (1977) Belief and the problem of women. In S. Ardener (ed.), *Perceiving Women*. London: J.M. Dent: 1–27.

Arditti, R. (1982) Feminism and science. In E. Whitelegg *et al*. (eds), *The Changing Experience of Women*. Oxford: Martin Robertson: 136–46.

Armstrong, K. (1993) *The End of Silence: Women and Priesthood*. London: Fourth Estate.

Armstrong, N. and Tennenhouse, L. (1987) *The Ideology of Conduct: Essays in Literature and the History of Sexuality*. London: Methuen.

Ashton, H. (1990) Women's ministry in the United Reformed Church. *MC* New Series, **XXXII**(3): 1–31.

Association for Inclusive Language (1988) *Women, Language and the Church*. London: Christian Women's Resource Centre.

Bacchi, C.L. (1990) *Same Difference: Feminism and Sexual Difference*. Sydney: Allen and Unwin.

Bachofen, J.J. (1967) *Myth, Religion and Mother Right: Selected Writings of J.J. Bachofen*. Translated by Ralph Manheim. Princeton: Princeton University Press.

Badinter, E. (1989) *Man/Woman: The One is the Other*. London: Collins.

Baker, J.A. (1981) *The Right Time*. London: Movement for the Ordination of Women.

Baker, S.W. (1980) Biological influences on human sex and gender. *Signs: Journal of Women in Culture and Society*, 6(1): 80–96.

Balbus, I.D. (1987) Disciplining women: Michel Foucault and the power of feminist discourse. In S. Benhabib and D. Cornell (eds), *Feminism as Critique: Essays on the Politics of Gender in Late-Capitalist Societies*. Cambridge: Polity: 10–27.

Barash, D. (1979) *The Whisperings Within: Evolution and the Origin of Human Nature*. New York: Harper and Row.

Barash, D. (1981) *Sociobiology: The Whisperings Within*. London: Fontana.

Bardwick, J.M. (ed.) (1971) *Psychology of Women: A Study of Bio-Cultural Conflicts*. New York: Harper and Row.

Barrett, M. (1987) The concept of 'difference'. *Feminist Review*, 26: 29–41.

Bartels, E. (1982) Biological sex differences and sex stereotyping. In E. Whitelegg *et al*. (eds), *The Changing Experience of Women*. Oxford: Martin Robertson.

Bauman, Z. (1990) *Thinking Sociologically*. Oxford: Blackwell.

Bauman, Z. (1992) *Intimations of Postmodernity*. London: Routledge.

Baxter, S. (1994) I'm not a feminist but . . . *New Statesman and Society*, 18 March: 12–13.

Beauvoir, S. de (1949/1988) *The Second Sex*. London: Picador.

Behr-Sigel, E. (1987) *The Ministry of Women in the Church*. Translated by S. Bigham. Redondo Beach, California: Oakwood Publications.

Bem, S.L. (1987) Masculinity and femininity exist only in the mind of the perceiver. In J.M. Reinisch, L.A. Rosenblum and S.A. Sanders (eds), *Masculinity/Femininity: Basic Perspectives*. Oxford University Press: 304–11.

Bem S.L. (1993) *The Lenses of Gender: Transforming the Debate on Sexual Inequality*. London: Yale University Press.

Benhabib, S. (1992) *Situating the Self*. Cambridge: Polity.

Benjamin, M. (ed.) (1991) *Science and Sensibility: Gender and Scientific Enquiry 1780–1945*. Oxford: Blackwell.

Birke, L. (1982) Cleaving the mind: speculations on conceptual dichotomies. In The Dialectics of Biology Group (ed.), *Against Biological Determinism*. London: Allison & Busby: 60–78.

Birke, L. (1986) *Women, Feminism and Biology: The Feminist Challenge*. Brighton: Wheatsheaf.

Bleier, R. (1984) *Science and Gender: A Critique of Biology and its Theories on Women*. Oxford: Pergamon.

Bloch, M. and Bloch, J.H. (1980) Women and the dialectics of nature in eighteenth-century French thought. In C.P. MacCormack and

M. Strathern (eds), *Nature, Culture and Gender*. New York: Cambridge University Press: 25–41.

Bly, R. (1991) *Iron John*. Longmead: Element.

Boff, L. (1987) *The Maternal Face of God: The Feminine and its Religious Expressions*. San Francisco: Harper and Row.

Bordo, S. (1992) Postmodern subjects, postmodern bodies. *Feminist Studies*, 18(1): 159–75.

Bordo, S. and Jaggar, A. (eds.) (1989) *Gender/Body/Knowledge: Feminist Reconstructions of Being and Knowing*. New Jersey: Rutgers University Press.

Braidotti, R. (1989) The politics of ontological difference. In T. Brennan (ed.), *Between Feminism and Psychoanalyis*. London: Routledge: 89–105.

Braidotti, R. (1991) *Patterns of Dissonance*. Cambridge: Polity.

Brennan, T. (ed.) (1989) *Between Feminism and Psychoanalysis*. London: Routledge.

Brennan, T. (1991) An impasse in psychoanalysis and feminism. In S. Gunew (ed.), *A Reader in Feminist Knowledge*. London: Routledge: 114–38.

Brighton Women and Science Collective (1980) *Alice through the Microscope: The Power of Science over Women's Lives*. London: Virago.

Brittan, A. (1989) *Masculinity and Power*. Oxford: Blackwell.

Brown, J.A.C. (1961) *Freud and the Post-Freudians*. Harmondsworth: Penguin.

Brown, P. and Jordanova, L.J. (1982) Oppressive dichotomies: the nature/culture debate. In E. Whitelegg *et al.* (eds), *The Changing Experience of Women*. Oxford: Martin Robertson: 389–99.

Browning, D.B. (1991) *A Fundamental Practical Theology: Descriptive and Strategic Proposals*. Minneapolis: Fortress.

Brownmiller, S. (1986) *Femininity*. London: Paladin.

Burke, C. (1981) Irigaray through the looking-glass. *Feminist Studies*, 7(2): 288–306.

Burnett, S. *et al.* (eds) (1978) *The Same God: Women, Men and Priesthood in the Church Today*. London: Movement for the Ordination of Women.

Butler, J. (1987) Variations on sex and gender: Beauvoir, Wittig and Foucault. In S. Benhabib and D. Cornell (eds), *Feminism as Critique: Essays on the Politics of Gender in Late-Capitalist Societies*. Cambridge: Polity: 128–42.

Butler, J. (1989) Gendering the body: Beauvoir's philosophical contribution. In A. Garry and M. Pearsall (eds), *Women, Knowledge and Reality: Explorations in Feminist Philosophy*. Boston: Unwin Hyman: 253–62.

Butler, J. (1990) *Gender Trouble: Feminism and the Subversion of Identity*. London: Routledge.

Bynum, C.W. (1989) The female body and religious practice in the later middle ages. In M. Feher *et al.* (eds), *Fragments for a History of the Human Body*. New York: Zone Books: 161–219.

Bynum, C.W. (1992) *Fragmentation and Redemption: Essays on Gender and the Human Body in Medieval Religion*. New York: Zone Books.

Caine, B., Grosz, E.A. and de Lepervanche, M. (eds) (1988) *Crossing Boundaries: Feminisms and the Critique of Knowledges*. London: Unwin Hyman.

Campbell, K. (ed.) (1992) *Critical Feminism: Argument in the Disciplines*. Buckingham: Open University.

Caplan, P. (1987) (ed.) *The Cultural Construction of Sexuality*. London: Routledge.

Carey, G. (1983) *Women and Authority in the Scriptures*. London: Movement for the Ordination of Women.

Carmody, D.L. (1994) *Responses to 101 Questions about Feminism*. London: Geoffrey Chapman.

Carr, A. (1990) *Transforming Grace: Christian Tradition and Women's Experience*. San Francisco: Harper and Row.

Carr, A. and Fiorenza, E.S. (1991) *The special nature of women?* London: SCM Press.

Chapman, R. and Rutherford, J. (eds.) (1988) *Male Order: Unwrapping Masculinity*. London: Lawrence & Wishart.

Charles, N. (1993) *Gender Divisions and Social Change*. Hemel Hempstead: Harvester Wheatsheaf.

Chetwynd, J. and Hartnett, O. (eds.) (1978) *The Sex Role System: Psychological and Sociological Perspectives*. London: RKP.

Chodorow, N. (1978) *The Reproduction of Mothering: Psychoanalysis and the Sociology of Gender*. Berkeley: University of California Press.

Chodorow, N. (1989) *Feminism and Psychoanalytic Theory*. Cambridge: Polity.

Chodorow, N. (1990) What is the relation between pyschoanalytic feminism and the psychoanalytic psychology of women? In D.L. Rhode (ed.), *Theoretical Perspectives on Sexual Difference*. New Haven: Yale University Press: 114–30.

Chung Hyun-Kyung (1991) *Struggle to be the Sun Again: Introducing Asian Women's Theology*. London: SCM.

Cixous, H. (1981) The laugh of the Medusa. In E. Marks and I. de Courtivron (eds), *New French Feminisms*. New York: Schocken Books: 245–264.

Cixous, H. and Clément, C. (1987) *The Newly Born Woman*. Translated by B. Wing. Manchester University Press.

Clanton, J.A. (1990) *In Whose Image? God and Gender*. London: SCM.

Clark, D. (ed.) (1991) *Marriage, Domestic Life and Social Change*. London: Routledge.

Coakley, S. (1988) 'Femininity' and the Holy Spirit? In M. Furlong (ed.) *Mirror to the Church: Reflections on Sexism*. London: SPCK: 124–35.

Cockburn, C. (1983) *Brothers: Male Dominance and Technological Change*. London: Pluto Press.

Colledge, W. (1989) That certain little something that makes a man male. *Independent*, 10 September: 10.

Collingwood, R.G. (1945) *The Idea of Nature*. Oxford: Clarendon.

Connell, R.W. (1985) Theorising gender. *Sociology*, **19**(2): 260–72.

Connell, R.W. (1987) *Gender and Power: Society, the Person and Sexual Politics*. London: Polity.

Connerton, P. (1990) Hungry ghosts. *London Review of Books*, **12**(8): 17–18.

Connor, S. (1989) *Postmodernist Culture: An Introduction to Theories of the Contemporary*. Oxford: Blackwell.

Cooey, P.M., Eakin, W.R. and McDaniel, J. (eds) (1991) *After Patriarchy: Feminist Transformation of World Religions*. New York: Orbis.

Coontz, S, and Henderson, P. (eds) (1986) *Women's Work, Men's Property*. London: Verso.

Coward, R. (1984) *Female Desire: Women's Sexuality Today*. London: Paladin.

Crawford, J. and Kinnamon, M. (eds) (1983) *In God's Image: Reflections on Identity, Human Wholeness and the Authority of Scripture*. Geneva: World Council of Churches.

Crews, F. (1993) The unknown Freud. *New York Review of Books*, 18 November: 55–66.

Cucchiari, S. (1981) The gender revolution and the transition from bisexual horde to patrilocal band: the origins of gender hierarchy. In S. Ortner and H. Whitehead (eds), *Sexual Meanings: The Cultural Construction of Gender and Sexuality*. New York: Cambridge University Press: 31–79.

Daly, M. (1978) *Gyn/Ecology: The Metaethics of Radical Feminism*. Boston: Beacon Press.

Dawkins, R. (1976) *The Selfish Gene*. London: Oxford University Press.

Daws, A. (1978) Theories of social action. In T. Bottomore and R. Nisbet (eds), *A History of Sociological Analysis*. London: Heinemann: 362–417.

Deaux, K. (1987) Psychological constructions of masculinity and femininity. In J.M. Reinisch, L.A. Rosenblum and S.A. Sanders (eds), *Masculinity/Femininity: Basic Perspectives*. Oxford University Press: 289–303.

Degler, C.N. (1990) Darwinians confront gender: or, there is more to it than history. In D.L. Rhode (ed.), *Theoretical Perspectives on Sexual Difference*. New Haven: Yale University Press: 33–46.

Delphy, C. (1987) Protofeminism and antifeminism. In T. Moi (ed.), *French Feminist Thought: A Reader*. Oxford: Blackwell: 92–97.

Derrida, J. (1978) *Writing and Difference*. Translated by A. Bass. London: Routledge and Kegan Paul.

Derrida, J. (1987) Interview: women in the beehive. In A. Jardine and P. Smith (eds), *Men in Feminism*. New York: Methuen: 187–203.

Dews, P. (1987) *Logics of Disintegration: Post-Structuralist Thought and the Claims of Critical Theory*. London: Verso.

Di Leonardo, M. (ed.) (1991) *Gender at the Crossroads of Knowledge: Feminist Anthropology in the Postmodern Era*. Berkeley: University of California.

Dialectics of Biology Group (ed.) (1982) *Against Biological Determinism*. London: Allison & Busby.

Dickason, A. (1977) The feminine as universal. In M. Vetterling-Braggin, J. English and F. Ellison (eds), *Feminism and Philosophy*. Totowa, New Jersey: Littlefield, Adams and Co.: 79–100.

Dinnerstein, D. (1987) *The Rocking of the Cradle and the Ruling of the World*. London: The Women's Press. (First published in 1976 as *The Mermaid and the Minotaur*. New York: Harper and Row.)

Doherty, T. (1993) (ed.) *Postmodernism: A Reader*. Hemel Hempstead: Harvester Wheatsheaf.

Douglas, M. (1970) *Purity and Danger*. Harmondsworth: Penguin.

Dowell, S. and Williams, J. (1994) *Bread, Wine and Women: The Ordination Debate in the Church of England*. London: Virago.

Doyle, J.A. and Paludi, M.A. (1991) *Sex and Gender: The Human Experience*. Second Edition, Dubuque, Iowa: William C. Brown Publishers.

Dupré, J. (1990) Global versus local perspectives on sexual difference. In D.L. Rhode (ed.), *Theoretical Perspectives on Sexual Difference*. New Haven: Yale University Press: 47–62.

Durber, S. and Walton, H. (eds) (1994) *Silence in Heaven: A Book of Women's Preaching*. London: SCM Press.

Durden-Smith, J. and de Simone, D. (1983) *Sex and the Brain*. London: Pan Books.

Easlea, B. (1980) *Witch-Hunting, Magic and the New Philosophy: an Introduction to Debates of the Scientific Revolution 1450–1750*. Brighton: Harvester Wheatsheaf.

Easlea, B. (1981) *Science and Sexual Oppression: Patriarchy's Confrontation with Women and Nature*. London: Weidenfeld and Nicholson.

Edwards, R.B. (1989) *The Case for Women's Ministry*. London: SPCK.

Ehrenreich, B. and English, D. (1979) *For Her Own Good: 150 Years of the Experts' Advice to Women*. London: Pluto.

Eistenstein, H. (1984) *Contemporary Feminist Thought*. London: Counterpoint/Unwin.

Eisenstein, H. and Jardine, A. (eds) (1980) *The Future of Difference*. Boston: G.K. Hall.

Elshtain, J.B. (1987) Against androgyny. In A. Phillips (ed.), *Feminism and Equality*. New York University Press: 139–59.

Elson, D. and Pearson, R. (1989) *Women's Employment and Multinationals in Europe*. London: Macmillan.

Epstein, C.F. (1988) *Deceptive Distinctions: Sex, Gender and the Social Order*. London: Yale University Press.

Erikson, V.L. (1993) *Where Silence Speaks: Feminism, Social Theory and Religion*. Minneapolis: Fortress.

Evdokimov, P. (1981) Ecclesia domestica. In *A Voice for Women*. Geneva.

Fabella, V. and Oduyoye, M. (eds) (1988) *Third World Women Doing Theology*. New York: Orbis.

Farganis, S. (1986) *The Social Reconstruction of the Feminine Character*. Totowa, New Jersey: Rowman and Littlefield.

Fausto-Sterling, A. (1985) *Myths of Gender: Biological Theories About Women and Men*. New York: Basic Books.

Featherstone, M., Hepworth, M. and Turner, B.S. (eds) (1991) *The Body: Social Process and Cultural Theory*. London: Sage.

Fee, E. (1983) Women's nature and scientific objectivity. In M. Lowe and R. Hubbard (eds), *Woman's Nature: Rationalizations of Inequality*. Oxford: Pergamon Press: 9–27.

Feher, M., Naddaff, R. and Tazi, N. (eds) (1989) *Fragments for a History of the Human Body*. Parts One, Two and Three. New York: Zone Books.

Féral, J. (1980) The powers of difference. In H. Eisenstein and A. Jardine (eds), *The Future of Difference*. Boston: G.K. Hall: 88–94.

Field-Bibb, J. (1991) *Women Towards Priesthood: Ministerial Politics and Feminist Praxis*. Cambridge: Cambridge University Press.

Firestone, S. (1971) *The Dialectic of Sex: The Case for Feminist Revolution*. London: Women's Press.

Flanagan, O.J. (1982) Freud: masculinity, femininity, and the philosophy of mind. In M. Vetterling-Braggin (ed.), *'Masculinity', 'Femininity' and 'Androgyny': A Modern Philosophical Discussion*. Totowa, New Jersey: Rowman and Littlefield: 60–76.

Flax, J. (1987) Postmodernism and gender relations in feminist theory. *Signs: Journal of Women in Culture and Society*, **12**(4): 621–43.

Flax, J. (1990) *Thinking Fragments: Psychoanalysis, Feminism and Post-Modernism in the Contemporary West*. Berkeley: University of California Press.

Flax, J. (1993) *Disputed Subjects: Essays on Psychoanalysis, Politics and Philosophy*. London: Routledge.

Ford, D. and Hearn, J. (1988) *Studying Men and Masculinity: A Sourcebook of Literature and Materials*. Manchester: University of Manchester.

Foucault, M. (1977) *Discipline and Punish: The Birth of the Prison*. Translated by A. Sheridan. Harmondsworth: Penguin.

Foucault, M. (1980) *Herculine Barbin*. New York: Random House.

Foucault, M. (1984) *The History of Sexuality: An Introduction*. Harmondsworth: Pelican.

Frank, A.W. (1991) For a sociology of the body: an analytical review. In M. Featherstone, M. Hepworth and B.S. Turner (eds), *The Body: Social Process and Cultural Theory*. London: Sage: 36–102.

Franklin, M.A. (ed.) (1986) *The Force of the Feminine: Women, Men and the Church*. Sydney: Allen & Unwin.

Franklin, M.A. and Jones, R.S. (eds) (1987) *Opening the Cage: Stories of Church and Gender*. Sydney: Allen & Unwin.

Freeman, D. (1983) *Margaret Mead and Samoa: The Making and Unmaking of an Anthropological Myth*. Cambridge, Mass.: Harvard University Press.

Frese, P.R. and Coggeshall, J.M. (eds) (1991) *Transcending Boundaries: Multi-Disciplinary Approaches to the Study of Gender*. London: Bergin and Garvey.

Freud, S. (1971) *The Complete Introductory Lectures on Psychoanalysis*. Translated and edited by J. Strachey. London: Allen & Unwin.

Freud, S. (1977) *Three Essays on the Theory of Sexuality and other works*. Edited by A. Richards, translated by J. Strachey. Pelican Freud Library, Vol. 7. Harmondsworth: Penguin.

Freud, S. (1986) *The Essentials of Psychoanalysis*. Edited with introduction by A. Freud, translated by J. Strachey. Harmondsworth: Penguin.

Friedan, B. (1963) *The Feminine Mystique*. Harmondsworth: Penguin.

Frith, G. (1993) Women, writing and language. In D. Richardson and V. Robinson (eds), *Introducing Women's Studies*. London: Macmillan: 151–76.

Frye, R.M. (n.d.) *Language for God and Feminist Language*. Edinburgh: Handsel Press.

Furlong, M. (ed.) (1984) *Feminine in the Church*. London: SPCK.

Furlong, M. (ed.) (1988) *Mirror to the Church*. London: SPCK.

Furlong, M. (ed.) (1991) *A Dangerous Delight: Women and Power in the Church*. London: SPCK.

Fuss, D. (1990) *Essentially Speaking: Feminism, Nature and Difference*. London: Routledge.

Gallop, J. (1989) Moving backwards or forwards. In T. Brennan (ed.) *Between Feminism and Psychoanalyis*. London: Routledge: 27–39.

Gallop, J. and Burke, C. (1980) Psychoanalysis and feminism in France. In H. Eisenstein and A. Jardine (eds), *The Future of Difference*. Boston: G.K. Hall: 106–21.

Gatens, M. (1991) A critique of the sex/gender distinction. In S. Gunew (ed.), *A Reader in Feminist Knowledge*. London: Routledge: 139–57.

Gatens, M. (1988) Towards a feminist philosophy of the body. In B. Caine, E.A. Grosz and M. de Lepervanche (eds), *Crossing Boundaries: Feminisms and the Critique of Knowledges*. London: Unwin Hyman: 59–70.

Geertz, C. (1990) Review article: A lab of one's own. *New York Review of Books*, 8 November: 19–23.

General Synod of the Church of England, Report of the Liturgical Commission (1989) *Making Women Visible: The Use of Inclusive Language with the ASB*. London: Church House Publishing.

Giddens, A. (1976) *New Rules of Sociological Method*. London: Hutchinson.

Gilligan, C. (1982) *In a Different Voice*. Cambridge, Mass.: Harvard University Press.

Glendenning, C. and Millar, J. (eds) (1992) *Women and Poverty in Britain: The 1990s*. Hemel Hempstead, Herts.: Harvester Wheatsheaf.

Goffman, E. (1977) The arrangement between the sexes. *Theory and Society* **4**: 301–31.

Goffman, E. (1979) *Gender Advertisements*. San Francisco: Harper & Row.

Goldenberg, N.R. (1976) A feminist critique of Jung. *Signs: Journal of Women in Culture and Society*, **2**(2): 443–49.

Goldenberg, N.R. (1977) Jung after feminism. In R. M. Gross (ed.) *Beyond Androcentrism: New Essays on Women and Religion*. Missoula, Montana: Scholars Press/American Academy of Religion: 53–66.

Goldenberg, N.R. (1993) *Resurrecting the Body: Feminism, Religion and Psychoanalysis*. New York: Crossroad.

Gossmann, E. (1991) The construction of women's difference in the Christian theological tradition. In A. Carr and E.S. Fiorenza (eds), *The Special Nature of Women?* London: SCM Press: 50–59.

Gould, S.J. (1984a) Triumph of a naturalist. *New York Review of Books*, 19 March: 58–71.

Gould, S.J. (1984b) Similarities between the sexes. *New York Times Book Review*, 12 August: 7.

Gould, S.J. (1992) *Bully for Brontosaurus*. Harmondsworth: Penguin.

Graham, E.L. (1993) Gender and intimacy. In E. James and A.R. Webster (eds), *Intimacy and Sexuality*. Christian Action Journal, 20–21.

Graham, E.L. (1994) Towards a theology of desire. *Theology and Sexuality*, **1**(1): 13–30

Graham, E.L. and Halsey, M. (eds) (1993) *Life Cycles: Women and Pastoral Care*. London: SPCK.

Griffin, S. (1980) *Women and Nature: The Roaring Inside Her*. New York: Harper and Row.

Grimshaw, J. (1986) *Feminist Philosophers: Women's Perspectives on Philosophical Traditions*. Brighton: Wheatsheaf.

Gross, H.E. *et al.*, (1979) Considering 'A biosocial perspective on parenting'. *Signs: Journal of Women in Culture and Society*, **4**(4): 695–717.

Grosz, E.A. (1989) *Sexual Subversions: Three French Feminists*. Sydney: Allen and Unwin.

Grosz, E.A. (1990) Conclusion: a note on essentialism and difference. In S. Gunew (ed.), *Feminist Knowledge: Critique and Construct*. London: Routledge: 332–44.

Grosz, E.A. and de Lepervanche, M. (1988) Feminism and science. In B. Caine, E.A. Grosz and M. de Lepervanche (eds), *Crossing Boundaries: Feminisms and the Critique of Knowledges*. London: Unwin Hyman: 5–27.

Gunew, S. (ed.) (1990) *Feminist Knowledge: Critique and Construct*. London: Routledge.

Gunew, S. (ed.) (1991) *A Reader in Feminist Knowledge*. London: Routledge.

Halperin, D.W. (1990) *One Hundred Years of Homosexuality and Other Essays on Greek Love*. London: Routledge.

Hampson, D. (1990) *Theology and Feminism*. Oxford: Blackwell.

Hanmer, J. (1993) Women and reproduction. In D. Richardson and V. Robinson (eds), *Introducing Women's Studies*. Macmillan: 224–249.

Haraway, D. (1987) Contested bodies. In M. McNeil (ed.), *Gender and Expertise*. London: Free Association Books: 62–73.

Haraway, D. (1990) Investment strategies for the evolving portfolio of primate females. In M. Jacobus, E. Fox Keller and S. Shuttleworth (eds), *Body/ Politics: Women and the Discourses of Science*. London: Routledge: 139–62.

Haraway, D. (1991) *Simians, Cyborgs and Women: The Reinvention of Nature*. London: Free Association Books.

Harding, S. (1986) *The Science Question in Feminism*. Milton Keynes: Open University Press.

Harding, S. (ed.) (1987) *Feminism and Methodology*. Milton Keynes: Open University Press.

Harding, S. (1989) Feminist justificatory strategies. In A. Garry and M. Pearsall (eds), *Women, Knowledge and Reality: Explorations in Feminist Philosophy*. Boston: Unwin Hyman: 189–201.

Harding, S. (1991) *Whose Science? Whose Knowledge? Thinking from Women's Lives*. Buckingham: Open University Press.

Harding, S. and Hintikka, M.B. (eds) (1983) *Discovering Reality: Feminist Perspectives in Epistemology, Metaphysics, Methodology, and Philosophy of Science*. Dordrecht: Reidel Publishing.

Hargreaves, D.J. and Colley, A.M. (eds) (1986) *The Psychology of Sex Roles*. London: Harper and Row.

Haste, H. (1992) Splitting images: sex and science. *New Scientist*, 15 February: 32–34.

Hawkesworth, M.E. (1989) Knowers, knowing, known: feminist theory and claims of truth. *Signs: Journal of Women in Culture and Society*, **14**(3): 533–57.

Hearn, J. (1988) *The Critique of Men: Current Lessons for the Theory and Practice of Men*. University of Manchester: Hallsworth Research Fellowship Working Paper, No. 1.

Heilbrun, C.G. (1973) *Towards Androgyny: Aspects of Male and Female in Literature*. London: Victor Gollancz.

Hekman, S.J. (1990) *Gender and Knowledge: Elements of a Post-Modern Feminism*. London: Routledge.

Hewitt, N.A. (1992) Compounding differences. *Feminist Studies*, **18**(2): 313–26.

Hite, M. (1988) Writing – and reading – the body: female sexuality and recent feminist fiction. *Feminist Studies*, **14**(1): 121–42.

Hodge, J. (1988) Subject, body and the exclusion of women from philosophy. In M. Griffiths and M. Whitford (eds), *Feminist Perspectives in Philosophy*. London: Macmillan: 152–68.

Hollingdale, R.J. (ed.) (1977) *A Nietzsche Reader*. Harmondsworth: Penguin Classics.

Holloway, R. (ed.) (1991) *Who Needs Feminism? Men Respond to Sexism in the Church*. London: SPCK.

Holm, J. (ed.) (1994) *Women in Religion*. London: Pinter.

hooks, bell (1984) *Feminist Theory: From Margin to Center*. Boston, Mass.: South End.

hooks, bell (1991) *Yearning: Race, Gender and Cultural Politics*. London: Turnaround.

Hopewell, J.F. (1987) *Congregation: Stories and Structures*. London: SCM.

Horigan, S. (1988) *Nature and Culture in Western Discourses*. London: Routledge.

Hrdy, S.B. (1981) *The Woman That Never Evolved*. Cambridge, Mass.: Harvard University Press.

Hubbard, R. (1981) The emperor doesn't wear any clothes: the impact of feminism on biology. In D. Spender (ed.), *Men's Studies Modified*. Oxford: Pergamon: 213–35.

Hubbard, R. (1990) The political nature of 'human nature'. In D.L. Rhode (ed.), *Theoretical Perspectives on Sexual Difference*. New Haven: Yale University Press: 63–73.

Imperato-McGinley, J. *et al.* (1979) Androgens and the evolution of male gender identity among male pseudohermaphrodites with a 5-alpha-reductase deficiency. *New England Journal of Medicine*, **300**: 1236–57.

Irigaray, L. (1980) When our lips speak together. Translated by C. Burke. *Signs: Journal of Women in Culture and Society*, **6**(1): 69–79.

Irigaray, L. (1985) *This Sex Which is Not One*. Translated by C. Porter and C. Burke. Ithaca: Cornell University Press.

Irigaray, L. (1986) *Divine Women*. Translated by S. Muecke. Sydney: Local Consumption Papers.

Jackson, D. (1990) *Unmasking Masculinity: A Critical Autobiography*. London: Unwin Hyman.

Jackson, M. (1987) 'Facts of life' or the eroticisation of women's oppression? Sexology and the social construction of heterosexuality. In P. Caplan (ed.), *The Cultural Construction of Sexuality*. London: Routledge: 52–81.

Jacobs, M. (1991) Is anatomy destiny? In R. Holloway (ed.), *Who Needs Feminism?* London: SPCK: 149–60.

Jacobus, M., Fox Keller, E. and Shuttleworth, S. (eds) (1990) *Body/ Politics: Women and the Discourses of Science*. London: Routledge.

Jaggar, A. (1983) *Feminist Politics and Human Nature*. Brighton: Harvester.

Jalland, P. and Hooper, J. (eds) (1986) *Women from Birth to Death: The Female Life Cycle in Britain 1830–1914*. Atlantic Highlands, New Jersey: Humanities Press.

Janeway, E. (1980) 'Who is Sylvia?' On the loss of sexual paradigms. *Signs: Journal of Women in Culture and Society*, 5(4): 573–89.

Jardine, A. and Smith, P. (eds) (1987) *Men in Feminism*. New York: Methuen.

Jay, N. (1981) Gender and dichotomy. *Feminist Studies*, 7(1): 38–56.

Jones, A.R. (1981) Writing the body: Towards an understanding of 'l'écriture féminin'. *Feminist Studies*, 7: 247–63.

Jordanova, L.J. (1980) Natural facts: a historical perspective on science and sexuality. In C.P. MacCormack and M. Strathern (eds), *Nature, Culture and Gender*. Cambridge: Cambridge University Press: 42–69.

Jordanova, L.J. (ed.) (1986) *Languages of Nature: Critical Essays on Science and Literature*. London: Free Association Books.

Jordanova, L.J. (1987) Gender, science and creativity. In M. McNeil (ed.), *Gender and Expertise*. London: Free Association Books: 152–57.

Jordanova, L.J. (1989) *Sexual Visions: Images of Gender in Science and Medicine Between the Eighteenth and Twentieth Centuries*. Hemel Hempstead: Harvester/Wheatsheaf.

Jordanova, L.J. (1991) Competing views of sex. *Times Higher Education Supplement*, 3 May: 26.

Joseph, A. (1990) *Through the Devil's Gateway: Women, Religion and Taboo*. London: SPCK.

Kearney, R. (ed.) (1994) *Twentieth-Century Continental Philosophy* (Routledge History of Philosophy Volume VIII). London: Routledge.

Keller, E. Fox (1982) Feminism and science. *Signs: Journal of Women in Culture and Society*, 7(3): 589–602.

Keller, E. Fox (1983) Women, science and popular mythology. In J. Rothschild (ed.), *Machina Ex Dea: Feminist Perspectives on Technology*. Oxford: Pergamon: 130–46.

Keller, E. Fox (1985) *Reflections on Gender and Science*. New Haven: Yale University Press.

Kelly, T. (1986) Christian conversion and the feminine. In M.A. Franklin (ed.), *The Force of the Feminine: Women, Men and the Church*. Sydney: Allen and Unwin: 175–186.

Kelly, T. (1987) Discovering the feminine. In M.A. Franklin and R.S. Jones (eds), *Opening the Cage: Stories of Church and Gender*. Sydney: Allen and Unwin: 128–134.

Kessler, S.J. (1990) The medical construction of gender: case management of intersexed infants. *Signs: Journal of Women in Culture and Society*, **16**(1): 3–26.

Kessler, S.J. and McKenna, W. (1978) *Gender: An Ethnomethodological Approach*. New York: Wiley.

King, U. (1993) *Women and Spirituality: Voices of Protest and Promise* (2nd ed.). London: Macmillan.

King, U. (1994) *Feminist Theology from the Third World: A Reader*. London: SPCK.

King, Y. (1983) Toward an ecological feminism and a feminist ecology. In J. Rothschild (ed.), *Machina Ex Dea: Feminist Perspectives on Technology*. Oxford: Pergamon: 118–29.

King, Y. (1989) Healing the wounds: feminism, ecology, and the nature/culture dualism. In S.R. Bordo and A. Jaggar (eds), *Gender/Body/Knowledge: Feminist Reconstructions of Being and Knowing*. New Jersey: Rutgers University Press: 115–41.

Klein, V. (1946/1989) *The Feminine Character: History of an Ideology*. Third Edition, with introduction by J. Sayers. London: Routledge.

Kristeva, J. (1981) Women's time. *Signs: Journal of Women in Culture and Society*, **7**(1): 13–35.

Kristeva, J. (1982) *Desire in Language*. Translated by L.S. Roudiez. New York: Columbia University Press.

Kroker, A. and Kroker, M. (eds) (1987) *Body Invaders: Panic Sex in America*. New York: St Martin's Press.

Kruks, S. (1975) The philosophy of Merleau-Ponty. *Radical Philosophy*, **11**: 17–24.

Kurzweil, E. (1980) *The Age of Structuralism: Lévi-Strauss to Foucault*. New York: Columbia University Press.

Lambert, H.H. (1978) Biology and equality: a perspective on sex differences. *Signs: Journal of Women in Culture and Society*, **4**(1): 97–117.

Laqueur, T. (1990) *Making Sex: Body and Gender from the Greeks to Freud*. London: Harvard University Press.

Lawrence, M. (ed.) (1987) *Fed Up and Hungry: Women, Oppression and Food*. London: Women's Press.

Leclerc, I. (1986) *The Philosophy of Nature*, Studies in Philosophy and the History of Philosophy 14. Washington, D.C.: Catholic University of America.

le Doeuff, M. (1977) Women and philosophy. *Radical Philosophy* 17: 2–11.

Liebowitz, L. (1975) Perspectives on the evolution of sex differences. In R.R. Reiter (ed.), *Toward an Anthropology of Women*. New York: Monthly Review Press: 20–35.

Leonard, G., MacKenzie, I. and Toon, P. (1989) *Let God Be God*. London: Darton, Longman and Todd.

Lerner, G. (1986) *The Creation of Patriarchy*. Oxford University Press.

Lévi-Strauss, C. (1963) *Structural Anthropology*. Translated by C. Jacobson and B. Grundfest Schoepf. New York: Basic Books.

Lévi-Strauss, C. (1969) *The Elementary Structures of Kinship*. Translated by J.H. Bell *et al*. Boston: Beacon Press.

Levitas, R. (1983) Feminism and human nature. In I. Forbes and S. Smith (eds), *Politics and Human Nature*. London: Francis Pinter: 116–30.

Lewontin, R.C., Rose, S. and Kamin, L.J. (1984) *Not in Our Genes: Biology, Ideology and Human Nature*. New York: Pantheon.

Lips, H.W. and Colwill, N.L. (1978) *The Psychology of Sex Differences*. New Jersey: Prentice-Hall.

Lloyd, G. (1983) Masters, slaves and others. *Radical Philosophy*, **34**: 292–309.

Lloyd, G. (1984) *The Man of Reason: 'Male' and 'Female' in Western Philosophy*. London: Methuen.

Longino, H.E. (1987) Can there be a feminist science? *Hypatia*, **2**(3): 51–64.

Lovell, T. (ed.) (1990) *British Feminist Thought: A Reader*. Oxford: Blackwell.

Lowe, M. (1978) Sociobiology and sex differences. *Signs: Journal of Women in Culture and Society*, **4**(1): 118–25.

Lowe, M. (1983) The dialectic of biology and culture. In M. Lowe and R. Hubbard (eds), *Woman's Nature: Rationalizations of Inequality*. Oxford: Pergamon Press.

Lyndon, N. (1992) *No More Sex War: The Failures of Feminism*. London: Sinclair Stevenson.

Lyotard, J.F. (1984) *The Postmodern Condition: A Report on Knowledge*. Translated by G. Bennington and B. Massumi. Manchester: Manchester University Press.

McCloughry, R. (1992) *Men and Masculinity*. London: Hodder and Stoughton.

Maccoby, E.E. (1987) The Varied Meanings of 'Masculine' and 'Feminine'. In J.M. Reinisch, L.A. Rosenblum and S.A. Sanders (eds), *Masculinity/Femininity: Basic Perspectives*. Oxford University Press: 227–39.

Maccoby, E.E. and Jacklin, C.M. (1974) *The Psychology of Sex Differences*. California: Stanford University Press.

MacCormack, C.P. (1980) Nature, culture and gender: a critique. In C.P. MacCormack and M. Strathern (eds), *Nature, Culture and Gender*. New York: Cambridge University Press: 1–24.

MacCormack, C.P. (1981) Anthropology: a discipline with a legacy. In D. Spender (ed.), *Men's Studies Modified: The Impact of Feminism on the Academic Disciplines*. Oxford: Pergamon: 99–109.

McDade, J. (1994) Gender matters: women and priesthood. *The Month*, **CCLV**(1519): 254–59.

McFadyen, A.I. (1990) *The Call to Personhood*. Cambridge University Press.

McNeil, M. (ed.) (1987) *Gender and Expertise*. London: Free Association Books.

Makward, C. (1980) To be or not to be . . . a feminist speaker. In H. Eisenstein and A. Jardine (eds), *The Future of Difference*. Boston: G.K. Hall: 95–105.

Maloney, L.M. (1991) The argument for women's difference in classical philosophy and early Christianity. In A. Carr and E.S. Fiorenza (eds), *The Special Nature of Women?* London: SCM Press: 41–49.

Mantel, H. (1989) No cause for cerebration. *Independent*, 30 December: 13.

Martin, E. (1989) *The Woman in the Body*. Milton Keynes: Open University Press.

Mascia-Lees, F., Sharpe, P. and Ballerino Cohen, C. (1989) The post-modernist turn in anthropology: cautions from a feminist perspective. *Signs: Journal of Women in Culture and Society*, 15(1): 7–33.

Mason, M. (1990) Do women like sex? *London Review of Books*, 8 November: 16–17.

Masson, J.M. (1985) *The Assault on Truth: Freud's Suppression of the Seduction Theory* (2nd ed.) Harmondsworth: Penguin.

Mathieu, N.C. (1978) Man-culture and woman-nature? Translated by D. M. Leonard Baker. *Womens Studies International Quarterly*, 1: 55–65.

Maynard, M. (1993) Violence towards women. In D. Richardson and V. Robinson (eds), *Introducing Women's Studies*. London: Macmillan: 99–122.

Mead, M. (1935) *Sex and Temperament in Three Primitive Societies*. New York: Morrow.

Mead, M. (1943) *Coming of Age in Samoa*. Harmondsworth: Penguin.

Merchant, C. (1990) *The Death of Nature: Women, Ecology and the Scientific Revolution* (2nd ed.) San Francisco: Harper and Row.

Merleau-Ponty, M. (1945/1962) *The Phenomenology of Perception*. Translated by C. Smith. London: Routledge and Kegan Paul.

Messing, K. (1983) The scientific mystique: can a white lab coat guarantee purity in the search for knowledge about the nature of women? In Lowe, M. and Hubbard, R. (eds), *Woman's Nature: Rationalizations of Inequality*. Oxford: Pergamon Press: 75–88.

Midgley, M. (1988) On not being afraid of natural sex differences. In M. Griffiths and M. Whitford (eds), *Feminist Perspectives in Philosophy*. London: Macmillan: 29–41.

Miller, J.B. (1976) *Toward a New Psychology of Women*. Boston: Beacon Press.

Millett, K. (1970) *Sexual Politics*. London: Virago.

Mills, P.J. (1987) *Woman, Nature and Psyche*. New Haven: Yale University Press.

Minas, A. (ed.) (1993) *Gender Basics: Feminist Perspectives on Women and Men*. Belmont, California: Wadsworth.

Mitchell, J. (1971) *Woman's Estate*. Harmondsworth: Pelican.

Mitchell, J. (1974) *Psychoanalysis and Feminism*. Harmondsworth: Penguin.

Mitchell, J. (1984) The question of feminity and the theory of psycho-analysis. In *Women: The Longest Revolution*. London: Virago.

Mitchell, J. and Rose, J. (eds) (1982) *Feminine Sexuality: Jacques Lacan and the 'Ecole Freudienne'*. London: Macmillan.

Moi, T. (ed.) (1986) *The Kristeva Reader*. Oxford: Blackwell.

Moi, T. (ed.) (1987) *French Feminist Thought*. Oxford: Blackwell.

Moi, T. (1988) *Sexual/Textual Politics*. London: Routledge.

Moi, T. (1989) Patriarchal thought and the drive for knowledge. In T. Brennan (ed.), *Between Feminism and Psychoanalysis*. London: Routledge: 189–205.

Moir, A. and Jessel, D. (1989) *BrainSex*. London: Michael Joseph.

Money, J. and Ehrhardt, A. (1972) *Man and Woman, Boy and Girl*. Baltimore, Maryland: Johns Hopkins University Press.

Moore, H. (1988) *Feminism and Anthropology*. Cambridge: Polity.

Morawski, J.G. (1987) The troubled quest for masculinity, femininity and androgyny. In P. Shaver and C. Hendrick (eds), *Review of Personality and Social Psychology*. Vol. 7: 44–69.

Morgan, D.H.J. (1992) *Discovering Men*. London: Routledge.

Morley, J. (1984) 'The faltering words of men': exclusive language in the liturgy. In M. Furlong (ed.), *Feminine in the Church*. London: SPCK: 56–70.

Morley, J. (1988) *All Desires Known*. London: Movement for the Ordination of Women.

Mort, F. (1987) *Dangerous Sexualities: Medico-Moral Politics in England Since 1830*. London: Routledge and Kegan Paul.

Nelson, G. (1987) Men, feminism: the materiality of discourse. In A. Jardine and P. Smith (eds), *Men in Feminism*. New York: Methuen.

Nelson, J. (1992) *The Intimate Connection*. London: SPCK.

Nelson, J. and Longfellow, S.P. (eds.) (1994) *Sexuality and the Sacred: Sources for Theological Reflection*. London: Mowbray.

Norris, R.A. (1984) The ordination of women and the 'maleness' of the Christ. In M. Furlong (ed.), *Feminine in the Church*. London: SPCK: 71–85.

Nussbaum, M. (1990) The bondage and freedom of eros. *Times Literary Supplement*, 1–7 June: 571–73.

Oakley, A. (1972) *Sex, Gender and Society*. Aldershot: Gower.

Oddie, W. (1984) *What Will Happen to God?* London: SPCK.

Offen, K. (1990) Feminism and sexual difference in historical perspective. In D.L. Rhode (ed.), *Theoretical Perspectives on Sexual Difference*. New Haven: Yale University Press: 13–20.

Ortner, S.B. (1974) Is female to male as nature is to culture? In M.Z. Rosaldo and L. Lamphere (eds), *Woman, Culture and Society*. California: Stanford University Press: 67–88.

Ortner, S.B. and Whitehead, H. (1981) Accounting for sexual meanings. In S.B. Ortner and H. Whitehead (eds), *Sexual Meanings: The Cultural Construction of Gender and Sexuality*. New York: Cambridge University Press: 1–27.

Ounstead, C. and Taylor, D.C. (eds) (1972) *Gender Differences: Their Ontogeny and Significance*. London: Churchill.

Overfield, K. (1981) Dirty fingers, grime and slag heaps: purity and the scientific ethic. In D. Spender (ed.), *Men's Studies Modified*. Oxford: Pergamon: 237–48.

Parlee, M.B. (1975) Review article: Psychology. *Signs: Journal of Women in Culture and Society*, 1(1): 119–38.

Pateman, C. (1987) Feminist critiques of the public/private dichotomy. In A. Phillips (ed.), *Feminism and Equality*. New York University Press: 103–26.

Pattison, S. (1986) The use of the behavioural sciences in pastoral studies. In P. Ballard (ed.), *The Foundation of Pastoral Studies and Practical Theology*. Cardiff: Holi: 79–85.

Perry, C. (1991) *Listen to the Voice Within: A Jungian Approach to Pastoral Care*. London: SPCK.

Person, E.S. (1980) Sexuality as the mainstay of identity: psychoanalytic perspectives. *Signs: Journal of Women in Culture and Society*, 5(4): 605–30.

Phillips, A. (ed.) (1987) *Feminism and Equality*. New York University Press.

Plaskow, J. (1990) *Standing Again at Sinai: Judaism from a Feminist Perspective*. San Francisco: Harper and Row.

Plumwood, V. (1988) Women, Humanity and Nature. *Radical Philosophy*, 48: 16–24.

Plumwood, V. (1989) Do We Need a Sex/Gender Distinction? *Radical Philosophy*, 51: 2–11.

Plumwood, V. (1993) *Feminism and the Mastery of Nature*. London: Routledge.

Pryce, M. (1993) *Men, Masculinity and Pastoral Care*. Edinburgh: Contact Pastoral Monograph No. 3.

Rapp, R. (1979) Review essay: Anthropology. *Signs: Journal of Women in Culture and Society*, 4(3): 497–513.

Reinisch, J.M., Rosenblum, L.A. and Sanders, S.A. (1987) Masculinity/femininity: an introduction. In J.M. Reinisch, L.A. Rosenblum and S.A. Sanders (eds), *Masculinity/Femininity: Basic Perspectives*. Oxford University Press: 3–10.

Rhode, D.L. (ed.) (1990) *Theoretical Perspectives on Sexual Difference*. New Haven: Yale University Press.

Rich, A. (1976) *Of Woman Born: Motherhood as Experience and Institution*. New York: Norton.

Rich, A. (1980) Compulsory heterosexuality and lesbian existence. *Signs: Journal of Women in Culture and Society*, 5(4): 631–60.

Richards, B. (1989) *Images of Freud: Cultural Responses to Psychoanalysis*. London: J.M. Dent and Sons.

Richardson, D. (1993) Sexuality and male dominance. In D. Richardson and V. Robinson (eds), *Introducing Women's Studies*. London: Macmillan: 74–98.

Rieff, P. (1959) *Freud: The Mind of the Moralist*. London: Victor Gollancz.

Rogers, L.J. (1988) Biology, the popular weapon: sex differences in cognitive function. In B. Caine, E.A. Grosz and M. de Lepervanche (eds), *Crossing Boundaries: Feminisms and the Critique of Knowledges*. London: Unwin Hyman: 43–51.

Roith, E. (1987) *The Riddle of Freud: Jewish Influences on his Theory of Female Sexuality*. London: Tavistock.

Rosaldo, M.Z. (1974) Woman, culture and society: a theoretical overview. In M.Z. Rosaldo and L. Lamphere (eds), *Woman, Culture and Society*. California, Stanford University Press, 17–42.

Rosaldo, M.Z. (1980) The use and abuse of anthropology. *Signs: Journal of Women in Culture and Society*, 5(3): 389–417.

Rose, G. (1993) *Feminism and Geography: The Limits of Geographical Knowledge*. Cambridge: Polity.

Rose, H. (1982) Making science feminist. In E. Whitelegg *et al*. (eds), *The Changing Experience of Women*. Oxford: Martin Robertson: 352–72.

Rose, H. (1983) Hand, brain and heart: a feminist epistemology for the natural sciences. *Signs: Journal of Women in Culture and Society*, 9(1): 73–90.

Rose, H. (1986) Women's work, women's knowledge. In J. Mitchell and A. Oakley (eds), *What is Feminism?* Oxford: Blackwell: 161–83.

Rose, H. and Rose, S. (1976a) The problematic inheritance: Marx and Engels on the natural sciences. In Rose and Rose (eds), *The Political Economy of Science*. London: Macmillan: 3–13.

Rose, H. and Rose, S. (1976b) *The Radicalisation of Science*. London: Macmillan.

Rose, J. (1983) Femininity and its discontents. *Feminist Review*, 14: 5–21.

Rosser, S.V. (1992) Are there feminist methodologies appropriate for the natural sciences and do they make a difference? *Women's Studies International Forum*, 15(5/6): 535–50.

Rossi, A. (1977) A biosocial perspective on parenting. *Daedalus: Journal of the American Academy of Arts and Sciences*, 106(2): 1–31.

Rothschild, J. (ed.) (1983) *Machina ex Dea: Feminist Perspectives on Technology*. Oxford: Pergamon.

Rubin, G. (1975) The traffic in women: notes on the 'political economy' of sex. In R.R. Reiter (ed.), *Toward an Anthropology of Women*. New York: Monthly Review Press: 157–210.

Ruether, R.R. (1991) Women's difference and equal rights in the Church. In A. Carr and E.S. Fiorenza (eds), *The Special Nature of Women?* London: SCM Press: 11–18.

Ruether, R.R. (1992a) *Gaia and God: An Ecofeminist Theology of Earth Healing*. London: SCM Press.

Ruether, R.R. (1992b) *Sexism and God-Talk: Towards a Feminist Theology*. (2nd ed.). London: SCM Press.

Rutherford, J. (1988) Who's that man? In R. Chapman and J. Rutherford (eds), *Male Order: Unwrapping Masculinity*. London: Lawrence and Wishart: 21–67.

Samuels, A. (1985) *Jung and the Post-Jungians*. London: Routledge and Kegan Paul.

Sanday, P.R. (1981) *Female Power and Male Dominance: On the Origins of Sexual Inequality*. Cambridge University Press.

Santer, H. (1984) Stereotyping the sexes in society and in the church. In M. Furlong (ed.), *Feminine in the Church*. London: SPCK: 139–49.

Sawicki, J. (1988) Feminism and the power of Foucauldian discourse. In J. Arac (ed.), *After Foucault: Humanistic Knowledge, Postmodern Challenges*. New Brunswick, New Jersey: Rutgers University Press: 174–75.

Sayers, J. (1982) *Biological Politics: Feminist and Anti-Feminist Perspectives*. London: Tavistock.

Sayers, J. (1986) *Sexual Contradictions: Psychology, Psychoanalysis and Feminism*. London: Tavistock.

Sayers, J. (1987) Science, sexual difference, and feminism. In B. Hess and M.M. Ferree (eds), *Analysing Gender: A Handbook of Social Science Research*. California: Sage.

Schiebinger, L. (1987) The history and philosophy of women in science: a review essay. *Signs: Journal of Women in Culture and Society*, 12(2): 305–32.

Schiebinger, L. (1989) *The Mind has no Sex? Women in the Origins of Modern Science*. Cambridge, Mass.: Harvard University Press.

Scott, J. (1988) Equality-versus-difference: or, the uses of poststructuralist theory for feminism. *Feminist Studies*, 14(1): 33–50.

Segal, L. (1987) *Is the Future Female? Troubled Thoughts on Contemporary Feminism*. London: Virago.

Segal, L. (1990) *Slow Motion: Changing Masculinities, Changing Men*. London: Virago.

Seidler, V. (1987) Reason, desire and male sexuality. In P. Caplan (ed.), *The Cultural Construction of Sexuality*. London: Routledge: 82–112.

Selby, P. (1991) 'They make such good pastors'. In R. Holloway (ed.), *Who Needs Feminism?* London: SPCK: 125–34.

SHAFT (Self-Help Association for Transsexuals) (1981) *Guidelines for Transsexuals, Male to Female*. South Ascot, Berks.

Shapiro, J. (1981) Anthropology and the study of gender. *Soundings: An Interdisciplinary Journal*, **64**: 446–65.

Sharrock, W.W. (1986) Individual and society. in R.J. Anderson, J.A. Hughes and W.W. Sharrock (eds), *Classic Disputes in Sociology*. London: Allen and Unwin: 126–56.

Shilling, C. (1993) *The Body and Social Theory*. London: Sage.

Simons, M.A. and Benjamin, J. (1979) Simone de Beauvoir: an interview. *Feminist Studies*, **5**(2): 330–45.

Singer, J. (1976) *Androgyny: Towards a New Theory of Sexuality*. London: Routledge and Kegan Paul.

Slocum, S. (1975) Woman the gatherer: male bias in anthropology. In R.R. Reiter (ed.) *Toward an Anthropology of Women*. New York: Monthly Review Press: 36–50.

Smith, D. (1979) A sociology for women. In J. Sherman and E.T. Beck (eds), *The Prism of Sex: Essays in the Sociology of Knowledge*. Madison, University of Wisconsin Press.

Smith, D. (1987) Women's perspective as a radical critique of sociology. In S. Harding (ed.), *Feminism and Methodology*. Milton Keynes: Open University Press: 84–96.

Smith, J. (1983) Feminist analysis of gender: a critique. In M. Lowe and R. Hubbard (eds), *Woman's Nature: Rationalizations of Inequality*. Oxford: Pergamon Press.

Soble, A. (1982) The political epistemology of 'masculine' and 'feminine'. In M. Vetterling-Braggin (ed.), *'Femininity', 'Masculinity' and 'Androgyny': A Modern Philosophical Discussion*. Totowa, New Jersey: Rowman and Littlefield.

Spelman, E.V. (1982) Woman as body: ancient and contemporary views. *Feminist Studies*, **8**(1): 109–31.

Spence, J.T. and Helmreich, R.L. (1978) *Masculinity and Femininity: Their Psychological Dimensions, Correlates and Antecedents*. Austin: University of Texas Press.

Spence, J.T., Helmreich, R.L. and Stapp, J. (1974) The personal attributes questionnaire: a measure of sex-role stereotypes and masculinity-femininity. *JSAS Catalog of Selected Documents in Psychology*, 4: 43–44.

Stanley, L. (ed.) (1990) *Feminist Praxis: Research, Theory and Epistemology in Feminist Sociology*. London: Routledge.

Stanley, L. and Wise, S. (1993) *Breaking Out Again: Feminist Ontology and Epistemology*. (2nd ed.). London: Routledge.

Stanton, M. (1983) *Outside the Dream: Lacan and the French Styles of Psychoanalysis*. London: Routledge and Kegan Paul.

Stanworth, M. (1987) *Reproductive Technologies: Gender, Motherhood and Medicine*. Cambridge: Polity.

Stoller, R. (1968) *Sex and Gender*. New York: Science House.

Storkey, E. (1988) Sex and sexuality in the Church. In M. Furlong (ed.), *Mirror to the Church*. London: SPCK: 45–61.

Strathern, M. (1980) No nature, no culture: the Hagen case. In C.P. MacCormack and M. Strathern (eds), *Nature, Culture and Gender*. New York: Cambridge University Press: 174–222.

Strathern, M. (1987) An awkward relationship: the case of feminism and anthropology. *Signs: Journal of Women in Culture and Society*, 12(2): 276–92.

Sturrock, J. (ed.) (1979) *Structuralism and Since*. London: Paladin/Collins.

Suleiman, S.R. (ed.) (1986) *The Female Body in Western Culture*. London: Harvard University Press.

Synnott, A. (1993) *The Body Social: Symbolism, Self and Society*. London: Routledge.

Tamez, E. (1989) *Through her Eyes: Women's Theology from Latin America*. New York: Orbis.

Teitelbaum, M.S. (1976) *Sex Differences: Social and Biological Differences*. Garden City, New York: Anchor Books.

Terman, L.M. and Miles, C.C. (1936) *Sex and Personality: Studies in Masculinity and Femininity*. New York: McGraw-Hill.

Thistlethwaite, S.B. (1990) *Sex, Race and God*. London: Geoffrey Chapman.

Thorne, B., Kramarae, C. and Henley, N. (1983) *Language, Gender and Society*. Cambridge, Mass.: Newbury.

Tong, R. (1989) *Feminist Thought: A Comprehensive Introduction*. London: Unwin Hyman.

Townsend, P. and Davidson, N. (eds) (1982) *Inequalities in Health (The 'Black' Report)*. Harmondsworth: Pelican.

Turner, B.S. (1984) *The Body and Society*. Oxford: Blackwell.

Ulanov, A. (1971) *The Feminine in Jungian Psychology and in Christian Theology*. Evanston, Illinois: Northwestern University Press.

Ulanov, A. (1981) *Receiving Women: Studies in the Psychology and Theology of the Feminine*. Westminster: Philadelphia.

Van Leeuwen, M.S. (1987) The Christian mind and the challenge of gender relations. *The Reformed Journal*, 37: 17–23.

Vetterling-Braggin, M. (ed.) (1982) *'Femininity', 'Masculinity' and 'Androgyny': A Modern Philosophical Discussion*. Totowa, New Jersey: Rowman and Littlefield.

Wajcman, J. (1991) *Feminism Confronts Technology*. Cambridge: Polity.

Walker, B.M. (1981) Psychology and feminism – if you can't beat them, join them. In D. Spender (ed.), *Men's Studies Modified*. Oxford: Pergamon, 111–24.

Wallace, T. and Marsh, C. (1993) *Changing Perceptions: Gender and Development*. Oxford: Oxfam.

Webster, M. (1994) *A New Strength, A New Song: The Journey to Women's Priesthood*. London: Mowbray.

Weedon, C. (1987) *Feminist Practice and Poststructuralist Theory*. Oxford: Blackwell.

Weeks, J. (1977) *Coming Out: Homosexual Politics in Britain from the Nineteenth Century to the Present*. London: Quartet.

Weeks, J. (1985) *Sexuality and its Discontents: Meanings, Myths and Modern Sexualities*. London: Routledge and Kegan Paul.

Weeks, J. (1987) Questions of identity. In P. Caplan (ed.), *The Cultural Construction of Sexuality*. London: Routledge: 31–51.

Wehr, D. (1988) *Jung and Feminism: Liberating Archetypes*. London: Routledge.

Whitford, M. (1988) Luce Irigaray's critique of rationality. In M. Griffiths and M. Whitford (eds), *Feminist Perspectives in Philosophy*. London: Macmillan: 109–30.

Whitford, M. (1989) Rereading Irigaray. In T. Brennan (ed.), *Between Feminism and Psychoanalysis*. London: Routledge: 106–26.

Whitford, M. (1991) *Luce Irigaray: Philosophy in the Feminine*. London: Routledge.

Whitford, M. (ed.) (1992) *The Irigaray Reader*. Oxford: Blackwell.

Whitmont, E.C. (1980) Reassessing femininity and masculinity: a critique of some traditional assumptions. *Quadrant*, 13(2): 109–22.

Williams, Raymond (1976) Nature. In *Keywords: A Vocabulary of Culture and Society*. London: Verso: 219–24.

Williams, Raymond (1980) Ideas of nature. In *Problems of Materialism and Culture: Selected Essays*. London: Verso.

Williams, Rowan (1984) Women and the ministry: a case for theological seriousness. In M. Furlong (ed.), *Feminine in the Church*: 11–27.

Williams, Rowan (1989) *The Body's Grace*. London: Gay and Lesbian Christian Movement.

Wilson, E.O. (1978) *On Human Nature*. Cambridge, Mass.: Harvard University Press.

Winkler, J.J. (1990) *The Constraints of Desire: The Anthropology of Sex and Gender in Ancient Greece*. London: Routledge.

Wittig, M. (1981) One is not born a woman. *Feminist Issues*, 1: 47–54.

Witz, A. (1993) Women at work. In D. Richardson and V. Robinson (eds), *Introducing Women's Studies*. London: Macmillan: 242–302.

Wolf, N. (1991) *The Beauty Myth*. London: Vintage.

Wren, B. (1989) *What Language Shall I Borrow? God-Talk in Worship: A Male Response to Feminist Theology*. London: SCM Press.

Wren, B. (1991) Language change and male repentance. In R. Holloway (ed.), *Who Needs Feminism?* London: SPCK: 135–48.

Yanagisako, S.J. and Collier, J.F. (1990) The mode of reproduction in anthropology. In D.L. Rhode (ed.), *Theoretical Perspectives on Sexual Difference*. New Haven: Yale University Press: 131–41.

Young, P.D. (1990) *Feminist Theology/Christian Theology: In Search of Method*. Minneapolis: Fortress.

Index